HEARTH WITCH

Other books by Anna Franklin:

The Sacred Circle Tarot, by Anna Franklin, illustrated by Paul Mason, 1998

Midsummer, by Anna Franklin, Llewellyn 2001

Lammas, by Anna Franklin & Paul Mason, Llewellyn, 2001

The Illustrated Encyclopaedia of Fairies, by Anna Franklin, Vega, 2002

The Fairy Ring Oracle, by Anna Franklin, illustrated by Paul Mason, Llewellyn, 2002

The Oracle of the Goddess, by Anna Franklin, illustrated by Paul Mason, Vega, 2003

The Celtic Animal Oracle, by Anna Franklin, illustrated by Paul Mason, Vega, 2003

Real Wicca for Teens, by Anna Franklin & Sue Phillips, Capall Bann, 2002

The Little Book of Fairies, by Anna Franklin, illustrated by Paul Mason, Vega, 2003

Herb Craft by Anna Franklin & Sue Lavender, Capall Bann, 1995

Familiars, the Animal Powers of Britain, by Anna Franklin, Capall Bann, 1997

Pagan Feasts by Anna Franklin & Sue Phillips, Capall Bann, 1998

Personal Power by Anna Franklin, Capall Bann, 1997

Magical Incenses and Oils, by Anna Franklin, Capall Bann, 2000

The Wellspring, by Anna Franklin, Capall Bann, 1999

Fairy Lore, by Anna Franklin, illustrated by Paul Mason, Capall Bann, 2000

Working With Fairies by Anna Franklin, New Page Books 2006

Path of the Shaman by Anna Franklin, Lear Books 2007

Pagan Ritual, Path of the Priest and Priestess, by Anna Franklin, Lear Books 2008

Visit www.annafranklin.co.uk

HEARTH WITCH
Anna Franklin

Lear Books
www.learbooks.co.uk

First edition published in 2004 by Lear Books
Reprinted 2006 by Lear Books
This revised edition published by Lear Books 2008

Lear Books
Windrush High Tor West
Earl Shilton
Leicestershire
LE9 7DN
England

Printed by Booksprint

Cover artwork Anna Franklin & Kathy Cocks
Cover design Paul Mason

ISBN 0-9547534-1-0

Lear Books
www.learbooks.co.uk

CONTENTS

Introduction
THE EIGHTFOLD WAYS OF MAGIC

Hearth Witch is part of a series of eight books on the paths of magic in the Wicce tradition. I invented the term 'hearth witch' to describe the long disregarded magic and skills of women, who acted as domestic priestesses at the sacred hearths of their homes. Since the first edition of this book was printed the term seems to have gained currency, and there are now websites dedicated to hearthwitchery all over the internet. This is very gratifying and means that these ancient gifts are being recognised.

In the Craft, we seek to explore and combine all the paths to a greater or lesser extent, depending on the abilities and preferences of the individual witch. Some mastery of each of the paths is required, though each person will probably come to specialise in one particular aspect.

All cultures, world-wide, have recognised and practised magic. Even western society has, as part of its inheritance, folk tales of magicians who are capable of harnessing invisible powers and of understanding occult laws. The tribal shaman, village wise woman or cunning man served the community by healing the sick and mediating with the spirit world for the benefit of the people.

Wicce is a religion; it is not a game or a trick that you use to get something for nothing. The world-view of the Pagan is essentially different from the normally accepted materialistic approach of Western Society. Pagans hold that all life is sacred, that all life contains spirit, a living force within it: this includes people, animals, plants and even the Earth itself. We believe that divine spirit is not separate from creation but is contained within it, and within each of us. In other words, deity is manifest within nature, is imminent, present - we can go out and touch our gods.

We use an analogy to explain how everything is connected and call it 'the web', visualising a series of threads that link and give life to the cosmos – the forces of magic. Any vibration on any strand will eventually reverberate throughout the whole web. The conscious witch can read the web, and through its threads, perform her magic with full knowledge of the outcome.

We believe that there is a cosmic harmony that recognises the perfect balance of male and female, black and white, day and night, summer and winter, light and darkness, life and death, God and Goddess. Each cannot exist without its opposite. One is not good and the other bad, but both are equally necessary, like the two sides of a coin. This harmony is depicted in the ancient *ying/yang* symbol of a circle, which represents wholeness, divided into two interlocking halves, one white and one black. Within each half is the germ of the other, represented by the dots of opposite colour. When balance is lost, conflict and chaos manifest; when a body is out of balance a person becomes ill. Pagans always try to maintain the natural balance and this is sometimes achieved by using magic. The village wise woman, shaman or cunning man was the first person anyone in trouble would turn to as they would understand what had happened to disturb the concord and see what had to be done to put it right, using their skills as seer, magician and communicator with the Otherworld. Witches were the healers, not just of human bodies, but of the whole cosmic harmony.

This maintenance of balance gives the witch her code of honour and rules of conduct. Every deed contains the seeds of its own punishment or reward. In magic like attracts like, so malicious thoughts and evil deeds attract negativity to those who project them; a witch must understand the consequences of her actions. Magic itself is neither good nor bad, but a force that can be wielded for either. I was always taught that unselfish, helpful, sacred magic is *called* white, while selfish or evil magic is *called* black. Using magic is an honour but also a great responsibility. Because magic uses the sacred part of us, we use it only for sacred purposes. It is a real and powerful force that taps into the deepest powers at the heart of the cosmos. The fires of creation should not be stirred just because you want a pair of designer shoes; only a child would do so. The primary magic of the witch is the transformation of Self; what we call the Grail Quest. The English occultist Dion Fortune said that magic is the art of changing consciousness at will. To accomplish this we use the Eightfold Ways. All of the eight paths can be - and are - used as individual paths to expanded consciousness by different practitioners.

Eight is a magical number encompassing the four elements and the four directions. It is the number of solar increase, giving us the number of festivals within the Craft year- Samhain, Yule, Imbolc, Ostara, Beltane, Coamhain, Lughnasa and Herfest. It has many echoes: the musical scale is based on the octave; the periodic table is based on multiples of eight. In numerology eight is the number of balance, of dualism, reflected on the way it is drawn, one circle topping another-'8'. The sign of infinity is an eight on its side. In spiritual terms, eight represents new growth and new life.

We are used to experiencing the world through our five senses alone and our interpretation of reality is derived from them, our responses based on them. By our memory and experiences, we recognise the shape of the world as it superficially appears. The witch learns to expand his or her consciousness and understanding to take into account other, more subtle realms. From childhood, we are taught to suppress this ability- our instincts, intuition and clairvoyant powers. When people enter the Craft they must be taught to recover these other senses, to unlearn thought structures that have been instilled as they grew. The Eightfold Ways are the steps to liberation from earthly existence into a new consciousness; steps that help us cross to the spiritual plane. Each step teaches us how to expand the consciousness, to reveal what is hidden; and this is the *real* magic.

The Eight Paths are:

1. Wise Woman/Cunning Man or Hearth Witch- herbal knowledge (including simpling and wort cunning, magical herb craft, plant shamanism, wild food, kitchen magic etc), the hearth as altar and sacred centre, priest/priestess of the living flame, the natural world, understanding the tides of the year, natural magic and healing

2. Hunter or Greenwood Witch- this is nothing to do with killing animals - the object of the hunt is the soul of the witch. The hunter develops those qualities that will further his/her spiritual growth in a programme of exercise and meditations based on hunting magic- silence, concentration, stillness, woodcraft, finding the questing beast or white hart, hunting the Self.

3. Warrior - the warrior referred to is a psychic warrior, and his or her tools are mind, body and spirit. These must be trained to work in harmony. S/he explores chivalry and knightly values, the code of honour, the psychic warrior, western martial arts, the weapons of the warrior, encountering the guardian of the threshold, questing

4. Bard- the bard is the keeper of history and lore, a storyteller, but also much more than this. He or she works with vibration, rhythm, chants, rhyme, storytelling, myth, sacred scripts and magical languages, riddles, memory, ancestral knowledge and spell craft in order to vibrate the web of being.

5. Sacred Dancer- it is said that dance was the original form of worship, and it is an essential part of sacred ceremony. Dance is to movement what poetry is to language. Pagan temples often employed dancers and in some places the dance went on without cease for centuries, with one dancer taking the place of another, expressing the passing of the seasons and the cycles of life, representing the Goddess who created them. Sadly, the early Christian church frowned on dance and we lost this aspect of worship in the western world. The sacred dancer works with movement and energy, the dance of the year- the zodiac, the sun, moon, stars, vibrating the web, avatars, masks, invoking and healing through dance.

6. Priest/Priestess- in the Craft, every initiate becomes a consecrated priest or priestess working with ritual, creating sacred space, recreating the macrocosm in the microcosm, expressing the sacred through ritual using ritual drama, seasonal, monthly and specific rituals, invocation and evocation, preparation, consecration and, most of all, intention.

7. Shaman- the word means 'one who knows' and is applied to someone who has gone through a shamanic crisis during which he/she knows from experience that the world is alive and connected, and that we are surrounded by spirit. The shaman travels to various realms of consciousness to gain teaching from Otherworldly beings, necessitating the ability to move from the world of everyday consciousness limited by the five sense, to one of non-ordinary reality. Part of Craft training involves learning how to enter and maintain trance states through such things as drumming, meditation, dances and the use of herbs and incenses. The shaman works with spirits, familiars and guides.

8. Witch- The witch is concerned with revealing the sacred concealed within the manifest, using the Eight Paths of magic, the circle, natural cycles and Wheel of the Year. It is the goal of every witch to combine all of the previous paths into a greater one. Central to this is a relationship with the land, in a real, not symbolic manner, to observe and celebrate the wheel of the seasons, and become part of their ebb and flow. The spirits of the land are sought for their teachings and honoured for their work. The gods and goddesses are honoured as the powerful beings that they are. We first recognise what happens on the earth plane, and celebrate the coming of spring, the return of greenery and light, the warmth of summer, the harvest and so on. On a simple level these celebrations help to connect us to the Earth and recognise natural cycles. At the next level we recognise that the natural cycles are reflected in the psyche- times of growth, times of promise, times of waiting, times of decay. These ideas are incorporated into seasonal rituals of inner and outer courts- the seed of promise, the sacrifice of the harvest and so on. At the third level the inner court uses the rituals of the year to align with the ebb and flow of natural and magical energy, to become aware of being at one with the tides, being part of effecting their change. The cycles become vehicles of transformation on a fundamental level, each complete turning of the wheel moving the initiate along the spiral path towards the centre, journeying each year with the Sacred King from birth, purification, youth, marriage, consummation, harvest, death and into the underworld. The ritual circle is our map and our compass. It contains the stations of the year. It connects us to all possible realms, the Otherworld cities of the four elements, and the centre where the end and the beginning are one. The outward expression of transformation is presented as the achievement of a quest and marked by the degrees of initiation.

Chapter 1
WISE WOMEN AND CUNNING MEN

The Hearth Witch is the priest or priestess of the hearth fire which contains the living essence of the Goddess.[1] She sees the sacred within the physical, the magical in the mundane, and uses this knowledge to incorporate spiritual practice into her everyday life. The way of the Hearth Witch is an uncomplicated, direct form of magic, deceptively simple but unspeakably profound. She draws her strength from the sacred flame that burns in her hearth, from the ground that sustains her, the water that nourishes her and the inspiration of her breath. She finds her gods in the land around her: the spirits of water, stone and tree, Earth, moon, sun, stars and sky. She needs no watch, calendar or magical almanac to tell her when to work her magic, but works with the observable ebb and flow of the changing seasons, the rising and setting of the sun and the waxing and waning of the moon. A Hearth Witch is drawn to the traditional ways, to the rhythms of nature and the call of the wildwoods, and is not much interested in prancing naked around someone's city living room mumbling someone else's words from bits of paper. This book is about walking the talk. It isn't about image, heavy eyeshadow, big jewellery and black velvet dresses. It is about adopting a magical lifestyle and living life as a practising Pagan in the modern world. It is not written for those who chatter and pose, but for those who *do*.

The Hearth Witch of today inherits the mantle of the village wise woman or cunning man. She is part shaman, part seer, part herbalist, part spiritual healer, but all witch. Hers are the Old Ways of the countryside, once passed down from mother to daughter, father to son, crone to apprentice, magister to neophyte and then improved by a lifetime of study and daily observation of Mother Nature. It is as old as time and as new as the newest witch.

The path of the wise woman or cunning man is largely solo,

---

1 A hearth witch can be male or female, but I shall use the feminine pronoun to avoid the clumsiness business of 'he or she' and 'him or her' within the text.

though some, like me, may be active in a coven situation; others simply join with like-minded people to celebrate the festivals. It is not an easy path, since it is often lonely and requires a great deal of hard work, study, discipline and a fair amount of time spent just being cold and wet. Though there are many paths to magic, this is the path I follow most closely, the one that draws me. I live in the countryside and grow my own vegetables, fruit and herbs. I spend time in the fields and woods. If you do not feel the pull of Mother Nature than this is not a path you will be able to - or want - to follow; you won't understand it or see its value. If you measure success in terms of money and posessions it is not for you. But if the starlit night draws you from the comfort of home and fire, if your heart swells at the sight of a swathe of woodland anemones in the spring, you will already know what I mean.

Pagans believe that the divine is manifest within Nature, and that to truly commune with Nature is to encounter the gods, with all the gifts that confers. In the 21st century people often feel alienated and separated from the natural world; we feel a sense of loss without knowing the cause; we yearn for something without knowing what it is. The planet is treated as a resource to be exploited and destroyed, instead of a goddess, our Mother Earth. Such separation is a by-product of the monotheistic patriarchal religions that tell us that we are simply stewards of the Earth, and may take advantage of it and its creatures as we will; that since God is separate from creation, creation is not important, but rather a fallen condition, an evil state to be endured until we can escape it in death. Pagans, on the other hand, believe that we are already in paradise, that we are surrounded by sacred energy which nourishes us if only we are open to receive it. All the knowledge we need is written plainly on the landscape, waiting to be read, if only we have the eyes to see it.

For as long as I can remember, my moments of deepest joy and fulfilment have come from communion with Nature. For me, each tree, each stream and each rock has spirit: is alive. The land itself has consciousness, a guardian spirit that some call a *genius locus*. Every country, and every part of the countryside, has its own integral gods and goddesses: sometimes just the local deity of a well, sometimes the genius of the whole country, as Britannia (Brigantia) is of Britain, and Erin is of Ireland. The land is alive with the spirits that we call the Wildfolk, or fairies. I work with all of these beings in my magical life, and in my daily life I perform age-old rituals to petition fertility for my own patch of land in the English village where I live.

Though I have always been conscious of nature spirits, and have always been drawn to the Old Gods, I was not brought up as a Pagan. My adopted family was Roman Catholic and sent me to a convent school to be educated by nuns. There I felt lonely and out of place, but I devoured the classical library, reading of the Greek and Roman gods and goddesses, and when I prayed, I prayed to golden Aphrodite, or wise Athene. They seemed much more real and immediate to me than the jealous god I was supposed to believe in. I saw creatures in the woodland no one else could see, and found pleasure in lonely places with the wild creatures. My family said I was mad, and the nuns said I was damned. Then when I was eighteen I found other people who felt the same way as me - they were called witches.

WISE WOMEN

Even after the coming of Christianity to Britain, the village wise women and cunning men cared for the bodies and spirits of those around them, telling their fortunes, treating their bodily ailments, dowsing for their lost property, and physicking their farm animals. They were the midwives who brought new life into the world, and who laid out the dead at the end of life. Their natural magic, in harmony with the rhythms of life, centred and nourished the spirits of the whole community. They were honoured for their wisdom and knowledge: when they spoke, people listened.

Such men and women carried on the beliefs and traditions of the Druid priesthood and Saxon sorcerers, keeping the essence of the Pagan religion alive. The word Pagan is derived from the Latin *paganus*, simply meaning 'person of the countryside'. The practices of wise women and cunning men had much in common with shamans and witch doctors around the world - a belief that we are surrounded by spirits and that we can commune with them, that the land is alive and must be honoured and cared for, that our actions affect the world around us and we must seek to live in harmony with it, and that we are part of the ebb and flow of the seasons and must perform certain actions at the correct time. This Pagan legacy was apparent even into the early twentieth century when fen folk still made offerings to Yarthkins (East Anglian fairies) on rocks on the edge of fields and images of the corn deity were ploughed into fields to return fertility to the land. While most wise women and cunning men wouldn't have understood themselves to be Pagan, or welcomed the term 'witch', their practices certainly stemmed from the earlier beliefs of our Pagan ancestors.

There are reliable accounts of many hundreds of such people in Britain from the Middle Ages up to the beginning of the Twentieth Century when every village seems to have housed someone with a magical reputation of some sort. George Pickingill (1816-1909) was a well known cunning man who practiced his art in the Essex village of Canewdon. He traced his ancestry back to Julia the Witch of Brandon, who had lived in a village north of Thetford in Norfolk. He was a simple farm worker, yet the whole locality was in awe of his magical abilities. It was claimed that anyone who crossed him fell ill, and could only be restored to health by the touch of his blackthorn walking stick. It is reputed that he established nine covens in Norfolk, Essex, Hertfordshire, Sussex and Hampshire, each with a leader that had proved his or her hereditary witch lineage. Both Crowley and Gardener are said to have been initiated into one or other of these covens, and to have shared together what they had garnered of the old Pickingill rituals.

Also in Essex, from 1812 to 1860, nearby Hadleigh was the home of James Murrell, called Cunning Murrell, the seventh son of a seventh son. He had a magic mirror for locating lost property, a telescope for looking through walls and a copper talisman which could differentiate between honest and dishonest clients. On December 15 1860, Murrell predicted that he would die the next day, and the time of his death to the minute. True to his prediction, he died and is buried in an unmarked grave in Hadleigh churchyard.

The numbers of cunning men and women seem to have dwindled after the First World War, which changed the face of Britain forever, when men who had faced the horrors of the trenches were no longer impressed by the threatened evil eye of a cunning man.[2] According to Nigel Pennick, the last genuine cunning man was practicing in Cambridgeshire in the 1960s.[3]

These village shamans had many names including wise women, cunning men, blessers, witches, conjurors and currens. They didn't use athames and magic swords (which are a Gardnerian introduction into the Craft from ritual magic) but scrying glasses, crystals, keys, shears, sieves, pitchforks, brooms, divining rods, wax, bottles, paper and anything that came readily to hand from kitchen or farm. Their three most important festivals were May Day, Midsummer and All Hallows, the three spirit nights when the denizens of the Otherworld roam the Earth.

2   Nigel Pennick, pers comm
3   Nigel Pennick pers comm

THE BURNING TIMES

During the times of witchcraft persecution - the days we erroneously call The Burning Times - the wise women were the first to be accused of devil worship and evil magic.

The Catholic Church initiated the Inquisition in the twelfth century for the purpose of eliminating non-believers, with the Benedictine, Franciscan, Dominican and Jesuit Orders being most active in its prosecutions. Since the Church confiscated all the property of anyone convicted, you might think its motives were not entirely spiritual, and in this way it gained much of its great wealth. The Church recognised three classes of non-believers: heretics (the Cathars, Waldensians, Albigencians and Gnostic Christians); heathens (which meant all the old Pagan religions, included the old Greek, Roman and Egyptian Pagans), [4] and witches. For the Church, the practice of witchcraft by women was always evil, defined as *maleficium* or malevolent magical acts. From the twelfth to the fifteenth centuries Church lawyers merged this with ideas of demonology and diabolism to invent the notion that witches were devil worshippers.

In 1484, in response to reports that in the dioceses of Cologne, Mainz, Trier and Salzburg many women were engaging in sorcery "*to make the conjugal act impossible*", Pope Innocent VIII wrote the *Summa Desiderantes,* a letter in which he associated witchcraft with evil done in villages, charms, conjuring, abortion, black masses and so on, maintaining that witches formed the church of the devil. The Pope - a father of many illegitimate children - so feared the influence of witches on his virility, that he appointed two German Dominicans, Jakov Sprenger and Heinrich Kramer, to pursue witches. They wrote the infamous *Malleus Maleficarum,* which means "Hammer of Evil Doers" or "Hammer of the Witches". Sprenger and Kramer demanded the death sentence for all witches who caused impotence. They wrote (quoting St Thomas Aquinas) that "*woman is an imperfect animal, and always deceives.... All witchcraft comes from carnal lust which in women is insatiable.*" So popular was their book that it ran into nineteen editions and was a principle text for the Inquisition.

The real witch craze, however, lasted from about 1580-1660, and there are many theories as to why this seemingly insane panic spread across Europe during this period. Economic, political and religious unrest were all contributory factors. The splitting of the Christian church into Protestant and Catholic factions caused upheaval and uncertainty in many countries. In England, for example, under Henry VIII and his son Edward, Catholics

---

4   Edo Nyland 1997   http://www.islandnet.com/~edonon

were executed, while under the next ruler, Queen Mary, Protestants were executed. When she died and Elizabeth I came to the throne, Catholics were for the chop again; no wonder people were confused and frightened.

The majority of trials took place in the parts of Europe disrupted by religious controversy. The areas most heavily affected included western and central Germany, Switzerland, south eastern France and Scotland. Disordered by economic and military crises as well as the disturbance of the Reformation, Lutheran Germany was probably the worst affected. A rash of pamphlettes and publications about demons and witches appeared - when people are scared, they look for someone to blame.

A German law professor first posited the theory that the persecutions were a Church led campaign against remnants of a pre-Christian religion in 1828, and Margaret Murray expounded on this in the early twentieth century. She described a tradition of witchcraft that was centred on a horned deity called Janus, whom the church identified with the devil. Her theories are very unfashionable now, and scholars (British scholars at least) are generally in favour of the notion that there is no evidence of any Pagan survival in Europe- despite the evidence of indisputably Pagan practices, ideas and beliefs, and contemporaneous reports. Gratian, an Italian jurist, wrote in 1140 in *A Concordance of Discordant Canons* that witches were women who believed that they rode on beasts through the air (echoing shamanic journeys in other cultures) and travelled, on certain nights, to meeting places where they were presided over by the goddess Diana. He attributed witchcraft to the survival of pre-Christian beliefs.

Whatever the reasons for the witch craze, and they are complex, witches seem to have become the scapegoats of public fears. The worst excesses of the persecutions were in rural communities, where people were more superstitious and easily influenced. Mass accusations and prosecutions were not uncommon. Nothing focuses a group's attention and binds them together as much as a hate figure to revile and dread. In the twentieth century we had the Cold War, when people in the west were taught to think that the USSR was 'the evil empire' and the people of the east to think the west was the domain of 'degenerate capitalists' both defining enemies to foster an 'us and them' mentality. And what could be more frightening than powerful magicians in the employ of the devil himself working to bring evil into a community, with the Church the only hope of defence?

The gentle Christian Inquisitors asserted that in punishment of witches, "*eternal damnation should begin in this life, that it might be in some way shown what will be suffered in hell*'. Accused women were stripped naked and intimately probed by men searching for 'witch marks'. Then there were three degrees of torture prescribed. The mildest included being tightly bound, fed salty food and denied water, being stretched on the rack until muscles tore, or being raped by the torturer and his assistants. In the trails, anyone who confessed at this stage was deemed to have confessed 'without torture' since these were considered minor measures.

The next level of torture, or Ordinary Torture, usually consisted of the *strappado*, binding the prisoner's arms behind her back, tying heavy weights to her feet, and hoisting her to the ceiling, agonisingly dislocating her arms in the process. In 1608, a young German woman was hoisted up eleven times in one day without confession and was then tortured for a further ten weeks. Some torturers delighted in piercing the women with red hot skewers as they hung, or applying red hot brimstone to their genitals. In the Channel Islands, prisoners continued to be tortured even after sentencing to try to make them reveal the names of their accomplices. There, the rope was tied round the thumbs for hoisting, and then abruptly dropped so that the thumbs were torn off.

For those who still would not confess to working evil magic, there was the Extraordinary Torture. Again, the victims were hung from the ceiling, but extremely heavy weights (as much as 660 lbs) were hung from their limbs in order to tear them off. Every bone in the body was usually broken by this procedure. It could be repeated up to four times before death ensued - with or without confession. Other procedures included the cutting off of hands and feet, immersion in boiling water, or metal boots into which boiling lead was poured.[5]

If a person recanted her confession after being released from the torture chamber, she was taken straight back in; once accused there was little hope of escape. Figures for those executed for witchcraft range from 50,000 to 100,000, but there were probably many more lynched, drowned and tortured to death that are not recorded in these statistics.

A WAR AGAINST WOMEN

It is revealing to note that 80% or more of the accused were women. A Dominican father declared that any woman knew more magic than a hundred men. According to the *Malleus Maleficarum* "*There are more women than men found infected with the heresy of witchcraft* "and "*a woman is by her nature more quicker to waver in her faith and consequently quicker to abjure the faith, which*

---

5   Pickering, Davis, *Cassell Dictionary of Witchcraft*, Cassell, London, 1996

is the root of witchcraft" . The authors prayed *"Blessed be the Highest who has so far preserved the male sex from so great an evil"* adding that women were weak in themselves, and could only perform magic in league with demons.[6]

While any woman practicing fortune telling, midwifery or herbalism could be executed as a witch, male doctors, astrologers and alchemists were left unscathed - powerful women were obviously something to be feared and put down. Female healers and the Church had always been at odds. The fifteenth century Council of Trent specifically forbade women from having anything to do with medicine, a profession they were not to be re-admitted to until the late nineteenth century. While male, university trained doctors were sanctioned by the Church, if any women stood before a tribunal accused of practising medicine or healing it was automatically assumed that she must have achieved any cure by witchcraft and she was put to death [7] According to the *Malleus Maleficarum* *"If a woman dare to cure without having studied than she is a witch and must die"* – and women were not allowed to study. If a woman was accused of healing a patient, the tribunal would call in a male doctor to pronounce on whether she had achieved her cures by witchcraft, and thus he was given the power of life and death over his female rival. Male doctors were trusted implicitly by the authors of the *Malleus Maleficarum*: *"Although some of their remedies seem to be vain and superstitious cantrips and charms... everybody must be trusted in his profession."* And lest we be too smug in reminding ourselves how attitudes have changed, a similar mindset still exists today, whereby the word of a doctor like Harold Shipman (who killed hundreds of his patients and got away with it for years) is never questioned, while any woman who queries her treatment is like to have the words 'hysterical' or 'depressed' penned on her medical records.

In particular, the Inquisition targeted midwives, as according to the *Malleus Maleficarum* *"no one does more harm to the Catholic Church than midwives...the witch-midwives exceed all other witches in deeds of shame"* If a baby was still-born or miscarried, they said the midwife had killed the child to steal its soul, and that female midwives dedicated new born children to the devil. Preventing pregnancy or terminating a pregnancy was a capital offence.

This persecution of women was made possible by a long history of anti-female philosophy in the Christian Church. For the Christian

---

6   Jani Farrell Roberts, *The Seven Days of My Creation*, iUniverse Inc, Lincoln, 2002
7   ibid

thinker, God was male, and thus the only true gender was male.[8] From the very beginning, they argued that women were inferior to men, as Eve was made from Adam's spare rib, and being formed by a bent rib she was naturally flawed. Saint Thomas Aquinas (still an authority respected by the modern Catholic Church) proclaimed that every girl child is a defective male, conceived only because her father was ill, weak or in a state of sin at the time.

According to Christian mythology, women are responsible for the fall of humankind and its expulsion from paradise, since Eve was tempted to eat the fruit of the tree of knowledge and persuaded her husband Adam to do the same.[9] According to the Church, a midwife was guilty of sinning if she eased a woman's pain during childbirth as that suffering was imposed by Jehovah as a punishment on all women for Eve's transgression. Clerics reminded Queen Victoria of this when she asked for chloroform in the royal labour ward.

Under Pagan Celtic and Saxon law, women could be priestesses, teachers, chieftains, property holders, healers and judges. Christianity stripped women of all these rights and left them as mere chattels of their husbands and fathers who stood as responsible adults for women who, according to the *Malleus*, "*are intellectually like children*"; a belief that persists in some monotheistic patriarchal cultures to this day. Moreover, women were denied the role they had enjoyed in Pagan cultures as mothers and creators of life. Church scholars decided that the spark of life comes from the male sperm, and the woman merely serves as the soil in which it is planted.

The Church felt that women were more carnal than men, as was clear from their many 'abominations': women menstruate, get pregnant and give birth, all evidence of the sexual activity which was reviled as sinful by the Church. The *Malleus Maleficarum* was very unambiguous in its references to women's sexuality as an evil force. A woman was said to be impure "*during her monthly periods.*" Tertullian called women the 'devil's gateway'. Like Eve, all women were considered temptresses, inciting

---

8   This is still argued by people who deny that women can be Christian ministers.
9   This is a misreading of a far more ancient Mesopotamian Goddess myth. The name Eve, in Hebrew *Hawwah*, is from the Akkadian word *Hayah* meaning "to live". She is thus called Hawwah because she was Mother of All Living" according to Genesis. This was a title of the Sumerian goddess Ninhursag. In the Sumerian myth the god Enki (possibly cognate with Yahweh or Jehovah) was cursed by Ninhursag because he stole forbidden plants from paradise. His health began to fail and the other gods prevailed on the Mother Goddess to help him. To do this she created a goddess called Ninti (literally *nin*= lady, *ti*= rib i.e. lady of the rib, a play on words since the phrase also means "to make live"). He claimed his rib hurt him and she healed him.

men to seek the forbidden fruit of lust. If a woman was raped, it was considered to be her own fault. St Thomas Aquinas taught that women exerted an evil influence over men which caused them to have involuntary erections and thus distracted them from contemplating God.

Bonaventure (d 1274), a famous Franciscan theologian, said that *"because the sexual act has been corrupted (though original sin) and has become, so to speak, stinking and because human beings besides are for the most part too lustful, the devil has so much power and authority over them."* St Thomas Aquinas ruled that Satan had particular control over human sexuality because *"of the loathsome nature of the act of generation, and because through it original sin is transmitted to all men."* Kramer and Sprenger believed that *"All witchcraft comes from carnal lust, which is in women insatiable."* These respected Christian thinkers were afraid of the power of women, particularly their sexual power.

The motives of the accusers were not always spiritual. Dame Alice Kyteler was put on trial in Kilkenny in Ireland in 1324, accused of witchcraft. She was a wealthy woman, having inherited fortunes from her deceased husbands. The trial of Alice Kyteler was initiated by her stepsons who believed that they, not a woman, should receive all of their father's inheritance. Women without brothers or sons to share the inheritance accounted for 89% of the women executed for witchcraft in New England between 1620 and 1725.

It is noteworthy that most of the women accused were middle-aged or elderly. For the Christian Church, the only acceptable roles for a woman were wife and mother, and a woman's sole legitimate function was to reproduce. In such a society, any woman over childbearing age was considered useless and had no justifiable function. This made older women, especially the widowed and alone, an easy target for the witch hunters.

In Pagan lore, the image of the older woman is positive and powerful. We look to examples of elderly goddesses, the ones who are mistresses of witchcraft and magic, keepers of the secrets of life and death, such as the Celtic Anu who appears in my home country of Leicestershire as Black Annis. In Greek myth, the crone Hecate, the lady of the crossroad, is the goddess of witchcraft, a wise woman, a midwife, seer and shaman who travels the realms. It was she who helped Demeter in her search for Persephone.

Dictionaries describe the crone as an old, ugly, withered woman or ancient witchy female, or say that crone is a derogatory word for an old woman. It is a word derived from 'carrion' i.e. dead meat. In fairy tales the crone is always evil. However, this was not always the case. In previous ages, she was the respected elder, a woman with a lifetime's garnered wisdom, incorporating that of maiden, mother, middle age and old age. She was the keeper of history, the fount of lore, the healer and midwife, the one consulted in time of trouble because her experience told her what to do. She was the *Cailleach* or 'veiled one', the *coron* or 'crowned one'. She is the hag, another derogatory term now, but derived from *hagia*, which means 'the sacred one' (as in hagiography, the study of saints), or from *heilig* meaning 'holy'.

In Japan, older people are honoured as 'living treasures'. In our own society, with its heritage of patriarchal monotheism, old women are seen as useless. They (allegedly) have no sexual or maternal functions, and are only valid as grannies useful for the odd present or spot of babysitting. You only have to look at an evening's worth of television adverts to see how older women are perceived - lacking in wisdom or insight, narrow minded, and more than a little ridiculous, while anyone under twenty is portrayed as worldly wise, sassy and knowledgeable. The inference is that we live backwards; we are born with knowledge and lose it as we age!

Today's witches are trying to reclaim the title of Crone as an honourable and respected estate, in which an older woman is empowered to be herself: as wise, holy, rebellious, incorrigible, astute, funny, sexy, or irascible as she wishes.

Chapter 2
THE SACRED HEARTH

It is in our homes that the first resonance of the sacred lies and where we create a reflection of hallowed space. The business of the home rotates around the hearth- it is the place where people meet to cook, eat and talk together. It is the traditional place to house the shrine of the goddess of fire and the guardian *genius* of the dwelling, tended by the woman of the house as domestic priestess.

The hearth has been the centre of human life for at least 400,000 years. In Celtic tradition the *ty teallach* or 'hearth' was the heart of the home, and fire was often literally placed centrally in ancient dwelling places such as Bronze and Iron Age roundhouses. Imagine frozen, blustery winter days, when there was little work that could be done on the land, and when the hours of daylight were short and the nights long. Fire meant the difference between survival and death, between comfort and cold pain. It was the centre of activity, where everyone gathered to eat and cook, to sit and warm themselves, and listen to the stories of the bards. The Latin word for it was *focus*, since it is the focus of the home. We call our coven a hearth, because it is the spiritual nourishing place of its family of members.

Nowadays, most people do not have a big open fire where they cook and sit in the evenings. Many simply have an electric hob in the kitchen and central heating in the living room. This doesn't matter; remember that the hearth is a symbol for the hospitality and living spirit of the home. By connecting with the energies of the hearth, you can invite ancient magic into your life and learn to make your home a happier, more attractive place. Your home is your personal temple and this should not be overlooked; it is here that the magic begins. It doesn't matter whether you are living in a bed-sit in the middle of the city, or a pretty cottage in the countryside. The principle is the same. It is a refuge, a place of worship, the shrine of the sacred flame, and a celebration of life. You can use candles and oil lamps instead of a fire to symbolise the living flame and embody the light of spirit and the presence of Deity.

Consecrating Candles

Candles are anointed with essential or infused oil from a plant suitable to the purpose (see herbs) from the centre to the top and then the centre to the bottom with the words:

'Be to me the fire of moon,
Be to me the fire of night,
Be to me the fire of joy,
Turning darkness into light.
By the virgin waxing cold,
By the Mother full and bold,
By the Hag Queen, silent, old,
By the Moon, the One in Three,
Consecrated, Blessed Be.'

HOUSE SPIRITS

For the ancients, the hearth-place was also the altar of the household gods, where offerings could be made; when you being to think of your home as having indwelling spirit it can make a huge difference to the quality of life within it. You can use your mantelpiece as an altar, and many people do, or you can make a small shrine or niche beside it.   Every house has its own spirit, what we detect as an 'atmosphere' when we enter it. A witch should be aware of this spirit and make sure that it is honoured in the proper way. It was once the custom to make gifts to the spirit before entering a dwelling, offering it bread and salt. In bygone Rome this spirit was called the *Lar familiaris* ('household lar') and was given daily offerings of food and monthly gifts of garlands, all placed on the hearth shrine. The Lar protected the house and its wealth. Its presence was invoked on family occasions such as birthdays, weddings, births and deaths.

Legends of house spirits are found throughout the world, from the Hawaiian Menahune to the Scottish and northern English Brownie, the Spanish Duende, the German Hausmänner, the Russian Igosha, the Finnish Kodin-Haltia, and the North American Shvod and Cambodian Àràk.

The first thing that people did when they moved into a new house was to greet its resident spirit. For example, the Dĕduška ('Grandfather') is a Russian house fairy who appears as an old man covered in hair, often in the likeness of a family patriarch. He wears a red shirt, cloak and a red belt. He lives behind the oven or near the threshold of the house, in the cupboard, or in the stable, sometimes with his wife and children. He will protect the family, their home and their livestock from bad luck, keep the servants in order and do all kinds of chores about the place while everyone is sleeping. He is especially keen on spinning. To keep him happy he should be given something from each meal and white linen should be placed in his favourite room. The family that pleases its fairy will prosper in all things but the family that fails to do him honour or uses bad language in his presence will suffer his anger. He will revenge himself on the crops and cattle or leave the house altogether. The unprotected family will then fall ill and die.

To entice an alienated spirit home, the inhabitants must dress in their best clothes and go out in the evening and walk about their courtyard saying *"Děduška Domovoy come and live with us and tend our flocks"*. Salted bread is wrapped in white cloth and put in the hall or courtyard while the family bows to the four quarters, praising the fairy and asking him to forgive them and return.

Without a Děduška Domovoy a house is unprotected, so when a new home is built certain rituals must be performed to gain one. The first creature to cross the threshold is in some danger so a cat or cock is thrown inside. Some of the first bread baked in the house is broken and buried in the right hand corner of the attic with an invocation to a spirit to come and protect the place and obey a new master. The Děduška Domovoy is sometimes thought to be an incarnation of an ancestral spirit.

When a family moves house, they will make every effort to take their house fairy with them. At the old house an elderly woman will clean the cinders from the hearth into a pan which she covers with a cloth. She then opens all the windows and invites the fairy to leave this house and go to the new one. She takes the cinders to the new house where the master and mistress wait with bread and salt at the gate. They bow low, take the pan into the house, and empty the cinders into the new grate. The pan is broken and buried in a corner of the room.

There were very similar beliefs in Britain. Brownies are solitary fairies found in southern Scotland and the northern counties of England. They become attached to particular houses or families and while the humans are asleep, they work about the house or farm, cleaning, tidying up, or help with the brewing. When the cock crows it is to let the brownie know it is time to go to bed. The only reward they ask is a bowl of cream or best milk. They are very good at hiding and can make themselves disappear at will, but those who have seen them describe them as small, shaggy haired and ugly, with flat faces. They are often ragged in appearance, but they are offended by gifts of clothes and will promptly disappear forever if given a new suit, so if you have a helpful house fairy don't be tempted to reward it in this fashion. Brownies have a mischievous side and like to play tricks on humans, such as rattling the fire irons, smashing crockery, hiding objects, or making a mess. They are easily offended, and if they are mistreated they turn into destructive boggarts. House fairies often have a mischievous side and like to play tricks on the human inhabitants of a dwelling, particularly if they are not getting their due. Such pranks might include rattling the fire irons, smashing crockery, hiding objects, or just making a mess.

THE HEARTH GODDESS
The goddess of hearth and fire dwells within every hearth, whether large or small. In many ancient religions, a fire was kept constantly burning to represent the presence of the goddess. These would be put out and relit with great ceremony on special occasions.

Hestia
In Greek myth the hearth goddess is Hestia. She refused a throne on Olympus to look after the hearth, and never took part in the wars and arguments of the gods. Instead she was the calm centre, the safe haven of the home, where people could seek refuge and shelter. She was worshipped as that centre, whether the centre of the city, the house, even the centre of the world, the *omphalos* ('the navel') at Delphi. As the domestic hearth is the centre of the home, the hearth of the gods is the centre of the cosmos. According to Plato the twelve Olympian gods - who represent the twelve constellations of the zodiac - circle the House of Heaven, while Hestia remains at the centre, tending the hearth, which is called 'the Everlasting Place', the still heart of creation around which everything else revolves.

She is the gentlest and most principled of all the gods, and the hearth is both her altar and shrine. She represents security and the solemn duty of hospitality. She presided over all hearth and altar fires, and was worshipped every day with prayers before and after meals. Her hearth was in the care of the woman of the house and before each meal an offering thrown onto the fire. Each city had a public hearth dedicated to her, and in new cities the public hearth would be lit from that of another city; this ensured that every city had a living heart and spirit (which is something that new cities often seem to lack today).

Hestia was the first born of the Olympian deities and last to be released by her father Cronos (Father Time), who had swallowed all of his offspring to prevent them from usurping his throne. Thus it is said that she is both the beginning and the end- *alpha* and *omega*. Her name, according to Plato, means 'the essence of things'; a formless core symbolised by the flame, an essence that flows through everything that has life.

Vesta

Vesta is the virgin fire goddess of Rome, equivalent to the Greek Hestia. She refused a place in heaven, preferring to remain on Earth, tending the fires in homes and temples. She was worshipped in private households and every day, during a meal, a small cake was thrown on the fire for her; it was good luck if it burnt with a crackle. She was also worshipped in an important state cult, maintained in a sacred building on the Forum Romanum with a circular chamber housing an eternal flame that was never allowed to die out. It is said that the cult was founded by king Numa Pompilius (715-673 BCE) and the sacred fire burned until 394 CE. Vesta is usually depicted as an austere woman, wearing a long dress and with her head covered. In her left hand, she holds a sceptre. She represents shelter and the safety and security of life.

Vesta's temple was served by six chaste priestesses called the Vestal Virgins. When a position became vacant, the *Pontifex Maximus* ('high priest') would select a girl from candidates offered by the best Patrician families. She had to be between the age of six and ten, fair of face and without physical defect or blemish. The new priestess was then taken by the hand with the words *"I take you, you shall be the priestess of Vesta and you shall fulfil the sacred rites for the safety of the Roman people"*. Her hair would be cut, and then she would be dressed in bridal white, with a white fillet binding her hair and a white veil. During the period she was to serve as a Vestal, the priestess undertook to keep a vow of chastity. After thirty years, Vestals were able to leave and marry if they wished; their elevated positions and personal wealth ensured that they were much sought after as wives.

While in service the Vestal Virgins enjoyed enormous privileges: their person was sacred, they were free from the control of the *pater*, and they were allowed to own and dispose of property as they saw fit. They even had the prerogative of freeing criminals sentenced to death. When they went out, *fasces* were carried before them to symbolise their authority.

The Vestals' chief function was to tend the *ignis inextinctus* ('undying fire') and the priestess who neglected her duty was flogged. The Romans regarded hearth and home as sacrosanct, the foundation on which the stability of Roman society rested. The Hearth of Vesta symbolised the spirit and permanence of Rome itself: to offend against it was to bring bad luck to Rome. If the fire went out, it had to be rekindled in the ancient way, by the use of friction.

The cult of Vesta probably originated in tribal society when a fire was the central focus of the village. This may have been attended by women chosen as its priestesses, forerunners of the Vestal Virgins. Vesta symbolises the purity of fire, so it is appropriate that her priestesses should be virgins.

Brighid

Brighid is pan-Celtic goddess, appearing as Brighid or Brigit in Ireland, Brigantia in Northern England, Bride in Scotland, and Brigandu in Brittany. Her name is variously interpreted as meaning 'Fiery Arrow', 'The Bright One' and 'the Powerful One' or 'The High One'. She is a fire/dawn goddess born at sunrise when immediately a tower of flame emerged from her forehead that stretched from earth to heaven. She is the daughter of the Dagda ('good god') and the wife of Bres. Her face is either pied, half youthful and half crone, or half beautiful and half ugly.

Brighid is a triple goddess: the Brighid of poetry, prophecy and inspiration who invented Ogham; the Brighid of healing waters and midwifery; and lastly the Brighid of fire who oversees the hearth and the forge and who is the patroness of craftsmen and women. This triplication was represented by the Druidic sign of *awen* ('inspiration'), known as the fiery arrows of Brighid since it is represented by three shafts of sunlight. It was likely Brighid who inspired the line in the famous Song of Amergin: "*I am a fire in the head*". She also has aspects as a goddess of fertility, livestock and warfare.

Her festival is Imbolc (2nd February) also called *Oimelc* ('ewe's milk') which marked the first stirrings of spring when young sheep were born and when ewes came into milk. On this day, the first of the Celtic spring, she was said to use her white wand to "*breathe life into the mouth of the dead winter*" meaning the white fire of the sun awakened the land. In Christian times the festival became Candlemas, when church candles were blessed. Imbolc remained a popular occasion in Celtic areas and most of its customs are plainly Pagan. Brighid was invited into the home by the woman of the house in the form of a doll or corn dolly dressed in maiden white. Oracles were taken from the ashes of the hearth fire which people examined for a sign that Brighid had visited i.e. a mark that looked like a swan's footprint: if found, it was a lucky omen (the swan was an ancient attribute of the goddess Brighid). Many Irish homes still have a Brighid's cross hung up. This four equal-armed cross was originally a solar symbol.

The goddess's chief shrine was at Kildare (*Cull Dara* = 'Temple of the Oak') where a perpetual flame was kept burning behind a circular hedge of shrubs or thorns. It was tended by a college of nineteen virgin priestesses called Daughters of the Flame. Each day a different priestess was responsible for maintaining the flame from sundown till sundown. On the twentieth day, Brighid herself tended the flame. No man was allowed to enter the shrine or have contact with the priestesses; any male who did went mad. With the coming of Christianity, the priestesses became nuns of the abbey said to have been founded by 'Saint Brigit' and kept the flame burning for another thousand years, until the Vatican decreed it was merely a Pagan ritual and ordered it extinguished. During the Vatican modernisation program of the 1960's St. Brigit was decanonised.

Gabija

Gabija is the Lithuanian fire goddess and her cult has survived for thousands of years. She has been variously imagined as a cat, a bird and a winged woman dressed in red. Her name is derived from the verb *apgaubti*, which means 'to cover up' and refers to the practice of the mistress of the house vigilantly banking the fire at night so that it will neither go out, nor spread from the hearth.

Care was taken not to offend the goddess. The fire could only be extinguished with cold, clean water and people were not allowed to spit into it. When it was being lit, everyone had to remain silent. The goddess would be offered salt sprinkled on the fire (to make it crackle) with the words 'Sacred Gabija, be nourished' and a glass of clean water was placed on the hearth with the words 'Bathe and rest, Fiery One'.

She is attended only by women, particularly the head woman of the clan or house. She is invoked at all family rituals and occasions, since without her they would not be possible. She is also a mediator, carrying prayers to the other gods. Like Brighid, she had special festivals at the beginning of February dedicated to the renewal of the hearth fire and the household gods. During every Baltic festival a fire was lit in some form. An Eternal Flame once burned at Sventaragis Valley tended by priestesses known as *Vaidilutes*.

The fire was believed to be the connection with the world of the ancestors who continued to live in the hearth flame. A similar belief existed among the Celts who left offerings on the hearth for the departed spirits of the ancestors at Samhain.

Svasti

Svasti is the Hindu goddess of the home and its prosperity. Her symbol is the swastika, an emblem of the sun (similar to Brighid's equal armed cross) and also of the fire drill, two sticks which are rotated to create fire. Hindus believe that the cosmos was created by a similar twirling or churning method, when the gods and demons (i.e. two opposing forces or polarities acting together), churned the oceans to find *amrita*, the drink of immortality. The serpent Ananta ('Endless') uprooted the mountain Mandara and the gods took it to the ocean to churn the waters, using the serpent Vasuki as 'the cord'. First the constellations appeared and at last the physician of the gods bearing a bowl of *amrita*. The process of fire-lighting represents the act of creation, the generating of the divine spark of life and as a ritual act recreates the process of Cosmic Creation.

THE HEARTH AS COSMIC AXIS

As the dwelling place of the living goddess, the hearth was a holy place, a sacred centre, a threshold between this world and the realm of the gods. Its rising smoke took prayers to the gods of the Upperworld, while the gods of the Worlds Below could be contacted through the hearthstone.

The concept of the home being the centre of the every family's world, its navel connecting it to the Otherworld, is common. The Kogi Indians, for example, see the world in the form of a quartered circle, with other disc-like worlds both above and below. The circular ceremonial house of the Kogi has four fires, which represent this quartered earth. The conical roof symbolises the top half of the universe and, within its construction, contains symbols of the worlds above. A series of underworlds lies below the house. The Kogi priests, the Mamas, sit in the ceremonial house as though it were a womb, and they are at the foot of an umbilical cord which reaches down from the centre of the roof. [10] The Desana of South America drink hallucinogenic *yajé* and the house becomes a model of the universe, and the men's door the eastern entrance to the Earth we inhabit. Movement through the house becomes movement through the Cosmos. [11]

The Neolithic round-house with the fire at the centre, in the square hearth, the smoke escaping through the open roof, was also a representation of the cosmos- the walls of the hut were the circumference

---

10   http://www.indigogroup.co.uk/edge/ *The Cosmic Mill* Alby Stone

11   David Lewis Williams & David Pearce, *The Neolithic Mind*, Thames and Hudson Ltd, London, 2005

of the universe, the hearthstone was the earth, its four sides the four directions and the four seasons. The presence of the gods was manifested in the living fire, with the smoke ascending through the smoke-hole to the gods.[12] The belief that control of the cosmos and entry to its various realms can be gained by recreating it in miniature in a chosen spot is an ancient one, exemplified by the old Hermetic maxim 'as above, so below'. The creation of stone circles, temples, etc was an attempt to allow the priest, magician or shaman to manipulate the forces of the macrocosm by recreating it in the microcosm. According to Plato's *Laws*, the cosmic order is taken as the pattern for any temple or shrine.

In many tales, the hearth and chimney it is the entrance and egress of spirits. In lore, various fairies are said to live behind the hearth, or to come down the chimney. Remember the tales of Father Christmas? He originates in the stories of Siberian shamans whose spirits flew out through the smoke-hole of the hut to travel the Otherworld after they had taken the red and white fly agaric mushrooms, which give Santa his costume. [13]

FIRE MAGIC

We all have some kind of atavistic attraction to fire. Just watch a group of twenty-first century men at a barbecue - none of them will be able to resist poking it and giving the others their fire making tips like any caveman.

The discovery of fire was the most important advance of humankind. It transformed human existence; people could keep warm, cook their food, protect themselves and later use it to shape metals. It has been celebrated and used in festivals throughout the world and employed to encourage that big brother of all fire, the sun, with bonfires, rolling flaming wheels, torches and candles.

Fire is the most mysterious of all the elements. It seems almost supernatural in comparison to earth, air or water. In occult terms, fire

---

12   John Michell, *At the Centre of the World*, Thames and Hudson, London, 1994
13   The story that father Christmas wears red and white as the result of a Coca-Cola promotion is an urban myth, and it is more likely that, like the red caps of other fairies, his costume associates him with the fly agaric mushroom. Like the northern shaman, he enters the house via the smoke hole or chimney, or perhaps, like other fairies and spirits, his method of entrance and egress is via the hearth. It is usually claimed that he originated with St Nicholas, a fourth century bishop who saved three sisters from prostitution by leaving bags of gold in their stockings, which were hung up to dry. However, he has origins that are far more ancient. It is possible that he devolved from the Scandinavian/Germanic god Odin or Woden, who rode the skies at Yule wearing a red, bloody, flayed animal skin, punishing the wicked and rewarding the good. It seems likely that he passed into English folklore, traceable in the character that appears as master of ceremonies in the mumming plays, and as the King of Christmas.

rules creativity, life energy, the illumination within and the force of the spirit. Fire is the power of inner sight and creative vision, directing it and controlling it to make it manifest in the world, the dominion of Will. It is the glow of the candle flame, the warmth of the hearth, the burning heat of the desert, the incandescence of the sun: the fire that both purifies and destroys. Cattle were driven over the ashes of the Beltane and Samhain fires to purify them, and flaming torches were carried around the crops at Midsummer to protect them. It is an agent of transformation - the food in the cauldron is changed as it cooks, raw ores and metals are altered into useful objects on the blacksmith's forge, and it transforms the materials it consumes into ashes.

Once, a new bride and groom would be led to the hearth of their new home and the fire-irons put into their hands to symbolise their new status as mistress and master of the house. In the early days, making fire was difficult and involved time rubbing sticks together or trying to generate a spark with flint. For this reason, once lit the hearth fire was not allowed to go out and was kept burning all year round, banked up at night. It was unlucky if it did go out accidentally, and presaged ill for the household. In Ireland, the fire was kindled with invocations to Brighid and at night covered in a special way, with the embers divided into three equal sections with a peat laid between each section, each one touching a little mound in the middle. The first peat was laid down in the name of the God of Life, the second in the name of the God of Peace, and the third in the name of the God of Grace. The woman of the house then covered the circle with ashes, a process known as smooring, taking care not to put out the fire, in the name of the Three of Light. A protective prayer was then said over it.

Festival fires were often kindled in a special way, either by rubbing two selected woods together or by use of a lens. Sacred fires, such as that of Vesta, were kept burning all the time, except at certain times of year when they were put out and ceremonially re-lit. The Celts re-lit their hearth fires with brands called butterflies from the festival bonfire. The Beltane fire consisted of nine different woods.

On the Isle of Man it was deemed necessary to sweep the floor of the house on New Year's morning from the door towards the hearth, so that the good fortune of the family would be not swept away out of the door for the coming year. Although it was considered lucky to give and receive fuel for the fire, it was extremely unlucky to give kindling or light from your own fire to someone whose fire had gone out; in giving away your flame you were also giving away your blessing leaving yourself unprotected.

When moving to a new house it was often the custom to take live coals from the previous one to ensure the continuation of the life and spirit of the home and family. (You can repeat a similar custom by lighting a candle brought from your old home in the new one. This echoes the carrying of Hestia's sacred fire to new colonies and towns.)

OMENS FROM THE FLAMES

Various kinds of omens may be read from fire. We often gaze into the fire and see pictures there, and this is a very ancient form of divination. Dion Fortune wrote of the *Fire of Azrael* made from sandalwood, cedar and juniper logs used for the purposes of divination.[14]

Because the fire was so important, portents were often taken from the behaviour of the flames, a practice called pyromancy. For example, when a fire burns all on one side, or falls into two heaps in the grate, it foretells a parting of some kind. If it will not start in the morning it predicts quarrels in the house, and arguments are also presaged by a spluttering piece of coal. A coffin-shaped piece of coal flying out of the fire and into the room foreshadows a death, whereas a cradle-shaped piece means a birth. A cluster of bright sparks at the back of the chimney means good news on the way, and dull sparks mean bad news. Showers of gold sparks indicate money and blue flames in the fire indicate coming frosts.

WOODS FOR BURNING

I have a wood burning stove that heats my whole house in winter, and getting enough fuel to keep it going is a year-long quest. However, not all wood is equal, and some is hardly worth the effort of storing and burning. An old rhyme lists the burning potential of the various woods:

Logs to burn! Logs to burn!
Logs to save the coal a turn!
Here's a word to make you wise
When you hear the woodman's cries.

Beechwood fires burn bright and clear,
Hornbeam blazes too,
If the logs are kept a year
To season through and through.

Oak logs will warm you well,
That are old and dry
Logs of pine will sweetly smell
But the sparks will fly

Birch logs will burn too fast
Alder scarce at all,
Chestnut logs are good to last
If cut in the fall.

14   Dion Fortune, *The Sea Priestess*, Aquarian Press, London, 1972

Holly logs will burn like wax
You may burn them green,
Elm logs like to smouldering flax
No flame to be seen.

Pear logs and apple logs
They will scent your room,
Cherry logs across the dogs
Smell like flower of broom.

Beech logs for the winter time
Yew logs as well,
Green elder logs it is a crime
For any man to sell.

Ash logs, smooth and grey
Burn them green or old,
Buy up all that come your way
They're worth their weight in gold!

THE TOOLS

The Hearth Witch has no need of numerous swords and different coloured knifes. A knife *is* useful, but it doesn't matter what colour the handle is. It can cut, be used for ritual and any useful thing you need to do. I have a silver herb knife made from a sharpened silver fish knife, which I use to cut plants without earthing their power as iron or steel does. We use a cauldron, which is basically a cooking pot, a vessel of transformation that changes one thing to another it bubbles, whether this is food or herbal cures and potions. It represents the womb of Mother Nature which transforms whatever it contains, sprouting the seed and giving new life to the dead. A pestle and mortar is useful for grinding spices and making incenses. Male witches often carry a stang or forked stick to represent the God, or a stout blackthorn walking stick, which can also be used for magic.

Chapter 3
KITCHEN WITCHERY

Food is one of the most basic necessities of life. Food *is* life, a gift of Mother Earth, and we acknowledge that gift only when we treat it with reverence. Preparing, cooking and serving food is daily ritual of hospitality, love and sharing, and expresses the cycle of the seasons when fresh, seasonal food is used.

Food has always played a vital part in the worship of the gods. Its production was one of the central themes of ancient Pagan religions. Mysteriously, a small seed planted in the dark earth would shoot and grow into something that could provide a sustaining meal. It was as though by placing it in the womb of Mother Earth she would nourish and sustain it, magically transforming it, just as a woman nurtures the seed in her womb to produce a child.

Corn was often seen as a god who awakens in the spring, matures in the summer and dies in the autumn with the harvest. As he dies, he sheds his seed which is replanted in the belly of Earth Mother, ready to shoot again in the spring- an eternal cycle of life, death and rebirth. Myths of such dying or sacrificed vegetation gods are common throughout the world. They are always born of a virgin mother (the all-powerful Goddess who needs no outside agency to give life) and killed by the Goddess as harvest mother herself, or sacrificed on or in a tree.

Because of the importance of this myth cycle, bread made from the corn [15] came to symbolise all other food within ritual. Eating bread and drinking wine was an important part of the rites of harvest goddesses and vegetation gods. An ear of corn was the central mystery of Eleusis in the worship of Demeter, and bread was eaten in the rites of Artemis and Cybele (and other earth and moon goddesses), often baked in circles and marked with a cross, representing the four solar festivals of the equinoxes and solstices, and the four phases of the moon (waxing, full, waning and dark moon), and the four phases of the moon goddess- maiden,

---

15   A generic word for cereals crops in Europe, not just maize as in the USA, which the settlers called Indian corn.

mother, crowned one and crone. This is still seen today in our hot crossed buns, eaten at Easter, which was once the springtime observance of the resurrection of the vegetation god.

Cakes and Wine

The dedication of the cakes and wine is one of the central points of any Craft ritual. It is the partaking of the sacrificed God of the Corn and the body of the Goddess as Mother Earth, from whom all life stems, recalling that we owe our Divine Parents for our lives and sustenance. The custom is far more ancient than Christianity.

All plants which had the ability to change consciousness were considered sacred, but wine is more palatable than most and the vine grows in a spiral pattern, a very ancient symbol of immortality. Wine was thought to feed not the body but the spirit with the divine inspiration of the god, freeing the imbiber from mundane thoughts and conventions, altering levels of consciousness, and awakening the powers of the primal self within.

When bread and wine are consecrated they become the food of the spirit. Eating a thing imparts something of its essence to the consumer, and during the ceremony of bread and wine we absorb the spirit of the God and Goddess. Bread represents the earth and wine the heavens, bread the solid, wine the liquid, bread the body and wine the blood, and the taking of the two together signifies the union of opposites.

The Making of the Cakes

Traditionally these are made from meal, salt, honey and wine and are shaped as crescent moons. I use different ingredients at the various festivals and esbats and some of my recipes follow. They are put to bake with the words:

> *"Let the cakes be baked in the name of the Goddess for now is the time of the…feast, when the secret worshippers meet once more. Before the Goddess we shall drain the cup. Before the Goddess we shall serve the secret rites. Before the Goddess we shall feast and rejoice. In the holy name of the God and in the holy name of the Goddess."*

The Wine

The wine should preferably be home made (recipes below) and is placed on the altar with the words:

> *"Let the wine be made ready in the name of the God and in the name of the*

Goddess. Let it be placed on the altar beneath the sign of the pentagram that the worshippers shall drink of it. Before the God and the Goddess we shall consume and be consumed by the wine of wisdom and blessing. Before the Lord and Lady we shall consume the cakes and wine. Before the God and the Goddess."

SEASONAL FEASTS

In addition to sharing the cakes and wine, it is the custom to feast at the Eight Festivals and other ritual occasions of the Craft year. In the past people were acutely aware of the passing of the seasons and what each had to offer in terms of foods and herbs. Humankind was bound to the Wheel of the Year, which determined times for planting, times for weeding, times to gather seeds and times for harvest. During the summer and autumn a variety of plentiful food would be available, but during the winter there would only be stored produce. In the months that were counted as early spring (the end of January and February) even stored produce- unless the harvest had been particularly good- would have been largely consumed, and only the return of spring and the greening of the land could save the population from starvation.

In a time when food is always available in the shops we tend to forget the importance of the agricultural and pastoral year which was everything to our ancestors. The festivals of the Craft attempt to make us more aware of the natural cycles and our part in them. In our seasonal celebrations, and in our feasts, we try to honour and reflect these magical connections of herbs and plants with the seasons.

Whether you are cooking for a festival or just for supper, treat it as a conscious act of magic and reflect that when you eat, you take in the life energy of the food you are eating, not just its vitamins and minerals.

Kitchen Protection

To keep your home and family safe and happy, take a sprig of each of the following herbs:

Sage for wisdom
Rosemary for remembrance
Lemon Balm for joy
St John's wort for protection
Lavender for peace

Tie the herbs with a red thread, making sure that some herbs are tied one way, and some the other, so that you are left with a bunch with herbs sticking out both sides, instead of one end herbs, the other stalks. As you tie them say:

> I tie this sage for wisdom, to know what is truly important
> I tie this rosemary for remembrance, so that I might never forget it
> I tie this lemon Balm for joy, that I might celebrate it
> I tie this St John's wort to protect it
> And I tie this lavender to keep it in peace and harmony

Fresh Herbs

Grow a row of fresh herbs on the windowsill to use in cooking, and also to bring positive green energy into the kitchen.

SEASONAL FOOD

Think about where the ingredients come from, what they contain, and buy local foods in season if you can; it will help you to harmonise with the Wheel of the Year. Here are some traditional seasonal recipes for the Eight Festivals:

IMBOLC 1st February

Elizabethan Curds

8 oz curd cheese
½ tsp powdered cinnamon
Pinch grated nutmeg
1 tbsp rosewater
2 tsp sugar
Beat the ingredients together. Serve with cream.

Cheese Spread

8 oz cream cheese
2 oz dried dates, stoned and chopped
1 oz chopped walnuts
Small handful fresh parsley, chopped
Small handful fresh chives, chopped
2 oz sunflower seeds
Pinch of salt

Combine all the ingredients, except the sunflower seeds and shape into a ball. Roll in the sunflower seeds and chill for a couple of hours before serving.

Oatcakes

4 oz medium oatmeal
1 tsp butter
½ tsp salt
½ tsp bicarbonate of soda
Hot water
Mix the oatmeal, soda and salt. Make a well in the centre and pour in the melted fat and enough hot water to make soft dough. Turn onto a surface dusted with oatmeal and form into a smooth ball. Knead and roll out thinly. Cut into 8 pieces and put on a baking sheet.

Bake at 350 F/ 180 C/ gas mark 4 until the edges curl. The oatcakes should be toasted under the grill just prior to eating.

Potato Bread

8 oz potatoes, boiled and sieved
½ pt water the potatoes were boiled in
1 ½ lb wholemeal flour
2 tsp sugar
3 tsp salt
1 oz fresh yeast
Mix the potatoes, potato water, sugar and butter. Cool to lukewarm and crumble in the yeast. Leave in a warm place 10 minutes. Add the flour and salt gradually, mixing with your hands. Knead until smooth and not sticky. Cover and leave in a warm place until doubled in size. Knead again and divide in two. Place in two loaf tins, leave in a warm place to rise again. Bake at 450F/ 230 C/gas mark 8 for 15 minutes. Reduce the heat to 375 F/ 190 C/ gas mark 5 for 35-45 minutes until brown and hollow sounding when tapped.

Winter Soup

1 small white cabbage
1 onion
1 leek
1 oz butter
1 pint milk
1 oz quick-cook rice
Seasoning to taste
2 pints water

Croutons
Shred the cabbage and put into some salted boiling water for 10 minutes. Melt the butter and add the chopped onion and leek. Cook for 5 minutes over a low heat. Add the cabbage and cook for a further 5 minutes. Add the water, bring to the boil, reduce the heat and simmer 20 minutes. Season to taste. Add the milk and rice, and cook 15 minutes. Serve with croutons or squares of toast.

Leek and Potato Savoury

1 lb potatoes
2 leeks
1 oz butter
Parsley sauce
Parsley
Seasoning to taste
2 oz cheddar cheese
Cut the peeled potatoes into pieces and boil until tender. Melt the butter in a pan and gently fry the chopped leeks. Combine the leeks and potatoes in the sauce, with the fresh chopped parsley. Sprinkle the grated cheese over the top and melt under a hot grill.

Imbolc Pottage

½ cup lentils
1 ½ pt water
1-2 bay leaves
1 cup grated sheep's cheese
1-2 cloves, ground
Grated nutmeg
Pinch powdered mace

39

1 oz ground almonds

Fresh ground pepper

Rinse the lentils in fresh water and place in a pan with the water, bay leaves, salt and pepper.

Simmer gently until the lentils soften. Add the sheep's cheese and spices. Continue to cook until the pottage begins to thicken. Stir in the almonds and serve.

Brighid Cakes

1 lb. plain flour

4 oz margarine

4 oz sugar

2 oz chopped candied peel

¾ pt milk

Pinch of salt

1 tsp. bicarbonate of soda

1 tsp. cream of tartar

4 oz sultanas

Sieve the flour and salt, cream of tartar and bicarbonate of soda into a bowl. Rub in the margarine, then add the sugar, peel and sultana. Add the milk and knead into a dough. Place in a greased 7" tin and bake at 200ºC/400ºF/gas mark 6 for 60 minutes. Turn the oven down to 180ºC/350ºF/gas mark 4 and bake for another 30 minutes. Turn out and cut into smaller pieces to serve.

Farls

4 oz medium oatmeal

¼ level tsp salt

Pinch baking powder

½ oz butter

3 tbsp hot water

Mix the dry ingredients together. Melt the butter and pour this over the dry ingredients, then mix with enough hot water to make stiff dough. Knead the dough on a board sprinkled with oatmeal. Roll out into a 7 inch circle. Cut into 4 pieces. Cook on a hot, greased frying pan for 5 minutes a side.

OSTARA around 21st March

Egg Mornay

6 hard boiled eggs

1 tbsp mixed herbs

8 oz mild cheddar cheese

Pinch black pepper

2 tsp salt

¾ pint white sauce

Shell the eggs, cut them in half lengthways and remove the yolks. Put the yolks into a bowl with the sauce, herbs, salt and pepper and mix them together well. Fill the egg whites with the mixture. Grease an oven proof dish, put a thin layer of sauce on the bottom, and put the stuffed eggs onto it. Cover with the rest of the sauce and grated cheese. Bake at 180ºC/350ºF/gas mark 4 for 15-20 minutes.

Leek & Cheese Pie

8 leeks

4 carrots

Margarine

6 oz rolled oats

8 oz grated cheese

Wash and chop the vegetables.

Cook them in water until soft. Grease a deep dish and sprinkle the bottom of the dish with rolled oats. Add a layer of vegetables then a layer of grated cheese and continue to build up the layers in this manner until the dish is full finishing with a mixed layer of cheese and oats. Carefully pour six fluid ounces of the vegetable water or stock over the top and bake in a hot oven at 200°C/400°F/gas mark 6 for 30 minutes.

Figgy Pudding

This was traditionally served during Lent.
5 oz flour
3 oz vegetable suet
4 oz dried figs or dates
½ tsp cinnamon
½ tsp ginger
1 tsp bicarbonate of soda
Pinch grated nutmeg
2 tbsp golden syrup
1 large egg, beaten
4 tbsp crème freche
Mix the dry ingredients. Warm the golden syrup and stir in the beaten egg and crème freche. Add this to the dry ingredients and stir. Spoon into a greased pudding basin and put a round of greaseproof paper on the top. Steam for 2 hours.

Lenten Pie

1 lb puff pastry
6 eggs, hard-boiled and chopped
6 apples, peeled and cored
4 oz raisins
1 oz candied peel
2 cloves, crushed
Pinch ginger
Pinch nutmeg
Pinch salt
1 tbsp brandy
1 tbsp white wine
Juice of an orange
Milk to glaze
Mix the eggs, apples, fruit and spices, add the brandy and wine. Line a pie dish with the pastry and spoon in the mixture, pouring the orange juice over it. Fit a pastry lid, brush with milk and bake at 200C/400 F or gas mark 6 for 50-60 minutes or until golden brown.

Hot Cross Buns

1 ½ lb. plain flour
Pinch salt
2 tsp. mixed spice
2 oz butter
½ oz fresh yeast/ 1 sachet dried yeast
½ pint warm water
1 oz caster sugar
2 oz currants
2 oz mixed peel
1 egg, beaten
To make the crosses:
3 oz plain flour
4 tbs. water
For the glaze:
2 tbs. caster sugar
1 tbs. milk
Sift the flour, salt and spice into a bowl. Stir the started yeast into a well made in the flour mixture.

Add the dry ingredients and the egg. Knead well on a floured board. Return to the bowl and cover with a clean cloth and leave in a warm place to rise for around an hour. Knead lightly again. Divide into 16 pieces and roll each piece into a ball. Flatten with your hand. Place on a baking tray and cover with a cloth and leave to prove for 30 minutes. To make the crosses mix the flour and water to make a paste. Place in a piping bag and pipe a cross onto each of the risen buns. Bake the buns at 220°C/425°F/gas mark 7 for 15 to 20 minutes. Meanwhile make the glaze by dissolving the sugar in the milk. Bring to the boil and remove from the heat. Brush the buns with the glaze as soon as they come out of the oven. *These are traditionally eaten on Good Friday, but cakes marked this way are pre-Christian, the cross on the round bun representing the quartered circle, the four directions and solar increase.*

Simnel Cake

4 oz butter
4 oz brown sugar
5 oz plain flour
1 oz ground almonds
3 eggs
6 oz currants
4 oz raisins
Grated rind and juice of ½ lemon
½ tsp. mixed spice
½ tsp. baking powder
6 oz marzipan

Cream the butter and sugar and gradually add the beaten eggs. Fold in the flour, almonds, spice and baking powder. Stir in the lemon juice and rind and the dried fruits. Grease and line an 8" cake tin and spoon in half the mixture. Smooth down and put in a layer of rolled out marzipan. Add the rest of the cake mixture and bake at 180°C/350°F/gas mark 4 for 2 hours. Decorate the top with 13 marzipan balls. *This is a traditional Easter cake, the 13 decorations of the top supposedly representing Jesus and the twelve apostles, but actually a much older representation of the 13 lunar months of the year.*

18th Century Pancakes

4 oz flour
Pinch salt
2 eggs
7 tbsp milk
3 tbsp cream
1 tsp sugar
Pinch nutmeg
1 tbsp brandy
Oil for cooking
Sift together the flour and salt. Make a well in the centre and break the eggs into this well.. Combine the milk and cream. Add half of this into the well with the egg. Beat together until smooth. In a separate bowl, combine the remaining milk and cream with the sugar, nutmeg and brandy. Beat until smooth. Combine the two mixtures, once

again beating until smooth. Cover the bowl and allow the mixture to rest for 30 minutes. Put just enough oil in the pan to coat thinly and heat until very hot. Drop in spoonfuls of the mixture and fry until cooked, turning once (this takes only around 30 seconds a side). In England, the traditional accompaniment is a generous sprinkling of lemon juice and sugar, but if you like you could serve the pancakes with cooked fruit, fresh or dried fruit and cream.

Festival Biscuits

4 oz butter
3 oz brown sugar
1 egg, separated
7 oz plain flour
1 tsp mixed spice
2 oz currents
½ oz candied peel
2 tbsp milk
White sugar for sprinkling
Cream butter and sugar; add egg yolk then gradually the sifted flour and spices. Add the fruit and peel, and finally the milk. Use your hands to pull it together into soft dough. Roll out on a floured board to ¼ inch thick. Cut out with pastry cutters, and place on a baking sheet and brush with the egg white to glaze. Bake at 200C/ 400 F/ gas mark 6 for 10 minutes. Take out and sprinkle with sugar and return to the oven for 10 minutes until brown.

Egg Caudle

1 pt tea
½ pint sherry
2 egg yolks
1 oz sugar
Pinch grated nutmeg
Heat everything gently in a pan, do not boil. Serve hot.

BELTANE I st May

Beltane Pottage

1 tbsp split peas
1 tbsp lentils
1 tbsp pearl barley
2 pt water
1 leek
½ cup chopped cabbage
3 tbsp chopped mixed fresh herbs of your choice
Salt and pepper
Soak the pulses and barley overnight in some water. Next day, add fresh water and boil and boil for 30 minutes. Discard this water. Add 2 pints of fresh water and simmer until tender.
Meanwhile, finely chop the herbs and vegetables. Add them to the pulses with some pepper and salt. Cook until the vegetables are tender.

Pottage was a traditional meal made by people in Britain for hundreds of years. It was a popular breakfast dish throughout the seventeenth century and was the main food given to the poor in workhouses - the gruel referred to in Dickens' Oliver Twist was probably pottage. The word

*pottage is probably derived from the
Latin* porrum, *meaning 'a leek' and
this became* 'porray' *in Middle English
and later the word became pottage and its
meaning was extended to any thick, green
broth.*

Clipping Pudding

8 oz short grain rice
1 pt milk
½ tsp powdered cinnamon
3 tbsp sugar
1 egg, beaten
4 oz currants
4 oz raisins/sultanas
1 tbsp butter
Grated nutmeg
Wash rice in cold water put it in a
pan with the milk, cinnamon and
sugar. Simmer gently until the rice
is tender. Stir in the egg, dried fruit
and butter. Pour into an ovenproof
dish and sprinkle with nutmeg to
taste. Bake at 350F/ 180 C/ gas
mark 4 for around 20 minutes or
until a skin has formed on top.

Brac

Brac is a Celtic word for bread.
12 oz mixed currents, raisins and
sultanas
6 oz Demerara sugar
½ pint cold tea
1 egg, beaten
12 oz self raising flour, sifted
Soak the dried fruit in the tea overnight.
Add the egg and flour. Mix and spoon
into a greased loaf tin and bake for 90
minutes at 180 C/ 350 F/ gas mark 4.

St George's Wine

6 pints dandelion flower heads
3 lb. sugar
2 lemons
1 orange
1 lb. raisins
1 cup of black tea
1 gallon water
Yeast and nutrient
Gather the flowers when you are
ready to use them fresh. Boil the
water and pour over the flowers,
stand for 2 days, stirring daily.
Boil with the sugar and citrus fruit
rinds for 60 minutes. Put it back
in the bin and add the citrus fruit
juice. Cool to lukewarm, add the
tea, yeast and nutrient. Cover the
bin and leave in a warm place for
3 days, stirring daily. Strain into a
demi-jon and add the raisins. Fit an
airlock. The flavour of this wine is
much improved with keeping, and
it should not be drunk for at least
a year.

Hawthorn Liqueur

Fill a jar with hawthorn flowers and
an ounce or two of sugar. Fill with
brandy and leave for three months
in the airing cupboard. Strain into a
clean bottle.

May Cup

Handful woodruff flowers
1 pint cider
1 pint mead
Place all the ingredients together in
a jug and leave for 2 hours. Strain

and serve.

This is an old British alternative to the German Mai Bowl.

COAMHAIN around June 21st

Herb Soup

2 pt stock
10 chopped spring onions
1 cup chopped celery
1 cup chopped spinach
½ cup shredded lettuce
2 tbsp chopped sorrel
4 tbsp chopped mixed herbs (choose from: chervil, borage leaves, violet leaves, rosemary, parsley, sage, thyme, mint, fennel, basil, or your own favourites). Put the spring onions and celery in a pan. Add the stock and simmer for 10 minutes. Add the herbs, spinach and lettuce. Simmer a further 5 minutes. Season to taste.

Herb Tart

For the pastry:
4 oz flour
2 oz butter or margarine
Pinch salt
Enough cold water to bind
For the filling:
1 tbsp olive oil
1 small onion
2 tbsp chopped parsley
3 tbsp mixed fresh herbs (whatever you have available)
3 eggs
½ pt cream
Pinch nutmeg

Salt and pepper

Sift the flour and salt into a bowl. With your fingertips, lightly rub in the shortening until the mixture resembles fine breadcrumbs. Add just enough cold water to bind the ingredients together. Cover and refrigerate for 20 minutes. Roll out the pastry and line a quiche dish. Prick all over with a fork to keep the pastry flat whilst cooking. Bake blind for 15 minutes. Meanwhile, heat the oil and fry the chopped onion until transparent. Add the herbs and remove from the heat. In a bowl, beat the eggs, cream, nutmeg, salt and pepper together. Add the onion and herbs and mix together thoroughly. Pour this mixture into the hot tart pastry case and bake until the filling is set (around 30 minutes) at gas mark 4, 350 F, 180 C.

New Potatoes

1 lb new potatoes
1 onion
2 oz butter
4 tbsp plain yoghurt
Fresh, chopped parsley
Seasoning to taste
Cook the potatoes till tender in boiling, salted water. Chop the onion and fry gently in butter 5 minutes. Add the potatoes and toss with the onion until golden. Stir in the yoghurt and garnish with parsley before serving.

Summer Salad

1 lettuce
1 cucumber
¼ lb peas
Salt and pepper to taste
1 tbsp vinegar
½ tsp sugar
2 tbsp plain yoghurt
2 tbsp walnut oil

Cook the peas and toss in a little walnut oil. Cut the cucumber into fingers. Shred the lettuce. To make the dressing, put the sugar, salt and pepper in a bowl. Add the vinegar and mix well until the sugar has dissolved. Add the cream and oil. Arrange the salad and pour the dressing over.

Elderflower Fritters

8 heads of elderflowers
2 egg whites
¼ lb. cornflour
Water
Sugar

Mix the cornflour with a little cold water to form a thin paste. In a separate bowl, whisk the egg whites until fairly stiff. Add a little sugar and continue to whisk for a further minute. Carefully fold the egg whites into the cornflour paste to make a light frothy batter. Dip the elderflower heads into this batter and fry them until golden brown. Whilst still hot, roll the fritters in sugar and serve immediately.

Elderflower Milk Jelly

½ pint milk
1 tbsp elderflowers
1 tbsp honey
1 tsp powdered agar
1 tbsp cream
Pinch nutmeg

Heat the milk and add the elderflowers. Turn off the heat and leave for 20 minutes. Strain off the milk and return it to a pan with the honey and reheat, stirring continually. Mix the agar with the water and add to the milk, simmer 5 minutes. Take of the hob and add the cream. Pour into a mould and refrigerate to set. Sprinkle the grated nutmeg on the top.

Apricot Wine

4 lb apricots
1 gallon water
1 lb raisins
1 lb wheat
1 oz yeast

cover the apricots with cold water. Mash and stir. Leave for 10 days, stirring daily. Add the chopped raisins, sugar, wheat and yeast, sprinkled over the top. Ferment on the pulp for 21 days, and strain into a demi-jon until fermented out. Bottle.

Cheese & Thyme Bread

1 ½ lb wholemeal flour
1 tsp salt
1 oz fresh yeast
1 tsp honey

1 tsp sugar
1 oz Soya flour
½ pt warm water
1 tbsp sunflower oil
1 oz grated cheddar
2 tsp dried thyme or 4 tsp fresh thyme

Sieve the flour and salt into a bowl. Mix the yeast, honey, sugar and Soya flour. Add ¼ pint warm water and mix until the yeast has dissolved. Leave in a warm place for 20 minutes to activate- it will get frothy. Pour the yeast mixture into the flour, add the rest of the water and the oil and stir to form dough. Knead until smooth. Put in a bowl and cover with a cloth, leave in a warm place until doubled in size. Add the cheese and thyme and knead in. shape into loaves, or put in a bread tin, cover and leave to rise again in a warm place. Bake 35-45 minutes at 220C/ 425 F/ gas mark 7.

LUGHNASA 1ˢᵗ August

Apple Soup

2 pints vegetable stock
8 oz Bramley apples
½ level tsp curry powder
½ level tsp ginger powder
½ level tsp garam marsala
Croutons

Peel, core and chop the apples. Put them in a pan with the boiling stock and simmer for 15 minutes. Put through the blender or sieve, and then add the spices. Return to the pan and bring to the boil. Simmer 5 minutes and serve with croutons.

Sussex Potato Cakes

12 oz mashed potato
1 oz butter
2 oz cheese, grated
2 oz / 50 g plain white flour
1 level tsp dry mustard
1 egg, beaten

Put everything in a bowl and mix together until smooth. Heat a greased frying pan, drop spoonfuls of the mixture onto the griddle flatten slightly and cook, turning once. Cook 5 minutes a side or until brown.

Plaited Loaf

1 ½ tbs. sugar
½ oz yeast
6 fl oz milk
1 lb. plain strong flour
Pinch salt
3 eggs, beaten
For glaze:
1 egg beaten
Poppy seeds

Start the yeast with a little sugar and

47

the slightly warmed milk. Sift the flour and salt into a bowl. When the yeast is frothy add it to the bowl with the eggs and sugar. Mix to a smooth dough. Cover and leave in a warm place for an hour to double in size. Knead until smooth, divide into three strands and plait together. Place on a baking tray, cover and leave to prove for another 40 minutes. Brush with egg and sprinkle on the poppy seeds. Bake at 220°C/425°F/gas mark 7 for 15 minutes. Reduce the temperature to 190°C/375°F/gas mark 5 and bake for another 25 minutes.

Colcannon

1 lb cabbage or kale, chopped finely
7 fl oz milk or cream
2 small leeks, chopped
2 lb. potatoes, diced
Salt, black pepper and ground nutmeg to season
4 tbsp melted butter
Cook the cabbage or kale in a pan of boiling water until it is tender. Drain and keep warm. Heat the milk or cream with the leeks and gently simmer until soft. Boil the potatoes until tender then drain and mash them. Mix in the other cooked ingredients and season with salt pepper and nutmeg. Drizzle the melted butter over the top and serve. Should serve 4.

Courgette Casserole

1 lb courgettes
1 lb tomatoes
6 slices white bread, cut into cubes
2 oz butter
6 oz strong cheese
Fresh herbs- basil, oregano or parsley
Seasoning to taste
Slice the courgettes thinly. Skin the tomatoes (plunge them into boiling water for a second or two and the skins will come off easily) and slice thinly. Melt the butter and pour over the bread. Grease a pie dish and then start to layer up the courgettes, tomatoes, herbs, bread and sprinklings of cheese, seasoning as you go. Finish with a layer of bread. Bake at 375 F/ 190 c/ gas mark 5 for 1 hour.

Lammas Wool

4 large cooking apples
Honey
Nutmeg
4 pt of ale
Core the apples and fill the centres with honey. Sprinkle with nutmeg and bake in the oven for 40 minutes in a deep baking tin. Remove from the oven and pour the ale over the apples. Heat gently on the hob for a few minutes, spooning the ale over the apples. Strain off the liquid and serve warm. The apples can be served separately.
The apple harvest begins at Lughnasa. Lamb's Wool or Lammas wool (from the Gaelic La Mas Nbhal *or 'feast of the apple gathering)' is a hot spiced drink of cider and ale, with toast or pieces of*

apple floating in it. Each person takes out a piece and wishes good luck to everyone, before eating it and passing the cup on.

Cambridge Ale Cup

2 pts water
6 cloves
2 cinnamon sticks
Pinch grated nutmeg
1 oz sugar
Juice and grated rind of a lemon
2 pts beer
½ pt sherry
Slice of white bread toast

Simmer the water and spices for 20 minutes. Add the sugar, lemon, beer and sherry and heat through but do not boil. Pour into a heat proof punch bowl and float small pieces of toast on top.

Blackcurrant Wine

1 gallon blackcurrants
1 gallon water
4 lb sugar
1 oz fresh yeast
2 slices toast

Put the currants and water together and bring slowly to the boil. Simmer 20 minutes, strain. Put the sugar and 1 slice of toast into a bowl. Pour the boiling liquid over. Stir until the sugar has dissolved. When cooled to 20 C (lukewarm) add the yeast spread on the remainder of the toast. Ferment on the fruit for 14 days. Strain into a demi-jon until it has fermented out. Bottle. Improves with keeping.

HERFEST around 21st September

Wholemeal Loaf

3 lb. wholemeal flour
1 tsp. salt
1 oz fresh yeast
1 ½ pt. warm water
Method

Mix together the flour and salt and rub in the butter. Start off the yeast. Add to the flour mixture and stir in the water to make a dough. Knead well and return to the bowl. Cover with a clean cloth and leave in a warm place for 2 hours. Knead again, divide into 4 pieces and place in greased 1 lb. loaf tins. Cover again and prove for 30 minutes. Bake at 220°C/425°F/gas mark 7 for 30-40 minutes.

Hazelnut Tart

8 oz wholemeal pastry
1 onion
1 oz butter or margarine
3 oz ground hazels

49

2 eggs, beaten
¼ pt stock
1 tsp. Marmite
1 tbs. fresh sage, chopped
Salt and pepper
Line a flan dish with the pastry.
Cook the finely chopped onion
in the butter and add the other
ingredients. Pour into the pastry
case and bake in a moderate oven
at 350°F/180°C/gas mark 4 for 40
minutes.

Herfest Cakes
6 oz ground hazel nuts
2 fl oz honey
1 oz flour
1 tbs. grated lemon peel
1 beaten egg
1 tbsp. lemon juice
Blend the honey and ground nuts
into a paste. Mix in the flour and
lemon peel. Blend the lemon juice
and egg together and add to the
mixture. Drop small amounts onto
a greased baking tray and bake at
180°C/350°F/gas mark 4 for 20
minutes.

Country Bake
1 lb potatoes, boiled and sliced
4 oz mushrooms, sliced and fried in
butter
4 oz peas, cooked
4 hard boiled eggs, sliced
¼ pint milk
6 oz grated cheddar cheese
1 oz butter
Pinch grated nutmeg

Salt and pepper
Grease a pie dish. Add the
potatoes, mushrooms, peas and
eggs in layers. Pour the milk over,
top with grated cheese and bake at
400 FR/ 200 C/ gas mark 6 for 30
minutes.

Tattie Drottle
1 ½ lb potatoes, peeled and finely
chopped
½ lb turnips
½ lb swede
8 oz carrots
4 oz onions
2 pt stock
1 pt milk
Chopped parsley
Salt and pepper
Peel and finely chop all vegetables.
Put them in a large pan with the
stock and season to taste. Simmer
for one hour. Remove from the
heat, cool slightly Blend until
smooth. Return to the pan and
bring to the boil. Serve sprinkled
with a little fresh, chopped parsley.

Mushroom Pie
1 lb shortcrust pastry
1 ½ lb mushrooms, sliced
2 potatoes, cooked
1 stick celery, chopped
2 onions, sliced
½ pint vegetable stock
2 oz butter
1 oz cornflour
1 tsp Marmite

1 bay leaf
Pinch thyme
Seasoning to taste
Melt 1 oz butter in a pan, and use
it to fry the mushrooms, onions,
celery and bay leaf over a low heat
for 5 minutes. Strain any juice off
and retain this. Melt the other 1 oz
butter in a pan, add the cornflour
and then gradually the stock,
seasoning, yeast extract and thyme
to make a sauce. Add the vegetables
and mix. Allow to cool. Roll out the
pastry to cover the base of a pie
dish. Spoon in the mixture. Cover
with a pastry crust and brush with
milk to glaze. Bake at 425 F/ 220
C/ gas mark 7 for 30 minutes.

Apple Pudding
12 oz self raising flour
6 oz butter
Milk
1 lb. cooking apples, peeled sliced
and cored
5 oz sugar
Rub the flour and butter together.
Add 4 oz of sugar and mix in
enough milk to form a soft dough.
Lightly roll out to slightly more
than ½ inch thick in a circular
shape. Place on a greased baking
tray. Pile the apples in the centre
and sprinkle the remaining sugar
over them, then bring up the sides
of the dough and seal the edges
together with a little water. Bake in
a moderate oven at 350°F/180°C/
gas mark 4 until risen and golden
brown. Can be eaten hot or cold.

Cashew Nut 'Ice Cream'
8 oz chopped cashews
½ pint yoghurt
4 oz raisins
2 dessertspoons honey
Tsp vanilla extract
Heat the milk and honey until
dissolved. Add the nuts and raisins
and other ingredients. Stir well. Put
in the freezer until set.

Kickshaws
1 egg white
8-12 oz sugar
Few drops lemon essence
Blanched almonds
Red food colouring
Whisk the egg white until stiff.
Gradually whisk in the sugar,
food colouring and lemon essence
until the mixture reaches a thick
consistency that can be worked
with the fingers. Wrap a little
mixture around an almond to form
each kickshaw and place them on a
non-stick baking sheet. Bake for 20
minutes at 125C 250F, gas mark ½.
Do not allow to brown.
*The name of these sweets is derived from
the French quelquechose, meaning
'something'. They were little treats, also
sometimes called conceits.*

Hazel Nut Scones
12 oz wholemeal flour
4 tsp baking powder
½ tsp salt
2 oz hazel nuts, chopped

½ tsp sage
2 fl oz sunflower oil
1 large egg, beaten
7 fl oz milk
Mix the dry ingredients. In a separate bowl mix egg, oil and milk. Add the dry ingredients and mix to a soft dough with your hands. Roll out to ¾ inch thick. Using a pastry cutter, cut into rounds. Bake at 220 C/ 425 F/ gas mark 7 for 10 minutes.

Bramble Wine
6 lb. blackberries
1 lemon
3 lb. Sugar
Yeast
1 gallon boiling water
Wash the fruit, place in a brewing bin and pour boiling water over it. Leave it for 3 days, stirring regularly. Strain the juice, dissolve the sugar in hot water and add to the mixture, together with the lemon juice. Cool to 20°C and add the yeast. Transfer the must to a demi-jon and fit an airlock.

SAMHAIN (31ˢᵗ October)

Spicy Pumpkin Broth
1 lb cubed pumpkin flesh
2 onions, finely chopped
2 oz butter
2 ½ pints vegetable stock
2 pinches mixed spice
1 tsp lemon juice
In a large pan, soften the onion in the butter over a gentle heat. Add the pumpkin and cook for a further 10 minutes. Pour in the stock and add the mixed spice. Stir thoroughly. Cook gently for 40 minutes or until the pumpkin is mushy. Liquidize or press through a sieve. Just before serving, reheat and add the lemon juice. Serve with crusty garlic bread.

Punkie Turnips
4 turnips
6 oz/ 180 g cooked green lentils
2 oz / 60 g full fat soft cheese
2 red or green sweet peppers, seeded and cut into broad strips
1 tbs./ 15 ml tomato puree
Dash soy sauce
1 tsp. yeast extract
Pinch marjoram
Cook the turnips whole in boiling water for 30 minutes and drain, being careful not to damage the skins. Scoop out the centres and set the hollowed turnips aside. With a very sharp knife, or pumpkin carving tools, carve a face on one side. This is tricky because the turnip will be soft. Make the holes small enough to be completely covered from the inside by the strips of pepper, but large enough to be visible. Line the inside of the face with the strips of sweet pepper to hold in the filling and make the face appear to glow. Mix together the other ingredients and pile this into the hollowed out turnips, being

careful not to dislodge the pepper strips. Bake in a moderate oven at 180C/ 350F/ gas mark 4 for 30 minutes.

Turnips were used for lanterns in Britain long before the American pumpkin was known and they were called Punkie Lanterns in some areas of Somerset. These edible lanterns have glowing eyes and are delicious!

Stovies

1 lb potatoes as near same size as possible, peeled
1 tsp butter
1 tsp. margarine
2 onions, skinned and sliced
Salt to taste.

Put the potatoes into a pan, uncut, into a single layer if you have a big enough pan. Add just enough water to cover, sprinkle with salt and dot with pieces of butter. Cover and simmer very gently without burning until the potatoes are cooked. Meanwhile melt margarine in a large shallow pan and gently fry the onions until soft and golden, but not brown. Drain the potatoes and slice thickly. Add to the onions and cook for a few more minutes until the two are well combined. Serve with either cold meat or as a supper dish.

All root vegetables are suitable for eating at Samhain. Not only were they often the only vegetables available, they also represent Underworld connections at a time when the veil between the worlds is at its thinnest.

Toffee Apples

8 oz sugar
¼ pt boiling water
6 Apples
6 wooden sticks

Dissolve the sugar in the water and boil until the sugar caramelizes. Fix wooden sticks to the apples and dip the apples in the caramel. Stand on a greased baking sheet until cool.

Old Fashioned Cider

10 lb. sweet apples
10 lb. crab apples
Champagne yeast
Campden tablets

Pick over the apples and remove any bad or bruised parts and wash them. If you have a fruit juicer, use it to extract the juice from the apples. Alternatively, either use a cider press or improvise by putting the fruit in a strong plastic bag and hitting this with a large mallet to pulp the apples. Put the pulp in a muslin bag and add a couple of campden tablets. Press the apples thoroughly to extract as much juice as possible. Remove from the bag. Put the juice in a brewing jar (demi-jon) and add the yeast. Fit an airlock and leave in a cool room until the first rapid fermentation ceases. Rack off into a clean jar, add another campden tablet and leave for 8 weeks until the cider clears. Bottle in screw topped bottles- if you want sparkling cider

Lancashire Parkin

8 oz. medium oatmeal
8 oz. plain white flour
4 oz. butter
4 oz honey
8 oz. black treacle
4 oz soft brown sugar
4 tsp ground ginger
4 tbsp milk
2 level tsp baking powder

Grease an 11 inch x 7 inch cake tin. Pre-heat oven to 325 F/ Gas Mark 3/ 160 C. Blend together the flour, oats and ginger in a mixing bowl. Gently heat the butter, treacle and honey in a pan until the margarine has melted. Add the flour, oats and ginger and mix well. Gently heat the milk until lukewarm and stir in the baking powder. Add to the oatmeal mixture and beat well. Pour the mixture into the prepared cake tin. Bake in the pre-heated oven for one and a half hours. Cool in the tin for about 15 minutes then finish cooling on a wire rack.

St Catherine Cakes

4 oz butter
4 oz castor sugar
8 oz self raising flour
1 large egg
½ level tsp ground mixed spice
4 level tbsp ground almonds
2 oz sultanas

Cream the butter and sugar together. Gradually beat in the egg with a spoonful of the flour to prevent curdling. Sift in the rest of the flour and spice, add the almonds and currants. Mix well until the dough binds together. Knead lightly and roll out on a floured board to ¼ inch thick by 8 inches wide. Cut into ½ inch strips and twist round to make about thirty flattened spiral shapes - or Catherine Wheels.

St Catherine's Day is celebrated in November. She was reputed to have been martyred on a wheel, but many Pagans believe that she was originally a spinning goddess, whose wheel represents both creation and the turning of the year. These cakes are eaten in Devon on the saint's feast day, November 24th.

Gingerbread Men

1 egg
1 tbsp black treacle
7 oz castor sugar
4 tsp ginger powder
9 oz butter
1 ½ tsp baking powder
11 oz plain flour
Currants to decorate

Beat together the egg, treacle, sugar and spice. Melt the butter in a pan,

54

remove it from the heat. When it begins to cool blend it into the egg mixture. Sift together the baking powder and flour. Add this to the mixture and knead slightly with your hands. Wrap the mixture in foil and chill for thirty minutes in the fridge. Roll out the dough on a lightly floured surface to just under ½ inch thick. Using a gingerbread cutter, cut into gingerbread-man shapes. Add two currants for eyes, and three more on the body for buttons. Place on a greased baking sheet, making sure that you leave room for the biscuits to spread. Bake at gas mark 3, 170C, 325F for 15-20 minutes.

YULE around 21st December

Posset
A traditional winter warmer
1 pt milk
2 digestive biscuits
2 tsp sugar
Pinch grated nutmeg
½ pt dry white wine
Put the milk in a pan and crumble in the biscuits, sugar and nutmeg. Simmer 5 minutes but do not boil. Cool and pour in the wine. Heat through again, but do not boil.

Twelfth Night Cake
8 oz butter
8 oz brown sugar
1 tsp ginger
1 tsp cinnamon
1 tsp mixed spice
5 eggs, beaten
8 oz flour
½ tsp baking powder
8 oz currants
8 oz sultanas
1 oz mixed peel
1 oz glace cherries
2 oz chopped almonds
A little milk
One dried pea
One dried bean
Cream the milk and sugar. Add the eggs and sift in the flour, baking powder and spices a little at a time. Add the fruit, pea and bean and nuts, mixing well. Pour into a lined 8 inch cake tin and bake at 150 C/300F, gas mark 2 for 3-4 hours, until the cake is brown and a skewer pushed into the centre comes out clean. Cut out a crown of gold paper to surround the cake or decorate with red and green knots. Whoever pulls out the pea and bean are rulers of the feast.

Syllabub
¼ pt white wine
1 tbsp brandy
1 oz sugar
½ pint double cream
Pinch grated nutmeg
2 tsp grated lemon peel
Mix the wine and brandy and add the sugar, stirring until it has dissolved. Gradually whip in the cream until thick. Spoon into individual serving glasses and sprinkle with nutmeg and lemon peel.

Roast Potatoes with Chestnuts

1 lb. potatoes, peeled
Salt
Oil
4 oz peeled chestnuts

Cut the potatoes in half and par boil in salted water for four minutes. Put them in a roasting tin, sprinkle with salt, coat with oil and cook in a hot oven for 30 minutes. Add the chestnuts and continue cooking until the potatoes are done.

Creamed Sprouts

1 lb Brussels sprouts
½ oz margarine
½ oz cornflour
¼ pint milk
Salt
Pinch grated nutmeg
Chopped parsley

Cook sprouts and strain. Melt the margarine in a pan and add the cornflour, gradually add the milk to make a sauce. Add the seasoning and nutmeg. Add the sprouts and heat through gently. Served sprinkled with fresh parsley.

Nut Roast

2 oz chopped hazelnuts
1 oz walnuts, chopped
4 oz brown breadcrumbs
2 oz butter
1 oz cornflour
Seasoning to taste
1 large egg, beaten
2 tbsp milk
1 tsp Marmite
½ pint vegetable stock
Pinch oregano
Pinch thyme

Melt 2 oz butter; add the cornflour, and then gradually the stock to make a sauce. Add the herbs, marmite and seasoning. add the breadcrumbs and the nut, and stir in the egg. Spoon the mixture into a greased oven dish and bake at 375 F/ 190 C/ gas mark 5 for 40 minutes.

Brandied Apricots

16 oz dried apricots
8 oz sugar
¼ pint brandy

Soak the fruit in cold water overnight. Place the fruit and water in a pan and bring to the boil. Cover and simmer for 15 minutes. Strain the liquor into a measuring jug and return the fruit with ¼ pt. of liquor to the pan. Stir in half the sugar and bring to the boil. Simmer without stirring for a couple of minutes. Using a slotted spoon, remove the fruit and pack it into jars. Add the remaining sugar to the pan and stir until dissolved. Boil for four minutes and remove it from the heat. Cool the syrup and measure it. Add an equal amount of brandy. Pour the mixture into the jars, covering the fruit. Seal. This will keep for up to 6 months.

Decorated Biscuits

4 oz margarine
3 oz butter
2 oz icing sugar

5 oz plain flour
4 oz self raising flour
1 tbs. cornflour
Cream together the butter and margarine, fold in the icing sugar, then the flours and cornflour. Knead lightly to make smooth dough. Wrap in cling film and chill in the fridge for half and hour. Roll out the dough on a floured board to ¼ inch thick. Bake at 180ºC/350ºF/ gas mark 4 for 15 minutes. Transfer to a cooling rack. In Germany these biscuits are traditionally cut into tile shapes and decorated and hung on the tree. Before baking, extra dough can be cut out or piped onto the biscuits to make raised patterns and a hole for hanging can be made with a clean drinking straw. After cooling the biscuits can be iced with royal icing and painted with food colourings, threaded on ribbons and hung on the tree.

Wassail
2 ¼ pt cider
3 apples, grated
2 oz brown sugar
½ tsp. ground ginger
Grated nutmeg
Put a ¼ pint of cider in a pan and add the grated apples. Cook until the apple is soft and add the brown sugar, ginger and the other 2 pints of cider. Heat through but do not allow to boil. Add some grated nutmeg and pour into a large cup or bowl. This is passed from one person to another with the blessing "*Waes haelinch*" or 'good health'.
The wassail cup is a traditional Yuletide drink. Formerly it was mulled mead, to which whole fruits and seasonings were added.

PRESERVING

If you are growing your own vegetables you will know that you have a glut of produce in the late summer and early autumn and very little in the winter. Our ancestors overcame this by developing techniques for preserving food. Fruit and vegetables were bottles, dried, salted, and made into jams, chutneys, pickles and jellies. Wonderful treats could then be produced at Yule or Twelfth Night- an otherwise dark and gloomy time with nothing fresh to eat- apricots in brandy, mincemeat and candied fruits. Preserved food makes a wonderful gift too, tie a ribbon round the jar, or cut out a round of pretty cloth of paper to cover the lid.

DRYING

Several fruits and vegetables dry successfully. To dry apple rings, core good, unblemished apples, and cut the apple into rings 1/8 " thick. Put them into a bowl containing a solution of salt (1 ½ oz to 6 pints) and steep for 10 minutes. Thread them onto a bamboo cane over a heat source, such as a wood burning stove, Aga, cooker or in an airing cupboard (watch out for drips). They will dry in 2-3 days and feel slightly leathery. Take down and store in an airtight container. To dry chillies thread them on a cord using a needle, hang in a warm place to dry, then take down and store in an airtight container.

BOTTLING

Bottling preserves both colour and flavour. Kilner jars are best for the purpose (the ones with the hinged lids and rubber seals): they are a little expensive, but last for years. Apples should be peeled, sliced and blanched for 2 minutes in boiling water. Apricots and peaches should be halved and stoned. Cherries, damsons and soft fruits can be bottled whole. If you decide to stone them, do this over a bowl to catch the juice. Make syrup from 1 lb. sugar to each 1 pt of water. Bring the syrup to the boil and add another pint of water. Pack the fruit into scalded jars and pour the syrup over. Screw on the lids firmly, then loosen by half a turn to allow any expanding air to escape when the jars are being sterilised. Place them on a trivet in the bottom of a large saucepan, which should have sides taller than the bottles. Place card between the bottles to prevent them touching. Add warm water to cover the jars and gently heat it so that it begins to simmer after about half an hour. Continue simmering for according to the table below. Remove the bottles from the pan and tighten the lids. As the jars cool, carefully tighten the lids two or three times more to be sure of a good seal. Fruits can also be bottled in brandy. The syrup is made in the usual way with sugar and water but it is allowed to cool and an equal measure of brandy is added.

Sliced apples	2 minutes	Damsons	10 minutes
Blackberries	2 minutes	Plums	10 minutes
Currants	2 minutes	Peaches	10 minutes
Gooseberries	2 minutes	Apricots	10 minutes
Raspberries	2 minutes	Whole pears	40 minutes
Strawberries	2 minutes		

JAM

To make the best jam, you need to pick the fruit when it is just ripe and in perfect condition. Wash it and remove any stalks and cores. Some fruits have very little pectin, the enzyme responsible for making the jam set.

This is easily remedied by adding a chopped apple or the soaked rind of a lemon to your recipe, both being rich in pectin. To make jam, place the prepared fruit in a pan, with a little water if necessary. Bring it to the boil and simmer until the fruit is soft. This is when the sugar should be stirred in. The quantity will vary according to the individual recipe. Once the sugar has dissolved, the jam should be heated to boiling point. Continue boiling, stirring only occasionally, until the setting point is reached. To test for set, spoon a little jam onto a cold saucer. Leave a minute and tip the saucer. If the jam is set, it will stay put and will not trickle away. Remove the pan from the heat and allow it to stand for a few minutes. Remove any scum that has formed on the surface, together with fruit stones. A knob of butter added at this time will help to eliminate any scum that remains. Stir once and pour the jam into warmed jars (warming is necessary, as cold jars are likely to shatter. Cover the surface of the jam with a wax disc and put on the lid firmly. If lids are not available, cellophane covers can be used and held in place with an elastic band.

Blackberry & Apple Jam
4 lb. blackberries
1½ lb. cooking apples, peeled and cored
½ pt water
6 lb. sugar
Wash the blackberries and simmer with half the water. In a separate pan simmer the apples with the rest of the water. Mash the apples and combine with the blackberries, add the sugar and boil until setting point. Pour into warm jars.

JELLIES
In jellies only the juice is used and the fruit pulp is discarded. Jellies should be clear. Wash and roughly chop the fruit - there is no need to peel or core it. Simmer in a large pan (you may need to add a tiny amount of water is the fruit is not immediately juicy) until the juice is extracted. Strain through a jelly bag suspended from a hook or beneath a chair into a large jug or bowl. This will take quite a while, but do not squeeze the bag as this will force through fibres that will cloud the jelly. Return the juice to the pan and for every pint of juice, add 1 lb. of sugar. Bring to the boil and continue boiling until the setting point is reached (see jam). Remove the pan from the heat and allow it to stand for a few minutes removing any scum that has formed on the surface and pour the jelly into warmed jars as

with jam. Cover the surface of the jelly with a wax disc and put on a lid or cellophane cover, held in place with an elastic band.

Crab Apple Jelly

Gather as many crab apples as you want and remove the stems and chop the apples roughly. Stew them in their own juice until soft. Strain through muslin and collect the juice. Add one pound of sugar for every pint of juice and boil together until the setting point is reached. Bottle in clean warmed jars. Crab apple jelly turns a beautiful shade of pink.

FRUIT CHEESES

All types of fruit are suitable for making fruit cheeses. They may be spiced with ginger, cinnamon or nutmeg. The fruit should be washed, large fruit should be chopped - there is no need to peel or core them. Put the fruit in a saucepan and just cover with water. Simmer gently until soft. Rub the fruit through a sieve to obtain the pulp and put the pulp in fresh pan. Add an equal weight of sugar and simmer gently for about an hour. You can test whether it is ready by pulling a wooden spoon across the pan. It should leave a clear line. The cheese can be poured into moulds or small pots. Seal with a wax disc and keep the cheese for 2 months before using to allow the flavour to develop.

Damson Cheese

3 lb damsons

$\frac{1}{4}$ - $\frac{1}{2}$ pint water

12 oz sugar to 1 lb pulp

Wash the damsons and remove the stems. Simmer in the water until very soft. Push through a sieve using a wooden spoon. Weight the pulp and add the sugar. Boil gently until thick, stirring regularly. Brush straight sided jars with glycerine and pour in the damson cheese- this is so that you can turn the cheese out as w hole. You can serve it as a dessert, studded with almonds and with port poured over it.

FRUIT SYRUPS

Use any ripe fruits in good condition and wash them carefully. Mash the fruit in a bowl, put the bowl over a pan of simmering water until the juice begins to flow out. Mash them again. Strain through a jelly bag overnight. Measure the juice and add $\frac{3}{4}$ lb. sugar to each pint of juice and stir until the sugar dissolves in the cold juice. Strain again through a jelly bag and pour it into screw top bottles. The bottles must then be sterilised. Screw on the lids of bottles to be sterilised, without tightening. Place them on a trivet in the bottom of a large pan. Add warm water to cover the bottles up to the neck (the water must be higher than the top of the syrup inside the bottles) and gently heat the water so that it begins to simmer after about half an hour. Continue simmering for 30 minutes. Remove from the saucepan with tongues and tighten the lids.

Rose Hip Syrup
2 lb hips
Water
1 lb sugar
Pick red hips and mince them, and put straight into boiling water allowing 3 pt per 2 lb hips. Boil then remove from the heat. Stand 15 minutes. Strain though muslin (reserve the liquid) and return the hips to the pan add another 1 ½ pints of water. Boil, stand 10 minutes and strain. Reserve the liquid and combine it with the first batch and boil until reduced to 1 ½ pints. Add 1 lb sugar, stir until dissolved. Boil 5 minutes. Strain into bottles and seal immediately. Sterilise, boiling for 5 minutes.

PICKLES
Virtually any fruit or vegetable can be pickled, although the most famous pickling vegetable is the onion. Utensils can be of any material with the exception of copper and brass- vinegar reacts with these metals. The easiest method of pickling is to put your produce in vinegar with a blend of pickling spices which will vary according to the fruit or vegetable being pickled. For a mild flavour, use ½ oz each of cinnamon, cloves, mace, allspice and white peppercorns to every 4 pt. of malt or spirit vinegar. The vegetables should be soaked in brine overnight, then rinsed and packed into jars. The spices should be put with the vinegar in a saucepan. Heat it up and then pour over the vegetables, making sure to cover them completely. Screw the lid on tightly and leave to cool. Store in a cool dry place.

Pickled Cucumber
3 large cucumbers cut in fingers 3-4 inches long
3 tbsp salt
4 onions, sliced
1 pint white or malt vinegar

6 oz sugar

1 tsp celery seed

1 tsp mustard seed

Place the onions, cucumber and salt in a bowl and stand for an hour. Rinse thoroughly. Heat the other ingredients and cook for 3 minutes until the sugar has dissolved. Pack the vegetables into jars, and cover with hot vinegar. Seal immediately.

CHUTNEYS

The fruit and vegetables should be washed, peeled and cored and finely chopped. They are put into a pan with the vinegar and gently cooked until soft. More vinegar, sugar and spices are added and the whole is simmered for 1 - 2 hours uncovered to reduce until the chutney has thickened to the required consistency. It is then bottled in the same way as the jam. The flavour improves with keeping and they can be stored for up to three years.

Spicy Apple & Tomato Chutney

2 lb apples, peeled and sliced

2 lb ripe tomatoes, skinned and sliced

¾ lb onions, chopped

1 clove garlic, crushed

½ lb raisins

¾ lb Demerara sugar

½ oz mustard seeds in muslin

½ oz curry powder

1 level tsp cayenne pepper

1 oz salt

1 ½ pts malt vinegar

Stew the apples in a little water. Add the other ingredients and bring to the boil. Reduce the heat and simmer until thick with no free liquid. Cool and spoon into clean glass jars and seal.

KETCHUPS AND SAUCES

Ketchups are made of the juice of one or two vegetables or fruits, the best known being tomato, but other vegetables can be used; mushrooms work well. The fruit or vegetables are simmered until soft, and then rubbed through a sieve to obtain a puree. For every pint of puree, add ½ pt vinegar and 2 oz sugar, and whatever spices are called for in the recipe. If you wish to retain the colour of the fruit or vegetable, then spirit vinegar should be used. Malt vinegar will give a brown colour. The ketchup is returned to the pan, simmered until it thickens, then it is poured into warmed bottles, which must then be sterilised and sealed. Sauces are made in the same way, but have more than two kinds of vegetable or fruit in them.

Mushroom Sauce
4 lb mushrooms
4 oz salt
4 cloves garlic
2 pints wine vinegar
½ tsp ginger
½ tsp cloves
Pinch pepper
4 tbsp brandy
Slice the mushrooms and layer in a bowl with the salt overnight. Wash thoroughly and put in a pan with the chopped garlic, vinegar and spices. Simmer for 60 minutes. Strain through a jelly bag and add the brandy. Pour into bottles and sterilise (see fruit syrups).

Chapter 4
THE STILL ROOM

Herbs have always been part of the wise woman's armoury. In the past, every woman had to be something of a herbalist and healer, responsible for her household's health, since professional medical help was either unavailable or too expensive - and possibly ineffective or dangerous to boot.

Nearly every home had a still room, so called because it usually contained a still for distilling flower essences used for medicinal purposes. Set aside from the kitchen and kept clean and sweet smelling with drying herbs and flowers, it was the place for making herbal infusions, powders, oils and poultices, inks, dyes, soaps, household cleaners and perfumes, as well as for brewing wine and ale, preserving fruit, making jams and jellies, pickles and chutneys. The woman of the house kept it under lock and key, and wrote down all her recipes in the same household book that recorded her mother's and grandmother's 'receipts'.

A girl was initiated into the secrets of these family formulas by her mother, along with her knowledge of folklore, stories, healing potions, minor surgery, gardening, brewing and wine making, spinning, weaving, dyeing, childcare, home management, animal husbandry, bee-keeping, fortune telling and cookery know-how. This didn't happen to me at home, and I don't suppose it happened to you. Such expertise is not valued in today's society, but it formed the pattern of women's lives for thousands of years and they developed highly skilful methods in all these areas, even though no historian wrote about them or accorded women status for their invaluable contribution to society; women's work and women's knowledge has always be derided and ignored.

I have created a still room in my house, lined with jars of herbs, resins, dried fruit peel and flower petals and bottles of essential oils. There I make my incenses, brew my wine, sloe and damson gin, and bottle my tinctures, salves, magical oils and other potions. My huge jam pan hangs from the ceiling, cupboards contain stored jams and wine and treats for Yule like home made sweets, while the freezer houses produce from the vegetable garden to keep us supplied during the winter.

Don't worry if you haven't got a utility room or scullery to dedicate as a still room, even the most basic kitchen contains all the facilities you need to make your own products.

THE GREEN HOME

None of us live in a rural idyll, and we have to buy most of what we eat and use from shops and supermarkets. If you can, buy locally produced goods, especially organic vegetables, support farmer's markets and farm shops.

Any self respecting (and Earth respecting) Pagan avoids actions that harm the environment. Our law is *'an' it harm none, do what you will'* with the emphasis on not harming any thing, person, animal, self or planet, and every Pagan must weigh their consumer decisions against their consciences and the Rede. When you shop consider the following in relationship to any purchase:

- Does it endanger your health or the health of others?
- Does it damage the environment during its manufacture, use or disposal?
- Does it have wasteful or non-recyclable packaging?
- Does it use materials from threatened environments or species?
- Does it involve animals testing?

CLEANING PRODUCTS

Commercial cleaning products are hazardous chemicals - toxic, corrosive, irritating and flammable. Many people find that they are sensitive to their constituents which can be neurotoxic, and can suffer from headaches, muscular pains, blocked sinuses and chronic fatigue as a result. And think what those traces of bleach, disinfectant and detergent are doing to your digestive system! When they are flushed down the loo, or washed down the sink, they pollute our environment causing death to river dwelling animals and fish.

The good news is that proprietary chemicals are not necessary to keep your home spotlessly clean. People in the past managed perfectly well with none of our modern products. Below are some natural recipes that you might like to try. If not, remember that you can obtain ecologically friendly household products from health food stores and most supermarkets. If you are determined to stick to your old chemicals, use them in a more dilute form - most people use them many times more concentrated than is necessary to achieve optimum results.

Antibacterial Spray
1 pint water
10 drops pure essential oil of lavender
10 drops essential tea tree oil
Pour the water into a spray bottle. Add the essential oils and shake. Use on surfaces to kill bacteria- just spray on and wipe over.

Vinegar
White spirit vinegar in a 5% solution can kill 99 percent of bacteria, 82 percent of mould, and 80 percent of viruses- it is also completely safe, unlike commercial antibacterial sprays which are toxic in large does. Make a stronger solution to clean lime scale from taps and appliances and to clean windows effectively without smearing. Use in the kitchen and bathroom to eliminate mould- spray on neat and leave to dry, and then rub off.

Lemon Juice
Got an oily dark ring around the bath? Squirt it with lemon juice, leave it for 30 minutes, and then just rub it off and rinse. Add 2 fl oz lemon juice to 1 fl oz liquid soap to make an effective floor cleaner. Add the solution to a bucket of hot water and mop the floor as usual.

Scouring powder
1 oz baking powder
1 oz borax (available from pharmacies)
1 oz salt
Place in a jam jar; pierce the lid and use as you would any commercial scouring powder.

Bicarbonate of Soda
Bicarbonate of soda has numerous household uses, but it should be used fresh- replace old boxes frequently. If you want to clean a bottle that has contained oil, fill it full of warm water and bicarbonate of soda, shake it and leave for a few minutes, shake again, and rinse with clean water. Bicarbonate of soda will clean many surfaces without scratching: mix to a paste with water and use to scrub grills, hobs, fridges, deep fat fryers, chip pans, irons, plastic buckets, bowls and sinks, barbecues, stained tea and coffee cups etc. Place a saucer of bicarbonate of soda in the bottom of your fridge to prevent odours. If your kitchen bin or your shoes and trainers are a bit smelly, sprinkle bicarbonate of soda in them. Place some

in the bottom of the cat litter tray and an open box beside it to absorb the odours. If the cat or the baby is sick on the carpet clean up as much as you can before sprinkling with bicarbonate of soda and scrubbing with clean water. Finish by sprinkling with bicarbonate of soda to absorb lingering pongs and vacuum when dry. Don't bother to buy fragrancers for your vacuum cleaner, just add some bicarbonate of soda to the bag, and use instead of carpet deodoriser powders. If you have burned the bottom of a saucepan, add an inch or two of water and bring to the boil. Turn off the heat and sprinkle in plenty of bicarbonate of soda, leave overnight and it will clean up easily in the morning. To clean tarnished copper pans, sprinkle bicarbonate of soda on half a lemon and use this to clean the pans. Combine bicarbonate of soda and white vinegar with plenty of hot water to get dirty windows sparkling, rinse with clean water and allow to dry. Add to your washing machine instead of fabric softener.

Furniture Polish
12 drops lemon essential oil
3 tbsp lemon juice
A few drops olive oil
Dip a soft duster in the mixture and wipe over wooden furniture.

Beeswax Wood Polish
3 oz beeswax
½ pint real turpentine (not turps substitute)
1 oz pure soapflakes
¼ pint water
10 drops lemon oil
In a double boiler heat the turpentine and flaked wax until dissolved. Boil the water, add the soap and allow to dissolve and cool a little. Pour into the wax and stir continuously as it cools and emulsifies. Add the lemon oil and pour into jars.

Nut Polish
A fresh nut is oily enough to polish furniture beautifully. Cut it in half and rub over the surface. Walnuts work particularly well, and a single walnut is enough to polish a coffee table, but you can use hazels, almonds, chestnuts and beech nuts.

Herb Polish
As well as nuts, some herbs are oily enough to impart a polish to wooden furniture. Try the leaves of the mock orange (*Philadelphus coronarius*), and just follow up with a clean duster afterwards. The Elizabethans used handfuls of lemon balm.

Leather Polish
4 oz beeswax
1 pint real turpentine (not turps substitute or white spirit)
1 pint water
1 oz pure soap flakes
20 drops lavender oil
Boil the water and add the soap

flakes, allow to cool a little. Warm the turpentine in a double boiler and add the shredded wax to dissolve. Remove from the heat and add the soap and water, stirring continuously until it is cold- it will emulsify. Bottle and label.

Scented Sachets for Drawers
2 tbsp orris root powder
1 tbsp dried lavender flowers
Few drops lavender oil
1 tsp ground cinnamon
Several squares of 4" x 4" cotton cloth
Thread
Mix the orris, lavender flowers and oil and cinnamon together. Place a couple of teaspoons full on each piece of cloth, gather it together and tie it up with the thread. If you are handy with a needle you can sew up oblongs of cloth into little pouches instead. These will scent your clothes drawers or you can hang one in the wardrobe.

Rose & Lavender Potpourri
Rose petal leaves
Scented geranium leaves
Dried lavender flowers
Orris root powder
Few drops geranium oil
Ground cinnamon
Whole cloves
If you are picking the flowers from the garden, you will need to dry the rose petals spread on paper for a few days. Mix the ingredients and seal together in a large jar for at least one month before using.

Pomander
Apple or orange
Cloves
Ribbon
2 tsp orris root powder
2 tsp nutmeg
Pomanders are usually made with oranges, though apples work equally well. The fruit must be fresh and unbruised. Press cloves all over the fruit, very close together so that the flesh is not visible between them; it is best to start at the base and work upwards and round in rows. Roll the pomander in the nutmeg and orris, wrap it up in tissue paper and put it in the airing cupboard for a few weeks until it hardens. Shake off the powder and tie a ribbon round it for hanging. These scent cupboards and wardrobes, and make excellent gifts at Yule.

Insect Repellents
Some plants repel flies and other insects. You can keep a sprig or two of these in your kitchen and still room, or place some in the wardrobe to protect against clothes moths. They include fleabane, elder leaves, southernwood and wormwood.

Rose Incense Cones
3 oz gum Arabic
2 oz storax

1 oz damask rose buds, dried and ground
1 oz salt peter
1 oz sandalwood powder
½ oz gum tragacanth
Rose water
Dissolve the tragacanth in a little rose water. Meanwhile, blend the other ingredients. Add the tragacanth. If the mixture is too slack, add more sandalwood so that you can shape it into pellets or cones.

NATURAL COSMETICS

I love making my own toiletries and beauty products. I've used my own formulas for many years and find that they work as well, or better, than bought ones.

Deep Cleanser

Use when your skin is tired and dull, it also helps reduce wrinkles
Small pot natural live yoghurt
2 tsp runny honey
1 tsp olive oil
1 small apple, peeled and cored
1 egg white
5 drops rosemary oil
5 drops lemon oil
Place all the ingredients in a blender and blend on a low setting. Massage the mixture over the face. Rinse thoroughly with warm water. Place any remaining mixture in a screw top jam jar and keep in the fridge for up to three days.

Cucumber & Honey Cleanser

This potion moisturises, cleanses and clarifies the skin.
1 oz runny honey
2 pints distilled water or rainwater
4 oz cucumber
Place the ingredients in a blender and blend on a low setting. Massage over the face and rinse with warm water.

Elderflower Cleanser

¼ pint natural live yoghurt
6 elderflower heads
1 tbsp runny honey
Wash the elderflower heads and cut off as much of the green stem as possible. Place them with the yoghurt in a pan and simmer over a very low heat for 30 minutes. Remove from the heat and leave for 4 hours. Reheat the mixture, then strain and add the honey, whipping as the mixture cools. Apply to the face with cotton wool, and rinse off with warm water. Keep in airtight jars in the fridge for up to 7 days.

Cleansing Milk

2 fl oz full fat cow's milk
2 fl oz runny honey
1 tsp wheatgerm oil
¼ oz fresh lettuce leaves
¼ oz fresh chamomile flowers
¼ pint distilled water or rainwater
½ oz fine cornflour
Place the herbs in the water and simmer for 10 minutes and allow

to cool. Place in a blender with the other ingredients. Massage into the skin with your fingers and rinse off with warm water. This will keep for 2 days in a screw top jar in the fridge.

Violet Milk
¼ pint milk
Handful violet flowers
Warm the milk, but do not boil. Pour over the fresh flowers, infuse for several hours, strain into a sealed bottle and keep refrigerated (it will keep for 3 days). Soak cotton wool in the milk and pat over the face twice a day to improve the complexion.

Heavenly Fluid
This sixteenth century recipe cleanses the skin and smoothes wrinkles.
3 oz rye breadcrumbs
2 egg whites
1 pint cider vinegar
5 drops benzoin oil
Put all the ingredients in a blender and blend on high speed for 1 minute. Strain through a muslin bag into a clean, screw top jar. Smooth over the skin and rinse with warm water. It will keep for 6-7 days in the fridge.

Eggy Cleanser
This will feed the skin as it cleanses and reduces wrinkles
1 egg yolk
1 tbsp cider vinegar

½ tsp sugar
4 fl oz extra virgin olive oil
Whip the egg yolk, as the sugar and vinegar and then the oil, a drop at a time, whisking vigorously until a paste is obtained. Use with a cotton wool pad and rinse off with warm water. Will keep for 3 days in the fridge.

Olive Oil Cleansing Cream
1 tbsp beeswax
2 tbsp lanolin
3 tbsp olive oil
1 tbsp sweet almond oil
Melt the wax in a double boiler, stir in the lanolin and oils. Remove from the heat and double boiler and beat until cool and creamy, spoon into clean jars. It will keep for several months. NB Some people are allergic to lanolin.

Pineapple Exfoliator
The enzymes in the pineapple will help to gently strip away dead skin cells and reveal fresh new skin beneath.
Take a fresh pineapple and pulp it in a blender. Apply to the face and leave for 30 minutes. Rinse off and moisturise.

Bran Facial Scrub
1 large egg
½ oz bran meal
2 tsp wheatgerm oil
2 drops calendula oil
2 drops chamomile oil
Beat the egg and add the bran and

oils. Massage into the face with circular movements, avoiding the eyes. Rinse with warm water. The mixture will keep for 2 days in a sealed jar in the fridge.

Apple & Marsh Mallow Mask
4 tsp runny honey
2 tsp almond oil
½ oz fresh mallow leaves
4 oz apple, peeled and cored
1 egg white.
Blend all the ingredients in a blender to make a thick paste. Add some rice flour if it is too thin. Immediately, spread the mixture over your cleansed face and leave on for 30 minutes. Rinse off with warm water and pat the skin dry before putting on a moisturiser.

Sesame Anti-Wrinkle Mask
1 tbsp lanolin
2 tbsp jojoba oil
2 tbsp sesame oil
1 tbsp wheatgerm oil
1 tbsp apricot oil
1 tbsp avocado oil
2 tbsp cider vinegar
4 drops lemon oil
In a double boiler melt the lanolin in the oils over a very low heat. Remove from the heat and add the cider vinegar. Keep whisking until the mixture is cool, add the lemon oil. Apply to the skin and leave for 1 hour before wiping off any excess. Use regularly to achieve the best effects. The mask should keep for a few weeks in an airtight jar. NB Some people are allergic to lanolin.

Herbal Steam Treatment
This is good for cleansing skin with spots, acne or clogged pores.
¼ oz chamomile flowers
¼ oz rosemary
¼ oz lavender flowers
¼ oz rosemary leaves
2 pints boiling water
Place a large fire-proof ceramic or metal bowl on a towel or mat and put the herbs into it. Pour the boiling water over them, leave to infuse a few minutes, and lean over the bowl, putting another towel over you head to keep in the steam. Let the steam cleanse your face until the water cools. The pores will be open, so after this you can apply a face mask or pat the skin with cold water to close the pores.

Linden Moisturiser
½ oz linden leaf buds (picked before they unfurl)
½ pint glycerine
3 fl oz vodka
¼ oz beeswax
½ oz cocoa butter
1 oz sweet almond oil
5 tsp jojoba oil
2 tsp runny honey
20 drops rose oil
20 drops jasmine oil
Put the crushed linden (lime) buds in a clean screw top jam jar

and cover with the glycerine and vodka. Leave for 2 weeks, shaking daily, and strain into a clean jam jar. Keep this in the dark and it will store indefinitely. Use 1 fl oz of the resulting linden maceration for this recipe. In a double boiler melt the wax into the oils then add the linden and honey. Remove from the heat and double boiler and continue to beat the mixture with a wooden spatula until the mixture is completely cool; it will thicken as it cools and is better for plenty of air being beaten in. When cool, stir in the essential oils and spoon into clean, screw top jars. Keep in the fridge.

Lanolin Night Cream

2 tbsp lanolin
½ tbsp runny honey
½ tsp glycerine
10 drops rose oil
1 tbsp wheatgerm oil
½ tbsp beeswax
3 tbsp rosewater

Place everything in a pan except the rosewater and rose oil. Place over a very low heat, beating with a wooden spatula until the wax has melted and the ingredients are blended together. Add the rosewater and continue to beat until smooth. Remove from the heat and continue beating until the mixture is cool and creamy. Add the rose oil. Bottle in an airtight jar. NB. Some people are allergic to lanolin; please test a little on the inner arm before use.

Mint Cream

For combination skin

Handful of fresh mint
½ pint boiling water
½ tsp powdered myrrh resin
3 tbsp cocoanut oil
2 tbsp jojoba oil
1 tbsp grapeseed oil
1 tsp beeswax

Infuse the mint in boiling water for 2 ½ hours. Strain and retain the liquid. Place the oils and wax in a double boiler and melt over a low heat. Separately warm the mint infusion again and dissolve the myrrh into it. Add this to the oils, remove from the heat and beat until cool and creamy.

Tomato Neck Mask

For an aging neck, cut a tomato into fine slices and spread over the neck and relax for an hour.

Nourishing Honey Mask

Spread honey all over your face and neck. Relax in the bath for 30-40 minutes, during which time the honey will be absorbed. Rinse.

Tooth Whitener

Crush or juice a strawberry and brush your teeth with the liquid. If you do this regularly it really does work.

Breast Firmer

1 pint boiling water
1 oz ladies mantle herb

Pour the boiling water over the herb and infuse for 20 minutes. Allow to cool a little and apply to the breasts with a warm flannel. Continue for 30 days.

Hand Cleanser

If you have dirty hands from working in the garage or garden, rub them over with half a lemon then wash with soap in warm water.

Nail Strengthener

Rub a little almond oil on your nails each night, using a cotton wool pad.

Lettuce Hand Cream

2 large lettuce leaves
½ pint boiling water
2 tbsp beeswax
1 tbsp lanolin
4 tbsp jojoba oil

Place the lettuce leaves in a pan and add the boiling water. Stand for 2 hours and strain. Melt the wax and lanolin in the oil in a double boiler over a very low heat. Whisk in the lettuce infusion and continue beating until the mixture is cool and creamy. Try adding the infusion a bit at a time as there may be too much liquid. Spoon into a clean jar and keep refrigerated. NB Some people are allergic to lanolin.

Elizabethan Hand Oil

¼ pint sweet almond oil
20 whole cloves

Put almond oil into a jar and add the cloves. Put the jar in the airing cupboard for three weeks. Strain off into a clean jar.

Foot Softener

2 pints boiling water
½ oz rosemary (fresh or dried)
Olive oil

Pour the boiling water over the rosemary herb and infuse for 15 minutes. Strain into a bowl large enough to soak your feet in and cool a little before soaking your feet for 15 minutes. Dry them off and then rub in plenty of olive oil and put on cotton socks and keep them on over night. Calloused and rough hands can be treated in a similar manner.

Soapwort Shampoo

1 oz soapwort root
½ pint distilled water
4 tsp castor oil
4 tsp salt
Few drops tea tree oil
2 oz brandy

Simmer the chopped root in the water for 15 minutes. Leave to cool a little then strain onto the salt and oils in a jam jar. Shake to dissolve the salt. Use as per a normal shampoo, though it won't lather much. You can make it without the brandy but it will not keep for more than a few days. It is good for greasy hair.

Chickpea Shampoo

2 oz chickpea flour
¾ pint distilled water

Gradually add the water to the flour in a pan and simmer very gently for 15 minutes. Use immediately- cool the mixture and work it through the hair and massage the scalp with it. Rinse very thoroughly.

Treat For Dry, Lifeless Hair

Few drops jasmine oil
1 egg yolk
1 tbsp. sweet almond oil
1 tbsp avocado oil
1 tbsp olive oil
4 tbsp runny honey

Mix the oils, egg yolk and honey and spread over the head, massaging into the scalp. Cover with a towel and leave for 30 minutes. Rinse with warm water, then shampoo as usual. You hair will be super-soft and shiny.

Dry Shampoo

5 oz dry semolina
Few drops lemon oil

In a pestle and mortar add the lemon oil to the semolina. Massage the mixture into the scalp and brush out. NB the semolina must be coarsely milled and not fine powder or it will be very difficult to get out. Maize flour works equally well.

Egg Shampoo

1 egg

¼ pint distilled water or rainwater

Whisk the ingredients together and immediately massage into the hair and scalp for at least 5-10 minutes. Rinse with lukewarm water (too hot and you will get scrambled eggs!) and add some lemon juice to the final rinse.

Nettle Anti-Grease Hair Lotion

4 oz fresh nettles
2 bay leaves
½ pint vodka
30 drops tea tree oil
1 pint cider vinegar

Wash the nettles and put them in a blender with the vodka and blend until pulped. Place in a jam jar and leave for two weeks, shaking daily. Strain into a clean jar and add the oil and cider vinegar. Regular use will help treat greasy hair. You can massage it into the scalp before shampooing, or use it between shampoos to remove grease by wiping the scalp and hair roots with a little on a cotton wool pad.

Anti Dandruff Hair Rinse

1 pint cider vinegar
1 oz fresh nettles
1 oz ivy leaves
½ oz sage leaves
½ oz rosemary leaves
½ oz thyme
2 fl oz vodka

Wash and pat dry the nettles and place, with the chopped herbs, vodka and cider vinegar, in a jam jar and leave for two weeks, shaking daily.

Strain into a clean jar. Shampoo your hair as normal, and add a tablespoon to the final hair rinse.

Anti Dandruff Scalp Treatment

Cider vinegar
½ oz marigold flowers
½ oz nettle
½ oz sage leaves
2 tsp wheatgerm oil

Place the herbs in a jar and cover with the cider vinegar. Leave on a sunny windowsill for 14 days, shaking daily. Strain into a clean jar and add the oil. Massage the mixture into the scalp regularly, using a cotton wool pad.

Camomile Lightener (Fair Hair)

1 oz camomile flowers
1 oz marigold flowers
Juice and zest of 2 lemons
½ pint water

Add the flowers and lemon zest to the water and simmer 10 minutes. Cool and strain through a muslin bag. Add the lemon juice. Apply the mixture to fair hair to lighten it. Cover with a warm towel and leave for 45 minutes, then rinse.

'Talcum' Powder

2 oz rice flour
1 tablespoon ground dried rose petals
2 tsp crushed dried lavender blossoms
½ tsp powdered myrrh
Small pinch powdered cloves
½ tsp dried, powdered rosemary
½ tsp powdered benzoin

Rub everything through a fine sieve and keep in a dark, airtight container.

Soapwort Soap

A handful of soapwort leaves, chopped and bruised
½ pint water

Boil together for 30 minutes. Strain off the liquid and retain this. It will be soapy and can be used for washing hands and woollen fabrics. Don't be alarmed by a slightly green stain on fabrics as it rinses out. This is also good for cleaning crystal and gem jewellery..

Aftershave

2 fl oz cider vinegar
2 fl oz witch hazel
2 fl oz vodka
6 cloves, powdered
1 oz sage

Put everything in a jar and leave on a sunny windowsill for 14 days. Strain into a clean bottle. You can experiment by using different herbs in the mix.

BATH TIME TREATS

For Fatigue

½ oz chamomile flowers
½ oz rose petals
½ oz white willow bark
1 pint water

Simmer the willow bark in the water for 15 minutes. Remove from the heat and add the flowers. Infuse 10 minutes, strain and add a cup to the bathwater.

Astringent bath

½ oz sage leaves
¼ oz yarrow
1 oz nettles
½ oz comfrey leaves
1 pint water
Boil the water and pour over the
herbs. Infuse 15 minutes, strain and
add a cup to the bath.

Elderflower Refreshing Bath

Tie an elderflower head in muslin and
hang beneath the hot tap as the bath
fills.

Herby Bath Salt

1 lb sea salt
1 oz lavender flowers
½ oz rose petals
Chopped orange peel
½ oz rosemary leaves, chopped
Few drops lemon oil
Blend together and store in an airtight
container for a moon before using to
develop the scent.

Purification Bath

1 lb salt
Few drops rosemary oil
Few drops frankincense oil
Blend together and store in an airtight
container. If you like, you can colour
this with a little blue food colouring-
only add a few drops or you will rise
from your bath looking like an ancient
Pict!

Cleopatra's Bath

2 oz dried milk powder

1 tsp powdered myrrh
5 drops cinnamon oil
4 drops frankincense oil
Blend together and store in an airtight
container.

Seventeenth Century Bath

1 part roses
1 part orange peel
1 part orange flowers
1 part jasmine flowers
1 part bay leaves
1 part rosemary
1 part lavender
1 part mint
Simmer together 15 minutes, strain
and a cup to the bath.

Relaxing Bath Bag

1 oz lavender flowers
1 oz peppermint
1 oz chamomile flowers
1 oz lemon balm
Tie in a muslin bag and allow the hot
water to run through it as the bath
fills.

Reviving Bath Oil

25 ml almond oil
10 ml wheatgerm oil
5 drops orange oil
5 drops Melissa oil
5 drops rosemary oil
Blend in a dark bottle. Add a
teaspoon to the bath after it has
run.

Chapter 5
GARDEN MAGIC

This section might not interest everyone, as not everyone has a garden, but I include it for those who do. I love to grow as much of what I eat as possible. I know that it has been grown organically, and that it has not been covered in toxic insecticides and weed killers. I have a good size back garden and an allotment but even if you only have a window box or a kitchen windowsill, it is still worthwhile to grow some herbs of your own.

Traditionally the wise woman's garden contained plants for healing, plants to attract and feed familiars, plants to contact the spirits, plants for divination and spells, and trees like rowan and holly for protection. Gardening helps us to attune to the ebb and flow of the earth's energy in its seasonal turning.

Clearing the Ground

Both my present allotment and garden had been sadly neglected when I bought them. They were knee high in couch grass, brambles, thistles, horsetails, docks, dandelions and other weeds. I didn't have the time or energy to devote to clearing this by hand, and I knew I wasn't going to use weed killers, so I bought a heavy duty petrol strimmer and flattened the lot. Then I covered the allotment in black plastic bought from a builder's yard and left it for a year- all 150 ft X 29 ft of it. If you are going to do this, the plastic has to be black to keep light from the ground and prevent weeds from growing, though old bits of carpet and lino will work equally well for smaller areas.

The first year I uncovered a third of the allotment. Then we made several deep beds from wooden frames. I decided to do this, as with ME I could no longer cope with a conventional method of allotment gardening as I had in the past, which involves a lot of back breaking digging several times a year. If you are making deep beds remember that the idea is that you do not dig them over frequently in a conventional fashion, and that you should be able to weeds them without standing on them. Mine are

4 ½ feet wide by 12 ft long. The paths between them we sowed with grass seed. I continued to expose more of the allotment every year and adding more beds for five years, until it is now all under cultivation. I recommend this method if you have never had an allotment before, as you will be discouraged by the amount of work involved. Each winter, after all the crops have been harvested, the beds are manured and covered with oblongs of black plastic weighed down with old tyres and left till spring.

Preparing the Soil

Once the ground has been cleared you need to determine what kind of soil you have. It will be obvious whether it is very stony, sandy or heavy clay that sticks together, but you need to know how acid or alkaline it is. To do this you can get a PH tester kit from the garden centre and follow the instructions. Take time to know and understand the requirements of your herbs. Pennyroyal, violets and thyme are quite happy to grow between cracks in paving slabs. Feverfew, pellitory, houseleeks and wall germanders will grow next to a wall. Some plants like shade, including alexanders, angelica, chervil and woodruff. A clay soil supports foxgloves, mint and parsley, while broom, lavender and thyme will be happier on a sandy soil.

Though herbs generally prefer a poor soil, most flowers and vegetables need added nutrients. Soil usually needs to be improved with plenty of organic matter to enrich its nutrient content, and help it to retain water. This is done by adding manure or compost. I get my manure from the ponies belonging to my neighbour or from the dairy farm down the road. This needs to be well rotted before it goes on, or it may be too 'hot' and will burn young plants. I also add home compost, and every garden, however small, should have its own compost heap. You can buy a plastic bin or make a wooden box from palettes, and throw in all your uncooked kitchen waste - eggshells, vegetable peelings, rotten fruit, non seeding weeds, leaves and other soft garden matter. Do not add meat, cheese, cooked food, seeding weeds and perennial weeds. There are supposed to be all sorts of secrets to good composting, but I just keep adding stuff on the top and getting nice crumbly compost out of the bottom.

The ash from my garden fires is rich in potash, and the fruit trees and bushes get a good dressing of this every spring.

What to Grow

This will depend on how much space you have. Even if you only have a windowsill you can grow a few herbs. In a small paved back yard you can put in some pots and growbags to raise tomatoes, salad leaves or even runner beans scrambling up a trellis. The flavour of food just picked and eaten within minutes is completely different to that of food purchased from the supermarket which may be days or even weeks old. You are getting the full life force of the plant when it is fresh, and the satisfaction in knowing you have grown it yourself is worth all the effort.

It is possible to be self-sufficient in fruit and vegetables on a plot 40 ft by 40 ft with some good planning and a big freezer. I have a small orchard with apple, pear, plum and cherry trees, soft fruit bushes including gooseberries, raspberries, redcurrants, blackcurrants and loganberries, rhubarb and two strawberry beds. In my deep beds I grow potatoes, celery, carrots, Jerusalem and globe artichokes, cauliflowers, sprouting broccoli, Brussels sprouts, calabrese, onions, leeks, asparagus, squashes, peas, broad beans, French beans, runner beans and garlic, as well as a variety of herbs. In my polytunnel I grow tomatoes, peppers, chillies, aubergines, melons, cucumbers and other less hardy plants and herbs, including a now sizeable lemon verbena bush. My salad crops I keep in the garden, since this is easier to water, and these keep me in salad for eight months of the year. (One year I am going to get it together to grow salads for the other four months in the polytunnel, but I haven't yet.)

MOON GARDENING

I'm experimenting with gardening according to the phases of the moon. While the moon is a constant presence in the night sky, it is ever changing. As she waxes and wanes, pulling with her the tides of the sea, she influences all that is living. As the moon waxes the energy flows upwards into the leaves and stalks of the plant, as it wanes the virtue travels to the roots. Plants to be harvested for their roots should be planted and gathered at the waning moon, and plants required for their flowers, leaves and fruits should be planted and gathered at the waxing moon.

Waxing Moon

The waxing moon is a good time for planting. It is a time for beginnings, things that will grow to fullness in the future. As the earth breathes out, sap rises and growth above soil is favoured. A waxing moon is the best time to sow and plant anything which yields a harvest above the soil, including flowers and blooms. In the first week following the new moon sow leafy vegetables and plants whose flowers and seeds are the edible part. Lawns also grow well when planted at the waxing moon. Do not prune during the waxing moon, as the sap is rising in plants, and they will 'bleed' heavily - as do humans who undergo surgery at the waxing moon. Re-pot plants during the waxing moon, as they will recover and grow better than if done at the waning moon.

Full Moon
The full moon is a good time for positive magic - healing, blessing and so on. Growth above soil reaches its peak now. The concentration of active ingredients in herbs and plants is highest at full moon, when they should be picked. Yule trees which are felled on the traditional day - the third day before the eleventh full moon of the year – will keep their needles for longer than those felled later. Sow potatoes.

Waning Moon
The waning moon is a time of winding down. As Mother Earth breathes in with the waning moon, her receptivity increases. This is a good time to prune trees and shrubs – they will 'bleed' less and recover more quickly. It is also a good time to weed and hoe to banish unwanted plants and pests. The energies of the waning moon are good for root crops. Sow root vegetables such as carrots and turnips just after the full moon, along with lettuce which seems to respond better to waning moon energies. Do not sow flowers at this time. Do not plant anything in the week before the new moon. Cleaning out the greenhouse and clearing beds is best done at the waning moon.

The Dark Moon
If possible, do no work in the garden during the dark moon.

Elder Leaf Aphid Killer
1 pint elder leaves
2 pints boiling water
Infuse for 2 hours. Strain and use to spray plants with aphid colonies.

Wormwood Slug Deterrent
1 oz wormwood
1 pint water
Pour the boiling water on the herb. Infuse 20 minutes and strain. Spray on the ground ion spring.

Chapter 6
THE LAND BEYOND

Mother Nature seems to have been the earliest deity worshipped by humans, often shown as a woman with large nurturing breasts and heavy, childbearing thighs; a symbol of fertility and plenty. Her pregnant womb may have been represented by mounds such as Silbury Hill, her womb by caves and wells. Phallic standing stones, maypoles and so on were the fertilising force of the God thrust into her body. People saw the Lord and Lady reflected in the landscape around them.

Once you have attuned to your own home and hearth, you should turn your attention to your local area, whether you live in a city or the middle of a field. The house itself is a reflection of the land around it. It stands in a specific place that has particular energies; it connects to the underworld and sky. Rather than shutting out the outside, open the windows and let it in, try to reconnect. Once a house would have been built of local materials with local methods, but now this is often no longer the case, its connection to the land is often lost. You can restore this by bringing in pebbles, stones and plants from the neighbourhood area.

It is in the wild places that the Hearth Witch communes with her gods. Many Pagans and New Agers flock to stone circles, long barrows and standing stones to perform workings, demanding that they give up their energy, often without finding out what kind of energy they possess or ascertaining whether they are willing to give it up. Worse still, some of them leave crystals in these sites to supposedly charge them, disrupting and deflecting not only the energy flow of the site but the energies for miles around. There is enough disruption from roads and buildings without us ignorantly adding to it. Some irresponsible people leave rubbish at the sites, the remains of fires and candles or even damage the monuments themselves. A little knowledge is a dangerous thing.

As Pagans, we believe that the *whole* Earth is sacred. There is magic to be found on the city streets, in parks and houses as well as fields, meadows, woodlands and rivers. The so-called 'sacred sites' mark places where the ancients found concentrations of earth energy, but every place has its own spirit, its own power, its own soul. The essence is different in different places, so one set of instructions on how to work with this spirit this will not help you much.

The first step is to find out about the character of your locality. Its spirit will be affected by its geology, its history, its towns, cities, roads and trackways, the plants, animals and people; all these contribute to the whole that is the *genius locus*. It may have known sacred sites, it may not. You can try tracking its ancient associations by looking at the place names-sometimes you will actually find the names of the gods in the landscape, such as Lir in Leicester and Woden in Wednesbury, Lud in London, Grim (an aspect of Odin) in Grimley. Some alleged saints are ancient gods and goddesses in disguise.

Natural springs, wells and water sources have always been regarded as holy; water is necessary to sustain and maintain life. Many have been regarded as healing; especially of they flow from east (the place of sunrise) to west (the place of sunset). At the summer solstice, spring equinox, Imbolc, Ostara, Beltane and Lughnasa they become empowered with healing energy. If there are tales of water fairies, or offerings of pins and coins being made, you will know that its spirit is well known. Look out for wells dedicated to the Goddess under the names of Bride (Brighid), St Anne (Anu) and St Helen (Elen). Sacred wells and springs may be called Holywell (holy well), and placed where they once existed called the Holywell Pub, or Holywell Road. The traditional way of appealing to the spirit of a holy well is by offering a pin or coin, or for healing by tying a *cloutie* (a piece of cloth) to a nearby hawthorn: as the cloth rots, then so the disease withers. Don't tie on plastic tape, bits of carrier bag and other rubbish. People who do are not making an offering, but adding to pollution and showing their ignorance of magical practice. Even old pub names like the Green Man can offer clues – unless they have been changed in the last few years to *The Tart and Strumpet* or *The Firkin Rabbit*. Some places have stories of spirits (white ladies and so on) appearing spontaneously to people throughout the years; look out for these tales, as they might point you in the direction of a land spirit. Local folktales offer clues to old mysteries. Regional earth mystery groups are often a good source of such information, as is the library.

You must contact the guardian deities of the land in order to gain permission to work and meditate there. When Australian aborigines visit a new place they first sing up the land, to greet it and announce their visit

in a respectful way. When working with a new site, you should approach
in silence and with deference, demanding nothing - this is not your right.
Some places welcome you with open arms and are happy to work with
humans on many levels; other places will permit certain activities but not
others. Some may be protected by elemental spirits and barrow wights who
will cause accidents in order to drive people away.

Any place regarded as holy will have had spirit manifested there
at some point, will have a sacred atmosphere, will be an entrance to the
Otherworld. Our ancestors recognised these places, but we find it more
difficult since we have not had the training and have lost many of the stories
that would tell us where they are. A place inhabited by a god or spirit is
sometimes discernable by its characteristics: perhaps the strange way the
trees are twisted, especially low or high plant growth, an unusual rock or
those places our ancestors marked with rings of stone, menhirs and cairns.
Places where many contacts between humans and the Otherworld have
taken place are often regarded as holy ground or a sacred site. Some of these
places now have Christian churches built over them. [16]

Look out for places where the land looks or feels different, where
animals behave differently, or where birds or insects may lead you; try
to look with eyes open to the sacred rather than the mundane. Try to
maintain a feeling of reverence and observation.

Take the magical journey we call the *Witch Walk*, in which you ask
the Gods that each thing that happens to you on that journey will have
meaning, whether it be the flight of birds, a strange tree formation, or a
chance meeting with another person who tells you something important.
In order to do this you need to learn to quiet the questioning part of
your mind and accept this as a magical reality and not take the path of
dismissing it and explaining it away. When you can learn to do this, you will
be amazed at the depth of knowledge that can be discovered on a single
walk. it is the wisdom that is part of your heritage as a witch. Learn to
accept it and use it.

THE LIVING SPIRITS OF THE LAND

Most Pagans are animistic and share a belief that humans, animals, trees,
plants, rocks, streams, rivers and places have *anima* or soul. Our ancestors
thought that as long as certain offerings were made and certain procedures
followed, the spirits would remain friendly and beneficent. If they were
neglected or offended, they would take their revenge. A river spirit might

16   Nigel Pennick, *Natural Magic*, Lear Books, 2006

rise up and drown humans crossing his domain. The spirit of the corn might cause the crops to fail; an apple tree might refuse to be fruitful.

Tree Spirits

Trees were objects of veneration in ancient times. The Celts and Teutons held trees and groves to be sacred to the spirits that inhabited them. While the life span of humankind is short, trees can live for many centuries. When all else fades in winter evergreens remain changeless in a changing world: strong enough to resist the death-time. Thus the tree became identified with the power of the deity or was seen as a deity itself. The cypress was the symbol of the Persian Abura Mazda, and in Greece, Artemis was represented by the willow, Apollo by the bay laurel and Athene by the olive. Representations of sacred trees are found in Chaldean and Assyrian temples, while in ancient Egypt several deities inhabited the sacred sycamore (*Ficus sycomorus*) which marked the boundary between this world and the afterlife. In England, mundane and Otherworldy boundaries were often marked with oak trees. Sticks or wands were (and still are) carried by elders, kings, heralds, and military leaders as a symbol of god given authority, derived from the sacredness of the tree, more especially the world tree or cosmic axis linking this world with the Otherworlds from which the king derived his power and authority.

As symbols of the god, or a god in actuality, trees were associated with fertility. At the festival of Dionysus in ancient Greece, anyone with a tree in their garden would dress it up to represent the god. At various other harvest and fecundity festivals trees would be decorated with wreaths and otherwise honoured. From this connection of the tree deity with virility comes the custom of carrying tree sprigs in a wedding bouquet, and such May Day observances such as the leaf-clad Jack in the Green dancer.

Many people instinctively feel that a tree has a spirit or consciousness. In the early days of Buddhism this was a matter of some controversy and it was decided that trees do not have souls like humans, but had certain resident spirits called *dewas* who spoke from within them. Among the Hindus these dewas are gods. Occultists use the term 'devas' to describe the resident spirit of a tree or other plant. We still honour the spirit of the tree when we decorate the evergreen Christmas tree and place the fairy, which represents its living spirit, at the top.

Vegetation Spirits

Early humans were hunter-gatherers, but during the Neolithic period became food growers, dependant on the yearly cycle of planting, germination, growth and harvest. In winter, the spirit of vegetation seems to die, to go down (as seed) into the underworld womb of Mother Earth until it is reborn the following spring. Ancient religion was largely concerned with entreating gods and nature spirits to provide food. Many nature spirits - or fairies as they were later called - are associated with vegetation, crops and the fertility of the land, having the power of either blessing or blighting. The German Kornböcke causes the crops to ripen; the Russian Polevik grows with the corn and after the harvest shrinks to the size of the stubble. The Russian Rusalki make the corn grow when they move through it. In Britain, the vegetation spirit is still portrayed on May Day by the Green Man. Green, of course, is the colour of growing things; after winter, the spring returns with a flurry of fresh green growth. Green is therefore a symbol of regeneration, the spirit of vegetation, hope, beauty, harmony and eternal life.

Fairies are very much associated with the colour green. They are often described as wearing green clothes, or even as having green skin. Good fairies like Puck and Robin Goodfellow – who might be seen as representing the powers of summer, growth, and life – retire from sight after Samhain, the start of winter, until spring returns. Evil fairies, representing the powers of blight, winter and death, such as the Scottish Unseelie Court, become very active. They are capable of stealing the spirit of the land, so that ears will not ripen on the corn, or cattle fatten. Good fairies re-appear again with the spring. Evergreens like holly and ivy were hung up by the Druids to preserve the green vegetation spirit throughout the winter.

Boundary Spirits

For the Celts boundaries of any kind were dangerous. These included such in between things as a crossroads, the shore between sea and land, midnight (the time between one day and the next) and Beltane, the threshold between winter and summer, and Samhain, when summer moves to winter again.

The place where the sun sets (or dies) is another kind of threshold, the entrance to the underworld of dead. At certain times, such as Beltane and Samhain, and certain places (where the human and Otherworld meet), it is possible to slip through the boundaries into the Otherworld.

The threshold is a dangerous place, neither inside nor outside, but a boundary between the two - a place between places. When a person crosses a threshold they move from one state to another and are in danger from the spirits that dwell *between*. . It was often believed to be the dwelling place of certain gods and spirits, such as the Indian Lakshmi and the Roman Lima and Limentius. Frazer recorded that the followers of the Philistine god Dagon took care not to tread on the threshold of his temple. [17] For this reason a bride – in a liminal stage of life - is carried across the threshold into her new house.

In Ireland primroses were scattered on the doorstep because malicious fairies are unable to pass them. In England, thresholds were made of holly wood, since no evil spirit could pass over them. In parts of Britain protective patterns ('step patterns') were drawn on the doorstep in salt, chalk, or reproduced in mosaic. These took the form of knot work and tangled threads, since spirits always travel in straight lines and would get caught in them.[18] Hearth stones were similarly decorated, as the hearth is a threshold too. In many cases, it was thought unlucky to tread on the doorstep itself, and people were always careful to step over it. To avoid offending these deities, corpses and pregnant or menstruating women had to leave by the back door.

Imagine then how much more dangerous and magical is a crossroads, a boundary between *four* places. The world over, they are places of mystery, danger and magic and the spirits of *between*. In Eastern Europe they are the haunts of vampires, in Japan evil spirits attack travellers there, and in India crossroads are ruled by Rudra, the god of evil powers. In England the evil omen of the black dog frequents crossroads, while in ancient Greece they were sacred to Hecate, the witch goddess of the Underworld; in many stories witches meet at crossroads.

Lares were the protective spirits of ancient Rome. The best known is the *Lar familiaris* ('household Lar'), which guarded the home, while the *Lares Compitales* guarded boundaries (a *compita* is the marker of a boundary). At important intersections marble altars stood, with temples housing statues of two *lares* accompanied by a *genius locus*. At small intersections there might be an altar of stuccoed brick against a wall on which would be a painting of two *lares*, dressed as Greeks with goblets, together with a toga clad *genius* holding a sacrificial saucer and cornucopia. Many boundaries run along a path or road and the *lares compitales* were worshipped at both rural and urban crossroads. Sometimes they were the chief deities of a hamlet. At the junction of two roads two *lares* would be

17   J.G.Frazer, *Folklore in the Old Testament, VOL 3*, Macmillan, London, 1918
18   Nigel Pennick pers comm

worshipped. The annual feast of the *Lares* was the *Compitalia*, celebrated soon after the winter solstice, when merrymaking accompanied the performance of theatrical farces. Some other elements of the festivals gave rise to later Christmas customs. The *Compitalia* called for the use of artificial light, and the *Lares* traditional sacrificial victim was the pig, traditional Christmas fare for centuries.

WORKING IN THE COUNTRYSIDE

Witches who get their learning from books are ignoring the greatest teacher of all, Mother Nature herself. Get out and observe the changing of the seasons, even if you live in a city. Learn to identify our native trees and plants. Stand on the earth, touch the stream, experience the wind and feel the warmth of the bonfire. However, you should always adopt a responsible attitude when working in the countryside and follow a few simple rules:

Safeguard against accidental fires- a dropped match or cigarette end can cause terrible damage to woodland that has taken hundreds of years to grow, and destroy wildlife over a large area; the karma for this is not going to be good! If you are going to light fires outdoors, make sure that you do so safely. Dig a proper fire pit so that the fire cannot spread and return the turf to it afterwards. Don't forget to put out any bonfires: smother the flames with soil or dowse with water. Don't leave jars and glasses where they can focus the sun's rays and start a fire.

Close gates- remember that cows, horses and other farm animals are a danger to themselves and others if they are wandering across the road. Fasten all gates behind you.

Keep your dog under control- a dog that is tractable at home may turn into a killer when faced with running sheep. Dogs kill 4000 sheep a year in Britain and if a farmer catches your dog molesting sheep, he is legally entitled to shoot it.

Take your litter home- leave no sign of your passing; take home all your paper, glass, candles, crystals and so on. Such things can be harmful to local wildlife, look unsightly, be disrespectful and interfere with natural energies. I always take a plastic bag to collect litter when I visit sacred sites and wild places to try to repay some of what they give me by tidying them up.

Do not pollute water- never throw litter or urinate into streams and ponds: this can kill wildlife.

Use stiles and gates to cross boundaries- cross in the appropriate places; you can damage a dry stone wall or fence by scrambling over it. Use the stiles and gates provided where possible. Walk along the edge of planted fields- never through the middle where you can damage crops. Farmers are more likely to be happy with your visits if you respect their property. Walk in single file if necessary.

Protect wildlife and plants- Loss of habitat and over-picking has lowered the stocks of many of our native plants. Don't take more than a few flowers or leaves from any plant. Cut them with a sharp knife. Never pick more than you need. Drop them into a flat basket or trug to avoid damaging what you do pick. Gather herbs on a dry day, preferably in full sun if you want the flowers to be open. Take flowers and foliage only from large patches of the plant. Be careful not to damage other vegetation when picking flowers. Under the Wildlife and Countryside Act (1981) which covers Britain, it is illegal to uproot any wild plant without permission from the landowner or occupier. The act contains a list of endangered plants, which are protected against intentional picking, uprooting and destruction and sale, and these are listed in Appendix 1.

WEATHER MAGIC

In the past country people could predict the weather with more accuracy than the modern TV weather man. They knew that the red sky at night meant a fine day in the morning, as stated in the one weather rhyme that everyone knows:

Red sky at night
Shepherd's delight
Red sky in the morning
Sailors take warning

An experienced Hearth Witch can smell the rain on the wind, and doesn't need to look at the sky for clouds. I went to a druid camp the other year, and on the final day an open market was held, where anyone who had brought things to sell could spread them out. If it is fine, we were told, the market will be in the open air in the flagged circle. If it is raining, we will hold it in the marquee. Come the day and it wasn't raining, so everyone set up their stalls in the flagged circle. Except me, I went into the marquee and grabbed the best spot. I sat there very much on my own for an hour, then the heavens opened and everyone came scrambling in. I am a witch; I know when it is going to rain!

Do we really need to know what the weather is going to do in this day and age when we buy our food from the supermarket, unless we want to walk to the shops? The farmer needs to know when the rain will spoil the harvest, so he can get it in before a storm, and when frost will blight the new shoots and take precautions. Hence the wealth of weather lore that everyone once knew. It is part of bridging the gulf that separates us from Mother Nature.

As a child I owned a pine cone which sat on a ledge outside the kitchen door. It opened when the weather was to be fine, and closed when rain threatened. Try it, it works. The scarlet pimpernel flower was once called the poor man's weather glass, since it closes its petals when rain threatens. The house cricket chirps when rain is due. You'll never see a bee when rain threatens, and other creatures such as kestrels, crows and swallows change their behaviour. When the kestrel hovers low over the ground it means that wet and windy weather is due and he is trying to hunt before it arrives. When rooks and gulls circle high in the sky, a gale is nigh. Mice come into the house before a cold spell. People have even noticed that cats are les playful when rain is due. The hens at the top of my garden always go into their nest box when rain threatens, and come out again when it is over. Cattle huddle together in fields or sheeted hedgerows when wet and windy weather is due.

It is said that one swallow doesn't make a summer, and swallows usually arrive mid April. If they come earlier it heralds a good summer. If they leave before their usual time of early October, it means that winter is coming early. If squirrels start to hoard nuts early it is a sign of a hard winter, and it is when leaves stay late on the trees. If frogspawn is early, it heralds a warm spring and summer. If it is laid near the edge of the pond, however, it heralds wet and windy weather.

If the rainbow appears in the morning, it means that rain will continue, but if it appears in the afternoon, there is good weather to come. The sky's colours in winter at sunset are indicative- pale yellow - wind and rain, pale green - frost or snow.

WITCH BOTTLE
Witches have traditionally fashioned witch bottles to protect their houses. Sometimes these are filled with sharp objects like nails and pins to frighten

away negativity, but this one uses coloured threads. It has always been believed that magic and Otherworldly forces travel in straight lines (hence the British idea of ley lines, or the Chinese concept of spirit paths). Should these forces come across anything twisted or curling, then they will be caught up in it and cannot escape.

Take a clear glass bottle or jar and fill it with coloured threads. The Old Ones always used red thread, but you could add other protective colours such as white, gold and silver. Bless the witch bottle with the words:

Let thy twisted, tangled thread,
Keep all evil things in dread
Caught in thy muddled encircling snare
Kept from my home and imprisoned there

Put the lid on the bottle or jar and place it by the front door or in a window that faces the street. Once a year take out the threads, burn them, and wash the jar. Dry it and fill it with new threads.

KNOT MAGIC

One of the first things that we encounter in life is a knot, when the midwife cuts and knots the umbilical cord. In times past, this was a magical act when she could bestow a good or bad fate on the child. Throughout history, the tying of the knot is associated with the binding of a spell, while the untying of a knot represents releasing magic or breaking enchantment. Knots were used to contain illness, secure love, confine evil spirits, weave blessings, control the weather, and bind curses.

Some of the magical implications of knot magic still survive in the English language where people speak of marriage as 'tying the knot', or in other words the couple are bound together. In certain marriage customs of some parts of the world, the couple's hands are actually tied together to symbolise this, just as they are in the Witch ceremony of handfasting. Then again, when we part from someone, we may speak of 'severing the bond'.

When the knot is tied, it is considered to be binding something up, or tying in the magic. When it is untied, it is considered to be releasing something, or releasing the magic. An ancient Mesopotamian magician might curse someone by reciting the curse while tying knots in a cord, which would then be buried to keep the curse in place. A disease might be cured by tying thread around an afflicted person's limbs, while the magician transferred the illness into the thread by a spell. The cord was then cut off and thrown away, taking the disease with it.

In many societies, women about to give birth would make sure that all knots in clothing and furnishings were untied so that the baby would slip easily from the womb. Jews forbade the tying of knots on the Sabbath in case they should constrict male potency. In a similar vein, Rome's high priest, the *Flamen Dialis*, was not allowed to wear any knot on his person, for fear of 'restricting' his power. Early Muslims offered prayers to Allah to be protected from all those who blow on knots (to imbue them with magical life). There are several Greek myths that speak of a hero being given a bag in which the winds are bound, and to release them he must untie the string that secures it. As untying something releases it, tying up binds it, so sympathetic magic to stop the flow of blood from wounds might consist of tying knots in a piece of cord.

More recently, English witches were believed to be able to tie up the winds by knotting strings, which would then be sold to sailors to provide good weather for sailing. However, they were also suspected of using know magic to also inflict illness and disability by closing eyes, mouths, or throats, or by restricting the movements of limbs with knot magic.

Initiation is the time a modern witch consecrates his or her magical cord, which is usually nine feet long and worn about the waist. Sometimes the neophyte is asked to fashion the cord themselves, plaiting it from new wool over many weeks or months, weaving enchantment into it. This cord is then used to measure the circumference of the magic circle, and for knot magic, either solo or in company with other members of the coven. Sometimes covens keep a set of cords in various colours for group spells.

The simplest form of knot magic is to tie nine knots in a cord, alternating them from each end and working towards the centre, concentrating on what it is you wish to achieve, then releasing it into the knot. There are several variations on the accompanying chant:

By the knot of one, the spells begun
By the knot of two, my wish come true
By the knot of three, the magic's free
By the knot of four, my will be law
By the knot of five, the spell will thrive
By the knot of six, the magic fix
By the knot of seven, my words to heaven
By the knot of eight, the magic create
By the knot of nine, this thing be mine.

Put the cord somewhere safe and leave it as long as you wish the spell to work. When you wish to undo the spell, undo or cut the knots.

You don't have to use a heavy cord for magic, but could use a thread or ribbon. It doesn't have to be nine feet long either, but does work best if the measurement is in some multiple of three- three inches, three feet, six inches, six feet, nine inches, nine feet (or nine centimetres for that matter) and so on. You might use different numbers of knots for different purposes, according to the laws of numerology:

- **One**: unity and wholeness, healing, sun magic
- **Two**: duality, choice, emotions, moon, choice
- **Three**: creativity, production, action, Mars
- **Four**: material matters, foundation, wealth, communication, Mercury
- **Five**: Expansion, growth, joyfulness, Jupiter
- **Six**: love, beauty, harmony, Venus
- **Seven**: limitation, ending, binding, Saturn
- **Eight**: dissolution, endings and beginnings, balance, Pluto
- **Nine**: the Goddess, truth, the meeting of all three planes of existence

You can enhance the magic by using a thread or ribbon of the appropriate colour:

- **Red**: life, vitality, health
- **Pink**:love
- **Blue**: healing, peace, spirituality
- **Black**: endings, negation of ego
- **Green**: growth, creativity, wealth
- **Orange**: optimism, joy
- **Yellow**: thought, mental activity
- **Purple**: power, assertion, confidence
- **White**: spirituality, protection

Use a little imagination, and the uses of knot magic are unlimited. For example, to bring two people together, use two threads in different colours to represent them. Loosely knot the two threads together, and then pull them tight. To protect a vulnerable person, you could obtain something that belongs to them, a button or earring perhaps, and tie it in a protective basket of knots. You might use threads of differing colours to weave in various strands of magic; green for growth, orange for joy, pink for new love and so on. Tie in beads to bring in extra elements of colour magic, feathers to represent messages and the element of air, and gemstones

according to their correspondences- amethyst for healing, rose quartz
for peace, and so on. Do a little research into the tying of knots, and use
different types of knots for different purposes.

Remember that knotting, weaving and braiding symbolises the
bringing together of disparate elements, and binding them together. After
a while, you won't need the cords at all but will be able to see the strands
of energy on the web and weave them as you will.

DOWSING

The cunning man was consulted in order to find lost objects, and often
used dowsing to achieve this. Dowsing is the intuitive use of pendulums or
rods to locate things and energies or answer questions. It is an art almost
anyone can master. Cunning men often used pendulums, either directly
dowsing over a specified location for a dropped ring for example, or over
a map. Dowsing may also be used to identify power spots, earth energies
and ley lines, either *in situ* or on a map. It may be used to pick out a useful
crystal or other object from a collection and so on and so on.

Dowsing is usually done with a pendulum, a forked stick or L rods.
The forked hazel stick is most often used to locate water, the forks held
in the hands. The tip of the stick will go down when the dowser locates
his objective. L rods consist of two bent pieces of metal held in the hands
which swing together when the objective is encountered. They are used to
locate water, minerals, ley lines, earth energies and illness in the body. They
can easily be made by cutting a section from a metal coat hanger about 9
inches long, plus one of the bends and four or five inches after the bend.
You will need two of these. Hold the shorter pieces loosely in the hands
pointing in front of you, parallel. Try walking over a spot where you have
placed a bowl of water. The two rods should cross over each other of their
own accord, then move back out as you clear it.

Pendulums are valuable divinatory tools and a pendulum is
nothing more than a balanced weight on the end of a thread or fine chain.
It does not need to be crystal, gold plated or expensive. One of the most
successful dowsers I know uses a button. A wedding ring or sewing needle
attached to a length of sewing thread has been used for centuries to try to
determine the sex of a newborn baby – rotating for a girl and swinging to
and fro for a boy. The method was used commercially in the nineteenth
century, with a small device containing a miniature pendulum, for sexing
chickens whilst still in the egg.

To use a pendulum you must determine your own responses. For
some a 'yes' response will be a clockwise swing, for others the pendulum

93

will go back and forth. Ask it some questions you know the answers to and determine the result.

Pendulums are extremely easy to make. Take a length of wire. Starting at the top and leaving an inch spare, wrap the wire around your chosen weight lengthways and bring it back up to the top. Twist the two ends and bring the longer end down around the weight again at 90 degrees from the first. Bring it to the top once more, twist again with the other end and fashion the remaining wire into a ring by wrapping it twice around a small knitting needle and cut of any excess. Thread the cord or chain through this ring and you have a pendulum.

MAKING A WALKING STICK, STAFF OR STANG

It is no coincidence that wizards and shamans everywhere are depicted with a staff, though its purpose is very rarely understood - it is not a fancy walking stick or an accessory to make the magician look more imposing. The staff is a portable world tree or *cosmic mundi*, which connects the magician to the three realms of the heavens, middle earth and the underworld.

The stang is a forked staff that represents the Horned God when placed in the circle. Cut the wood in winter when the sap is down. Remove any side twigs and branches. Leave the bark or remove as desired, burn on patterns with a soldering iron or a heated knitting needle. Allow the stick to dry out for several months before varnishing, if wished.

THE BROOM

Use twigs from the birch cut in the spring for the broom part, an ash pole for the shaft. The shaft should be smoothed and sanded. Carve a point in one end and bore a hole a couple of inches from this point. Insert a wooden peg into this. Gather the birch twigs around this and tie on the binding above and below the peg so that it is held on safely. Cut willow for tying when the tree is in leaf. Split these and put in hot water for 20 minutes to make them pliable.

RUSHLIGHTS

Cottages up and down the country were once lit with home-made rush lights, rather than candles or lamps. They are easily made from rushes with white spongy centres such as *Juncus effuses*. Soak them in water for six or seven hours and leave to dry outdoors in the sun. Peel the skin on one side, leaving it on the other. Heat wax in a dipping container and dip the rushes one at a time, allowing the wax to set in between each dipping. Aim to dip them four or five times in all. Clip the rushlight to the side of a bottle or candlestick using a bulldog clip.

HAG TAPERS
Many of the folk names for mullein, such as Hag Taper and Candlewick Plant, are a reference to the fact that it was used as a wick before the introduction of cotton. Dried pieces of the stalk were dipped into suet, tallow or pitch and used as candles. In Britain in the Middle Ages the stalks were dipped in suet to burn at funerals.

MAKING CANDLES
The best candles are made from pure beeswax, though paraffin wax is more common. Stearin is added to the wax at a rate of about 10% to harden it. The wax mixture must be heated in a double boiler or in one saucepan heated over another of simmering water. Commercially available dyes or children's wax crayons can be added to the melted wax to colour your candles. The diameter of the wick needs to be adjusted to take into account the size of the candle, If the wick is too narrow, the candle will puddle and go out. If the wick is too wide, the candle will smoke. The type of perfume that you can buy to scent candles is all synthetic, and is of no magical value. If you want to perfume magical candles you will need to add pure essential oil, which can be done just before the wax is poured.

There are many ways of shaping candles and you can be as creative as you like. Here are a couple of simple methods:

1) One of the easiest ways of making a candle is in a mould. There are many varieties commercially available, constructed from metal, glass, flexible PVC, rubber and plastic, though you can use household items such as yoghurt pots, tin cans and so on. Thread a wick through a small hole in the bottom of the mould and knot it. At the top of the mould suspend a twig and tie the other end of the wick to it. Pour in the melted wax and after a minute tap the sides of the mould to release any air bubbles. Stand the whole thing in a bath of cold water, placing a weight on top to keep it down. Check it after an hour and top up with more wax if necessary. When the candle has set remove it from the bath and cut off the know at the bottom and pull the candle out of the mould. Cut off the wick to the required length. If the bottom of the candle is uneven, 'iron' it off in a hot saucepan. The candle can then be painted, or you can make patterns in the surface with the back of a hot spoon or with a warm knife.

You can also decorate the candle with dried, pressed flowers: take your flowers and lay them on the candle then 'iron' all over with the back of a hot spoon.

2) An interesting candle can be made using a bucket of sand to form an irregularly shaped mould. Put some sand in the bottom of a bucket, and then place a wooden post on top. Supporting the post, pour in damp sand. Carefully remove the post and pour in melted wax. After a few minutes pour in some more. Don't worry about the wax seeping into the sand- it's supposed to. After a couple of hours insert a wick, threaded onto a wicking needle and top up with more wax. The candle will them take 5-6 hours to set completely, and you can then lift it carefully out of the bucket. Sand will still be adhering to the outside of the candle, and this looks very attractive.

MAKING FLOWER CHAPLETS
We wear these during summer festivals, particularly Imbolc and Beltane.
Thick florist's wire
Thin florist's wire
Green florist's tape
Flowers and greenery
First use the thicker wire to make a circle the diameter of your head. Then you can begin to attach the flowers and leaves with the thin wires, covering them with the florist's tape, which is green and slightly tacky.

NATURAL DYES
Different herbs, mosses, lichens, barks, berries, twigs and leaves can be gathered at different times of the year to make natural dyes. Dyeing with plant materials in an ancient and rewarding craft; it is full of surprises as you never quite know what colour you are going to get- it all depends on the freshness and concentration of the plant materials, the type of fabric you use, and the mordant (fixative) you use. The colours are softer and more subtle than chemical dyes, and can help you feel like part of the landscape.

For the ancient Celts, dyeing was a magical process, a women's craft with strict taboos on dyeing fabric in the presence of men.

Mordants
Most natural dyes need a mordant to make them fast. The word derives from a French term meaning 'to bite' and it refers to a chemical applied to

the fabric before dying that helps the dye adhere to the cloth and fixes it so that it doesn't wash straight out again. Some are poisonous and should be handled carefully. Always wear rubber gloves and work in a well ventilated space. Mordants can be obtained from pharmacies, specialist craft and dye suppliers.

Alum (aluminium potassium chloride/ potassium aluminium sulphate)

This is probably the most popular mordant, and works with a wide variety of dyestuffs. In the past it was obtained from stale urine, wood ash, oak galls, oak and alder chips and burnt seaweed. Alum brightens the colour of the dye. It is often combined with tartaric acid to produce fresher, clearer colours. Use 1 oz for every 1 lb. of dry fabric weight. And add 1 oz cream of tartar. Dissolve, add 2 gallons water, bring slowly to the boil, add the fabric and simmer 1 hour. Remove the fabric and drip fairy dry, now begin the dying process.

Iron (ferrous sulphate) or copperas

The ancients obtained this from bogs and iron ore. It makes colours more muted, or 'saddened' to use the correct term. Use 1/8 oz for every 1 lb. of dry fabric weight. Otherwise, boil the fabric first with the dye for 30 minutes. Lift it out. Ass ½ oz ferrous sulphate and 1 oz cream of tartar, ready dissolved, to the dye pot. Replace the fabric and boil for another 30 minutes.

Copper (copper sulphate) or verdigris

This is used to give a blue-green tint to a colour. Use ½ oz with ½ pint of vinegar for every 1 lb. of dry fabric weight. NB: Poisonous, handle with care!

Tin (stannous chloride)

For each 1 lb fabric add 1 oz cream of tartar and ½ oz of tin crystals. Dissolve them together in water and add to 2 ½ gallons of water. Heat and add the wet fabric. Bring slowly to the boil, reduce heat and simmer 1 hour. Take out the wool and let it drip fairly dry. You can now begin the dying process. Tin will brighten colours. Use ½ oz for every 1 lb. of dry fabric weight. NB: Poisonous, handle with care.

Chrome (potassium dichromate)

For each 1 lb fabric add ½ oz potassium dichromate. Dissolve them together in water and add to 2 ½ gallons of water. Heat and add the wet fabric. Bring slowly to the boil, reduce heat and simmer 1 hour. Begin the dying process straight away. NB Highly poisonous, handle with care. Use with the lid on the pot as the fumes are highly toxic. Always use rubber gloves when handling the material.

Substitutes
Simple household substances as vinegar, bicarbonate of soda, cream of tartar, and wood ash can provide a practicable and greener alternative. They will not produce a completely permanent dye, but will greatly reduce fading.

Preparing the Fabric
Natural dyes work best on natural materials such as cotton, silk, and wool. Although a natural fabric, linen takes dye less readily than other materials. Rayon is the only synthetic fabric with which natural dyes can be used successfully.

It is best to keep your dyeing utensils separate from your cooking ware, as some of the substances you will use are poisonous. Copper or brass kettles are reckoned best, though enamel is fine and obtainable from second hand shops- never use aluminium- clean them afterwards with white vinegar and a little sand for scouring. You will also need a plastic bucket to rinse the fabric, muslin for straining out the plant material, stirring sticks, measuring jugs and scales, a stove for heating the liquids, the dye plant material and mordant.

The fabric should be thoroughly washed and soaked overnight if necessary to remove residues of grease, preferably in rainwater. Give it a final rinse in warm water to which a tablespoon of vinegar has been added.

Adding the Mordant
If you are using a mordant it should be added at this stage. The mordant should be dissolved in a small quantity of hot water, and a further four gallons of water gradually added. Totally immerse the fabric in the liquid and gradually bring to the boil and simmer for an hour. An alternative method is to soak the cloth in the mordant mixture for twenty-four hours (though if using alum, it will need to be boiled). Remove the fabric from the solution and dye it immediately.

Dyeing the fabric

Use approximately 2 oz of the plant material for every 1 oz of fabric. The plant should be chopped or crushed place it in a large pan and bring to the boil. Simmer ½ -2 hours depending on the material- flowers will give up their colours quickly, while woods take longer. Turn off the heat and leave to cool a little, then add the fabric, bring back to the boil and simmer, stirring, until the fabric takes on a good colour. Wearing rubber gloves, rinse the fabric several times, gradually decreasing the temperature of the rinsing water. Hang up the fabric to dry naturally. You can repeat the dyeing process two or three times to increase the colour density of the fabric and improve its resistance to fading.

Plants to Use

Most plants will produce some kind of dye, but 'tinctorum' or 'tinctoria' in their Latin name indicates a plant that is long established as a dyestuff. Various parts of the plant can be used- bark, berries, flowers, juice, leaves, shoots, or roots, depending on the particular plant.

Dye Chart

Plant	colour	mordant
Alder bark	red-brown	alum
Alder flowers	green	alum
Alder twigs	brown	iron
Alkanet	beige	alum
Apple bark	green	iron
Bilberries	blue	iron
Bilberries	purple	alum
Bilberries	blue	iron
Privet leaves	blue	alum & salt
Birch bark	purple	iron
Blackberries	light grey	alum
Blackberry shoots	black	iron
Bayberry leaves	yellow- brown	alum
Parsley	green-yellow	alum
Birch leaves	green-yellow	alum
Apple bark	red-yellow	alum
Madder	dark red	alum & tartar
Bedstraw roots	red	alum & tartar
Walnut leaves	brown	alum
Iceland moss	light brown	none

Elder bark	black	iron
Blackthorn	orange	alum
Elderberries	purple	alum
St Johnswort	purple	none
Agrimony	yellow	alum
Ash inner bark	yellow	alum
Birch	yellow	alum
Bog myrtle	yellow	alum
Broom	yellow	alum
Marsh marigold	yellow	alum
Meadowsweet	yellow	alum
Nettle	yellow	alum
Crab apple bark	yellow	alum
Bracken	yellow	alum
Flag iris	blue	iron
Dock	beige	alum
Dyer's weld	green	chrome
Elder berries	pink-purple	alum
Elder leaves	yellow	alum
Elder shoots	green	chrome
Golden rod	yellow	alum
Gorse	yellow	alum
Heather	beige	alum
Horsetail	green	alum
Indigo	blue	none needed
Lichen	yellow/purple	none needed
Lily of Valley	green-yellow	alum
Madder root	orange-red	alum or iron
Marigold	brown	alum
Oak bark	brown	alum
Oak bark	yellow	tin or zinc
Oak bark	black	iron
Onion skins	yellow	alum
Pine	red-yellow	alum
Pine cones	beige	alum
Sloes	purple	alum
Sorrel leaves	yellow	alum
Sorrel root	red	alum
Sunflower petals	yellow	alum
Walnut shells	brown	alum
Woad	green-blue	none needed

Chapter 7
WORT CUNNING

"O, mickle is the powerful grace that lies
In herbs, plants, stones, and their true qualities..."
Shakespeare, Romeo and Juliet

In the past the wise woman was both healer and midwife. She achieved her cures by herb simples, domestic remedies and magic. Today her function has been taken over by dozens of different professionals- midwives, doctors, nurses, physiotherapists, counsellors, psychiatrists, teachers, therapists and so on.

Today's Hearth Witch takes on the role of healer, in whatever form this may manifest - she may be the person everyone tells their troubles to and who they ask for good advice. She may be a nurse or complimentary therapist, an aromatherapist, reflexologist or herbalist, she may be a Reiki master or spiritual healer. She may use magic to achieve healing. She may be a herbalist, but this is not a job for an amateur: do not dose people with potions until you have had some training and know what you are doing. Never use herbs that can harm as well as heal.

HEALTH AND HEALING
Herbs have been used since the dawn of time for healing ailments of the body. At one time all medicines were herb based; the word 'drug' is derived from the Anglo Saxon *dregen*, which means 'to dry', and refers to dried herbs. The wise woman often used herbs in conjunction with prayer, magic and incantations.

Though modern medicine still owes most of its cures to plant derivatives, the introduction of chemical drugs like sulphur, arsenic and mercury by Paracelsus eventually lead to the preponderance of chemical remedies and the orthodox approach of the modern day in which large doses of active chemicals are used to treat the symptoms of a given disease. However, many people are increasingly unhappy with this approach and believe that there is more to curing a disease than suppressing or eliminating its symptoms. Conventional medicine defines truth as mechanical, measurable and repeatable. Our bodies are merely organic machines and have to be treated as such; sickness and health are diametrically opposed. Conventional medicine would like to ban the use of herbs by non-medical professionals. They see plants as potential drugs, safe only in the hands of doctors. In Germany, only medical doctors, who often have little or no herbal training, are allowed to prescribe herbs.

Conventional medicine is based on the model of the healthy white male as the norm. Any deviation from the 'norm' is taken as something that needs correcting by drugs and surgery, including natural female states such as pregnancy and the menopause. In the 1950s pregnant women were given thalidomide to counteract nausea, which caused serious birth defects, and yet governments today continually talk about banning herbal remedies for nausea, such as ginger, which have a thousand year record for safety and efficacy. Menopausal women are routinely given Hormone Replacement Therapy to restore what is 'lost' (because an ageing woman is viewed as defective) which has been proven to lead to strokes and heart disease, breast and uterine cancer. They are often advised to undergo risky surgery to have their ovaries and uteruses removed, because they are now superfluous, while being discouraged from taking Soya and other plant based oestrogens which have meant that the unpleasant side-effects of the menopause have been virtually unknown in Japan for generations with no concomitant health risks.

And where has this reliance on the scientific drug based medicine got us? 70% of deaths in the USA and Britain are caused, not by illness or disease, but by the side effects of conventional medicine. Chilling isn't it?

The founder of homeopathy, Samuel Hahnemann, thought that the appearance of symptoms - such as rashes or a fever - was the means by which the body tried to rid itself of a disease, and the disease itself should be treated, rather than the symptoms suppressed, as still happens in much orthodox medicine. Disease is 'dis-ease' of the body, stemming from one or a number of causes, which might be physical, environmental, dietary, psychological, stress related or even spiritual. A problem in one of these areas will eventually affect the others; no problem exists in isolation and may have several causes and a variety of effects. Any treatment needs to address the whole being - not just the body, not just the mind and certainly not just the spirit. Even doctors are beginning to recognise that a patient's mental attitude can have a dramatic effect on recovery and serious illness survival rates, which is a small step in the right direction.

Any healing which aims to promote the full potential of an individual must address mind, body and spirit. You must make your body as strong as it can be with the correct diet, exercise, life-style and medicines, if they are necessary. You can make your mental attitudes strong and positive. You must recognise the spiritual in the material.

THE WISE WOMAN AS HEALER

All the chemical components of our blood and tissues are available from plants, which are natural chemical factories and energy powerhouses. From red plants we get iron, from sea plants iodine and so on. Some plants produce complex chemicals that appear to have no part in a plant's own metabolism, but have a profound effect on the humans and animals that ingest them. This can be no accident, but the reinforcing of Mother Nature's web which links us all together in a complex, interdependent eco-system.

The resurgence of interest in alternative medicine has led many people to be interested in herbs and herbal remedies. They are all natural aren't they? Well, no, sorry. The chemicals contained in plants can be synthesised or isolated and used in a conventional allopathic way. If you buy a jar of herbal tablets of the health food shop, read the label. If it says 'standardised' it means that the active ingredient has been stripped way from the rest, leaving something akin to an allopathic drug. The scientific drive to quantify active ingredients in herbs creates herbal products that are as dangerous as drugs. In a bid to be accepted by the medical profession, some herbalists seek to apply the scientific method, and concentrate on the so called active ingredient of a plant. For instance, most St. John's wort tablets and tinctures are standardised for hypericin. But the latest research shows that hyperforin is the real active ingredient. Most people who say they can't take St John's wort because they don't get on with it have tried the standardised variety; if they are put on the whole herb, they are fine. An article several years ago in *JAMA* on use of Ginkgo Biloba to counter dementia explained that no active ingredient from among the several hundred constituents present had been determined and it was, in fact, likely that the effect resulted from a complex, synergistic interplay of the parts. In other words, the whole plant contains a range of chemicals which seem to work in concert. [19] This is true of all herbs, for example, a diuretic normally robs the body of potassium, whereas the dandelion is one of nature's best diuretics and is also a rich source of potassium.

For the Hearth Witch, the plant as a whole is the key, and moreover, the life force or spirit of the plant is of as great an importance as any active ingredient. He or she works with locally grown plants, honouring the earth and using the resources of their locality as their healing allies in an ecologically sustainable fashion.

The Hearth Witch recognises that both health and illness are both part of life. We all suffer ill health at some time or another. The Hearth Witch does not see illness and disability as a personal failure to be whole, or as a karmic punishment for sin. There is no blame and no shame in being ill; it is part of the life pattern and can be an opportunity for growth. One of the first questions that people ask when they get sick is 'Why is this happening to *me*? What have I done to deserve this?' Some people suggest that illness is karmic, that in some way the sufferer deserves to be punished. I was once visited by a distraught patient; a so-called 'psychic healer' had told her that her Parkinson's disease was karmic. This was an unbearable burden on top of the pain and fear of the illness itself and an unforgivable sin on the part of the 'healer' who implied that the illness was her own fault, caused by negativity or sin, pollution of the mind, body or spirit. He went on to explain how he knew best, that she would only get well if she followed his advice without question, and bought several expensive crystals and exotic remedies from him.

An important part of the healing process is the empowerment of the patient. In the above case, the surrender of personal power to the so called 'healer' was every bit as destructive as that often engendered by the conventional doctor/patient relationship. Illnesses do have causes, even though they sometimes seem to strike out of the blue. We all know that if we live on junk food we will become obese, get digestive problems, cancer, heart disease and so on. If we smoke, we will, in all likelihood develop respiratory diseases, cancer or heart disease. This is cause and effect, if you like. But did you know that children today are six time more likely to get diabetes than their parents because of their high sugar diets? Or that childhood asthma is many time more common today than twenty years ago owing to air pollution? These children are not getting ill because the gods are punishing them, but because of the world we live in.

19   Susan Weed, www.susunweed.com

Not everyone can enjoy a perfect physique and perfect physical fitness. Some of us are born with disabilities or are damaged by accident or illness. While some physical diseases and mental conditions are curable, others are not. If you have lost a leg, a kidney or a thyroid it cannot be regenerated with present technology. Conditions such as arthritis and multiple sclerosis are regarded as degenerative life long diseases. Schizophrenia is not curable, but in most cases can be controlled by drugs. However, it is important to recognise that though you may have been damaged, you are still a whole person. You still have the full potential of your life force.

Healing is not accomplished by the healer but by the patient and healer working together. The healer helps the patient seek their own cure and works to increase, not diminish their personal power, their responsibility for the own health.

MEETING THE PLANTS

Only a few short years ago, every child would have walked to school picking rose hips to make itching powder, nibbling 'bread and cheese' (i.e. the hawthorn buds before they unfold in the spring), telling the time with dandelion clocks, using the buttercup test for whether you liked butter, throwing sticky buds and playing pooh sticks. Not too long ago, children knew most of their local plants and played in the open fields and parks. However, a couple of years ago I gave a talk on herbalism at a Pagan camp, and I was shocked to discover that while most people over forty could identify a good many common plants and trees, two out of every three people under twenty could not even recognise a simple dandelion.

If you want to work in the Hearth Witch tradition with herbs, then you must begin by getting to know the plants that grow in your local area, those vegetation spirits that live with you, along your local hedgerow, meadow, park, road or in your garden. Don't assume that medicinal plants are hard to find; dandelion, plantain and nettles (to name just a few) are as common in cities and suburbs as in the country. Get a good field guide to help you identify them and a reputable modern herbal to tell you what they may be used for. You will need to refer to the botanical name (usually Latin or Greek) since these names are specific while the same common name can refer to several very different plants. There are a dozen dissimilar plants referred to as bachelor's buttons, while "marigold" can be *Calendula officinalis*, a medicinal herb, or *Tagetes*, an annual flower used as a bedding plant.

Spend time with the plants, noting where they live, in sun or shade, on chalky soil or sandy soil and so on, their growth habits, when they flower, and when they set their seeds. Note the shape of the leaves, their texture and colour, their taste, if edible. In this way you will begin to learn from the plants themselves. Each plant is a living teacher and must be approached as an individual spirit, a vital life force which may become your ally if approached with love and respect. You must learn to speak its language by listening with an open heart and using the inner senses, as well as the everyday senses of taste, smell and touch. Don't expect to learn everything at once as it will likely be over several seasons that the plant reveals its nature to you. This is the wisdom that the old herbalists passed down to their apprentices, part of which is preserved in folklore and old wives tales. It is a knowledge that cannot be bought, and which cannot be learned from books but only by doing. Allow yourself to trust your inner wisdom, and you will uncover the instinctive knowledge of Mother Nature that lies deep within all our souls.

Witches use plant powers, but to capture them without dissipating them is not simple a matter of walking three times around a tree and saying 'can I have a branch?' lopping one off and leaving a coin in return. You might as well buy a dried herb off the shelf in the local shop, or pick up a dead twig from the forest floor. These instructions are based on folk magic, a distorted version of half forgotten lore, a shadow of the true knowledge. I learned this from Phil, my old High Priest, who insisted that first of all a relationship must be established with the particular tree or plant that you want to cut. Of necessity, this will be forged over a period of time; you must understand each other. He insisted that some plants are well disposed towards humankind, some need to be persuaded, some fought and some will never give you anything no matter what you do, and it would be dangerous to try. Few western magicians today understand or work with the Old Knowledge concerning plants.

Trees and herbs are not really 'used' magically. When properly approached they may share something of their life force, their spirit. True magical herbalism is not really a case of following a kind of cookbook approach, a pinch of this and a pinch of that. Individual herbs and plants can be befriended as allies to enable the practitioner to travel to Otherworldly places, and to become in tune with different energies. The Craft of the magical herbalist takes many years and absolute self discipline to master. The plant itself is always the teacher. Each plant must be correctly approached and harvested in perfect condition. It must always be respected as a living being: its life force is the essence of its power. This force is harnessed by taking the plant internally or externally, fresh or as an infusion, by smoking it or employing it in an incense or bathing herb, by using it as a magical condenser, and so on.

If the herb is approached with love and trust, its force will harmonise with the witch and share its secrets. If the plant is taken with the wrong motives, if it is mistreated or misused, it may cause discomfort, mislead or seek to gain control of the witch. If an enemy is made of the plant spirit, it can destroy. It is a common misconception that a plant needs to have hallucinogenic properties to facilitate expansion of consciousness. Only a small number of power plants are psychedelic, and these plant spirits are the most difficult to deal with and easily overcome the weak will of anyone stupid enough to use them for recreational purposes. Every plant, from the common daisy to the mighty oak, has its own power and vibration, and by taking time to gain the trust of the plant spirit, these can be shared.

The use of entheogenic (hallucinogenic) substances is central to a minority of shamanic traditions. The term entheogen was invented by Gordon Wasson, and means 'god containing' because these substances had the ability to allow people to unite the god-consciousness. The Aztecs of pre-Columbian Mexico revered psilocybin mushrooms so much that they named them *Teonanacatl*, meaning 'flesh of the gods' or 'divine flesh'. In Mexico and Guatemala, between 1000 and 500 BCE, people built temples to mushroom gods and carved mushroom stones. It is likely that at least some of the religions that speak of eating the flesh of the god mean the use of sacred plants.

Many early religions included the use of entheogenic plants as sacraments (i.e. Holy Communion with the gods), to evoke visions, or for divination and healing. Initiation to the Eleusinian Mysteries of ancient Greece probably involved the use of psilocybin mushrooms. Gilgamesh, the hero of an ancient Sumerian epic, went on a quest for a miraculous herb, which he eventually discovered only to have it taken from him by its guardian, the serpent. This may have influenced the Bible story which is told with a different slant- it is the serpent that actually offers the fruit of knowledge to Eve.[20] This 'forbidden fruit' may have been an entheogen which opened the mind to the god-state. Eating the fruit

20   *Soma and the Fly-Agaric*, (Ethno-Mycological Studies No. 2), by Wasson, R. Gordon, Cambridge, 1972

of the tree of life (the World Tree) unites man with the gods- eating it is forbidden in the Bible.

The Peruvian *mestizo* shamans use *ayahuasca* as a sacrament. In the Amazon, the ayahuasceros regard the giant serpent as the "mother spirit" of all the other spirits of the forest, of the river and the air. [21] In legend, ayahuasca was created when the great grandmother Cosmos Yewa Velo (the great maloca of quartz was formed. The great ancestral shaman, made of smoke of tobacco, and during in his encounter with the ancestral shaman of quartz, made the sacred ayahuasca plant, which is the umbilical cord of the Cosmos.

Traditional shamanic rituals involving hallucinogenic plants are carefully structured experiences, in which a small group of people come together with a respectful, spiritual attitude to share a profound inner journey of healing and transformation, facilitated by these allies, usually accompanied by music, drumming and chanting. The mushroom ceremonies of the Mazatec Indians of Mexico involve the participants sitting or lying in a very dark room, with only a small candle. The healer sings almost uninterruptedly throughout the night, weaving into her chants the names of Christian saints, her spirit allies and the spirits of the earth, the elements, animals and plants, the sky, the waters and the fire.[22]

USING YOUR PLANT

How do you extract the goodness from the plant and put it to use? You can't just eat all the herbs you want to use, and strangely enough, some dried herbs have more medicinally active constituents than fresh ones. Use some common sense and follow safety procedures. First make sure that you identify your herb correctly- if in any doubt at all, leave it alone. Make sure that you have looked up the method of preparation and the safe dosages. Pick your herbs from unpolluted locations- herbs from the side of a busy road will be covered with chemicals. Herbs may be used in a variety of ways, internally and externally:

Internal Remedies:

Dried Herbs in Capsules

This is usually the way you purchase herbs from a shop, and it is the worst way to take them, and the least effective. They are poorly digested, poorly utilized, often stale or ineffective, and quite expensive.

21   *The Reunification of the Sacred and Natural* by Ralph Metzner, PhD
22   *ibid*

Hot Infusion (Teas or Tisanes)
Many of a herbs components, such as its minerals, vitamins, sugars, starches, hormones, tannins, volatile oils and some alkaloids dissolve well in water, and for this reason, herbs are often taken as infusions or tisanes. Generally the difference between the two is simply of strength- an infusion is a medicinal dose, whereas a tea or tisane is weaker. Use one teaspoon of dried herb per cup or 1 oz per pint of boiling water. Pour the boiling water over the herb and infuse for 5-15 minutes.

Cold Infusion
Some herbs have properties which are destroyed by heat, so a cold infusion is made. Use a non metal container and put in 1 oz of the herb and 1 pint of cold water. Close the lid or cover with cling film and leave for 5-6 hours.

Decoction
Some seeds, roots, buds and barks etc. need to be boiled in water for a while. This is called a decoction. If they are dried they should first be pounded into a powered. Use 1 oz of dried herb or 2 oz of fresh herb to one pint of water. Bring the mixture to the boil in a non aluminium pan and simmer 10-15 minutes. Strain.

Tinctures
Plant constituents are generally more soluble in alcohol than water, so tinctures are made. Alcohol will dissolve and extract resins, oils, alkaloids, sugars, starches and hormones, though it does not extract nutrients such as vitamins or minerals. Brandy or vodka is usually used. Because a tincture is much stronger than an infusion or decoction, you only use a few drops -5-15) in a glass of water as a medicinal dose. Alternatively, a few drops may be added to a salve or bath. To make a tincture put 4 oz of dried herbs or 8 oz fresh herbs into a clean jar and pour on one pint of vodka or brandy. Seal and keep in a warm place for two weeks, shaking daily. Strain and store in a dark bottle.

Syrups
Some herbs are bitter tasting and are more palatable when taken in the form of a syrup, particularly for children. To make a syrup, for every one pint of infusion or decoction add 1 lb. of sugar and heat gently until the sugar is dissolved. This will need to be kept in the fridge.

Herbal Vinegars

By placing a few springs of herbs in vinegar, you can make herbal vinegar which is not only pleasant tasting, but also therapeutic. You can make a tincture with cider vinegar instead of alcohol (as per the instructions above for tincture) but bear in mind that this will not be as strong as one prepared in alcohol.

External Remedies

Baths

Add one pint of infusion or decoction to the bath water.

Ointments (Salves)

Herbs can be made into salves. Melt 8 oz petroleum jelly or other fat and simmer 2 tablespoons of the herb in it for 15 minutes.

Compresses

Prepare a clean cotton cloth and soak it in a hot infusion or decoction. Use this as hot as possible on the affected area. Change the compress as it cools down.

Poultice

Bruise fresh herbs and apply directly to the skin and cover directly with a cloth.

Cold Infused Oil

Fats and oils extract the oily and resinous properties of an herb, many of which are strongly antibacterial, antifungal, antiseptic, and wound-healing. These are applied to the skin or used with massage. To make an infused oil cut up the herb and cover with vegetable oil (olive, sunflower, almond etc.) in a glass bottle or jar, Leave in a warm place for 2-3 weeks, shaking daily. Strain into a clean jar. Infused herbal oils are available as is, or thickened into ointments. Unlike essential oils, they do not need to be diluted for use.

Essential Oils

These can be used in the bath, with massage or in an evaporator. They cannot be made at home, but are readily available from shops. They are very concentrated and must always be diluted with vegetable carrier oil. More about this later.

SIMPLES

The easiest, and often the most effective, way to use herbs for healing is as a simple i.e., one herb at a time rather than a blend. In this way you can, as Wise Woman Susan Weed puts it, match the uniqueness of the plant to the uniqueness of the patient. Combining herbs with the same properties is counter-productive and more likely to cause trouble than a simple. Remember too, that when you use one plant at a time it is much easier to discern the effect of that plant and if someone has a bad reaction to the remedy, it is obvious what the source of the distress is, and usually easy to remedy. The more herbs there are in a formula, the more likelihood there is of unwanted side-effects.

Preserving Herbs

Any fresh herbs can be dried. They should be picked and tied in small bunches. Dip the bunches in boiling water and hang them in the kitchen or a well ventilated shed to dry. Once dried out they should be crumbled into jars and stored in a dark place.

WISE WOMAN'S RECIPES

Herb Pillow

Oblong of cotton fabric
1 oz dried red rose petals
2 oz dried mint leaves
3 tsp powdered cloves

Sew the herbs into the cotton cloth to make a small pillow or bag. Use at the side of your regular pillow to promote restful sleep and a clear head. Use chamomile and lavender if you are having trouble sleeping.

Clove Oil Rub

This may be used for bronchial infections, colds, headache and backache

1 oz ground cloves
2 oz ground ginger
4 oz dried thyme
2 oz dried sage
2 oz dried rosemary
4 tsp cayenne pepper
1 pint vegetable oil

Put half of the herbs and spices into the oil in a jar with a tight lid. Put the container into a pan, fill with water up to 1 inch from the top of the pan and simmer for two hours. Cool. Strain the mixture through muslin. Discard the used herbs. Place the fresh ones in the jar and add the oil again. Simmer in the water bath for another 2 hours. Keep an eye on it as burnt oil is useless. Cool and strain. The mixture will keep for 1 year, or longer if you add wheatgerm oil at 5-10%. Pour into a clean bottle, label, and store in a cool, dark place.

Coltsfoot Tobacco

Coltsfoot leaves dried
1 part rum
3 parts water
1 part honey

Mix the rum, honey and water. Strip the mid ribs from the coltsfoot and pack the leaves into a container, sprinkling a little of the mixture between each layer. Press down tightly and put a weight on top. Leave for two days, then take out the block and shred it.

Dreambringer Smoke

1/8 part cinnamon
3 parts damiana
1 part crushed juniper berries
3 parts passion flower
3 parts wild lettuce
4 parts coltsfoot
2 parts catnip

Meditation Smoke

1/8 part cinnamon
3 parts damiana
1 part juniper berries, crushed
1 part rose petals
3 parts coltsfoot
3 parts catnip

Comfrey & Calendula Healing Salve

1 tbsp beeswax
1 tbsp lanolin
1 tbsp cocoa butter
1 1/2 tbsp infused calendula oil
1 tsp glycerine
1/4 tsp borax

2 tbsp comfrey infusion
6 drops pettigrain essential oil

Melt the beeswax. In a separate container melt the lanolin and butter and then stir into the beeswax. Warm the calendula oil and glycerine and then stir into the wax mixture. Dissolve the borax in warm comfrey infusion and add to the mixture. Stir well. When cool and thick add the essential oil and spoon into jars.

Daisy Salve

8 oz daisy flowers and leaves
8 oz petroleum jelly
1/2 oz beeswax

Melt the petroleum jelly and beeswax in a bowl over boiling water. Add the flowers and leaves. Simmer for two hours, and then strain into a pot.

Elderflower Salve

1/2 lb petroleum jelly
4 pints elderflowers (remove the stems)

Melt the petroleum jelly in a pan, add the flowers, and simmer 30 minutes. While still hot, strain through cheesecloth into small jars. This will sooth bites, sore and chapped skin and chilblains.

Wormwood Salve

1 lb petroleum jelly
1 oz wormwood
1 oz elderflowers
1 oz rosemary

In a double boiler, melt the petroleum jelly and add the herbs. Simmer for 30 minutes or until the jelly has taken on the scent of the herbs. Strain and bottle. This is good for rheumatism and lumbago. Do not use for extended periods.

Marigold Salve

½ lb fresh flowers
½ pint olive oil
2 oz beeswax
Warm the oil (do not boil) add the petals, avoid the green parts. Simmer very gently for 30 minutes and strain out the flowers. Add the wax and melt in. Remove from the heat and stir continually while it cools. Spoon into clean jars and label. This is good for burns and as an antiseptic cream.

Elderflower Water

1 pint of petals (removed from the green stems)
2 pints hot water
2 tsp honey
2 tbsp glycerine
2 tbsp witch hazel
Steep for 2 hours and keep refrigerated. This is a good lotion for the skin. Omit the glycerine and witch hazel and use for bathing sore eyes.

Honey and Lemon Cough Syrup

2 lemons
¼ pint runny honey
2 fl oz glycerine
Juice the lemons and strain it

through muslin to get a clear liquid. Add the honey and glycerine and mix together well. Bottle and refrigerate.

Cough Sweets

2 tbsp rosewater
2 tsp gum Arabic
Caster sugar
Cinnamon powder
Warm the rosewater and dissolve the gum Arabic in it. Mix together equal amounts of cinnamon and sugar, and work this into the gum paste, keep adding some until it becomes quite solid. You can shape this into little pastilles.

Queen Elizabeth's Electuary

1 pint honey
Bunch of hyssop, bruised
¼ oz liquorice root
¼ oz aniseed
⅛ oz elecampane root
⅛ oz angelica root
Pinch pepper
¼ oz fresh ginger root
Boil the honey and skim off the scum. Add the hyssop and simmer for 30-40 minutes. Strain off the honey and add the other ingredients. Simmer 10 minutes, then strain off and bottle. This is good for coughs, colds and indigestion.

Nettle Syrup

1 lb young nettle tops
2 pints water
Sugar

Boil for 1 ½ hours, then strain the liquid into a clean pan and add 1 lb sugar for every pint of water. Boil for 30 minutes and bottle in sterilised bottles. Keep refrigerated. The syrup is good for rheumatism.

Ginger Syrup

4 oz fresh ginger root
2 pints water
Rind of 1 lemon

Place everything in a pan and bring to the boil, and simmer for 45 minutes. Strain and to every pint of liquid add 1 lb sugar and the juice of 1 lemon. Boil 10 minutes. Cool and bottle. For coughs and colds, take 1 tablespoon in hot water.

Rose Petal Vinegar

Rose petals (red or pink)
White vinegar

Fill a glass jar with the rose petals. Cover with the vinegar and leave on a sunny windowsill for 2 weeks until the vinegar has turned a good red. Strain into a clean dark bottle and seal. For headache, pour some of the vinegar into a bowl and soak a clean flannel in it, wring out and apply to the forehead. Repeat as necessary. (You can also chill the bowl of vinegar in the fridge.)

Elderberry Rob

2 ½ lb elderberries
½ lb sugar

Simmer together in a saucepan until it thickens to the consistency of runny honey. Strain and bottle. Take a couple of tablespoons in warm water for colds, fevers and coughs. If you like, you can add a little whisky.

Garlic Salve

Take a jar of petroleum jelly and add a chopped clove of garlic. Place in the airing cupboard for 10 days. Remove and massage into the back and chest for bronchitis and chest complaints.

Horehound Cough Sweets

2 pints boiling water
1 oz dried horehound (*Marrubium vulgare*)
Demerara sugar
Cream of tartar

Pour the boiling water over the herb. Cover and infuse 30 minutes. Strain through muslin and squeeze out all the juice. For every two cups of infusion you have, add two cups of brown sugar and 1 tsp cream of tartar. When the sugar has melted, bring to the boil, continue boiling until setting point is reached (drop a little of the mixture into cold water and see if it hardens). Pour into a buttered swiss roll tin. Mark into squares and allow to set.

Oatmeal Bath Bag

Tie up some coarse oatmeal in a muslin bag, and tie it beneath the hot tap when running a bath. You can also use the bag in place of soap. This will benefit eczema.

HERB TEA BLENDS

All the ingredients for these tea blends should be dried. To make the blends up, chop and mix the ingredients well, and store in a tightly sealed tea caddy or dark container out of the light.   To brew the teas, boil the water and place two teaspoons of tea in a ceramic tea pot per person. Infuse 10-15 minutes and strain into cups. Sweeten with honey if desired, but do not add milk. Avoid metal teapots, particularly aluminium, and preferably use filtered water. If you want to make single cups, you can buy tea balls from kitchen shops. These look like two halves of a tea strainer clipped together, and you can fill them with enough herb to make a cup.

Agrimony Tea

1 oz agrimony
1 oz ground ivy
$\frac{1}{2}$ oz sweet marjoram
$\frac{1}{2}$ oz pennyroyal
$\frac{1}{2}$ oz lavender
$\frac{1}{2}$ oz rose petals
$\frac{1}{2}$ oz cowslip or primrose flowers

Coltsfoot Tea

1 oz coltsfoot leaves
1 oz fennel leaves
$\frac{1}{4}$ oz ginger powder

Elderflower & China Tea

1 lb China tea
3 oz elderflowers

Sleepy Tea

1 oz lemon verbena leaves
1 oz passion flower
1 oz hops
1 oz skullcap
2 oz peppermint
1 oz catmint

Goodnight Tea

1 $\frac{1}{2}$ oz ground valerian root

1 oz skullcap
1 oz passion flower
1 oz chamomile flowers
1 oz catmint

Pre-Menstrual Tea

1 oz uva ursi
1 oz white willow bark
1 oz hops
1 oz motherwort
4 oz raspberry leaf

Menopause Blend

2 oz red clover blossoms
1 oz sage
1 oz chamomile flowers
2 oz nettle
1 oz lemon balm

Women's Tea

1 $\frac{1}{2}$ oz raspberry leaves
1 oz motherwort
1 $\frac{1}{2}$ oz red clover
1 oz peppermint

Calming Tea
1 oz peppermint
½ oz lemongrass
1 oz lemon balm
½ oz catnip
1 oz camomile flowers
¼ oz lavender flowers

Shaman's Tea
½ oz sage
½ oz mugwort
1 oz catnip
½ oz skullcap
1 oz passionflower
¼ oz ginger powder

Hay Fever Tea
¼ oz elecampane (*Inula helenium*)
¼ oz cherry bark
¼ oz angelica root
¼ oz liquorice root

Clairvoyance Tea
1 oz peppermint
¼ oz dried orange peel

¼ oz rose petals
½ oz lemon grass
½ cinnamon stick, crushed
6 cloves, crushed
1 oz mugwort
¼ oz wild lettuce

Purification Tea
1 oz camomile flowers
½ stick cinnamon, crushed
½ oz fennel
¼ oz lavender flowers
½ oz lemon peel
¼ oz lime peel
¼ oz rosemary
¼ oz vervain

Peace Tea
1 oz rose petals
¼ oz lavender flowers
½ oz violet petals
½ oz meadowsweet
1 oz hibiscus flowers

ESSENTIAL OILS AND AROMATHERAPY

Essential oils have been used for thousands of years to treat illness and are very useful self help tools. They are readily available, and although quite expensive, a little goes a long way. They have a profound effect on mood and the emotions as well as the physical body. Different oils may be stimulating or calming, and can be used to aid depression, anxiety and stress. Always make sure that you buy 100% pure essential oils from a reputable supplier. Perfume oils are synthetic and have no therapeutic or magical effect.

How to use the Oils

Pure essential oils can be used in several ways:
1. In the bath- blend 20 drops of essential oil with 30 ml of vegetable

oil and add 2 teaspoons to the bath after it has run. Swirl it about in the water to ensure dispersion over the surface. As you get into the bath the oil will coat your skin, and the heat of the water helps its absorption. You will also breathe in the vapours. For an aromatherapy bath do not use soap- treat it as a therapy, not a wash.

2. Massage- most oils diluted with a base oil may safely be applied to the skin. Add 15-20 drops of essential oil to 30 ml of vegetable oil. An aromatherapy massage is a relaxing experience, designed to free the body from tension and apply healing oils to the skin. For headaches and migraine a suitable oil may be massaged just into the temples and neck or for treating arthritic knees a suitable oil may be used on the painful site and so on.

3. Vaporisation- all essential oils readily evaporate and many are antiseptic and make good air fresheners. Essential oils may also be used to create a relaxing or stimulating atmosphere. A purpose made oil evaporator can be used, or a few drops of oil can be added to a dish of water placed on a radiator.

4. In creams and lotions- oils can be blended with a lotion or your usual moisturiser. Add around 20 drops to 100 ml of lotion.

Do not take any of the oils internally, except on the advice of a qualified therapist. The oils are highly concentrated and can be damaging or even poisonous when taken internally.

Some Useful Oils:

Bergamot
Is strongly antiseptic and is used in the bath for cystitis, vaginal thrush and urinary infections. Add a few drops to a bowl of boiling water and inhale for bronchial infections. Use in massage or blended with moisturiser for wounds, eczema and psoriasis; it is especially effective when part of the cause is stress and depression. It helps ease the discomfort of chicken pox, shingles and cold sores. Do not apply to the skin before exposing yourself to strong sunlight.

Camomile
Is especially useful for women. Use in the bath or with massage to ease the problems of painful periods and menopausal symptoms. Rub into the skin to relieve muscular aches and pains, arthritis and rheumatism.

It is a very calming oil used to soothe anxiety and depression and relieve insomnia. It is also good for dry and inflamed skin, burns, dermatitis and broken veins. A camomile inhalation used for respiratory infections fights bacterial toxins. Camomile is a calming, soothing oil, safe enough to use on children.

Eucalyptus
The main use of eucalyptus is in the treatment of colds, sinus problems, asthma, coughs, bronchitis and catarrh- use in the bath or as a chest rub. It is also a good antiseptic and is used for cold sores, wounds and cystitis. It is beneficial for muscular pain, arthritis, and neuralgia. It can be used to stimulate the elimination of fluid retention and to bring down fevers. Use in an evaporator in the sick room to kill off air borne microbes.

Juniper
Stimulates the circulatory system and helps toxin elimination from the body. Blend with a cream or lotion for acne and oily skin or add a drop to the final rinse for greasy hair. It is very good for rheumatic pain and helps eliminate the uric acid build up that is a feature of conditions such as gout. Use in the bath or with massage for fluid retention, haemorrhoids, painful periods, anxiety, stress and insomnia. It is a gently stimulating oil.

Lavender
Is the most versatile and safest of all the oils, valuable in a large number of conditions, including high blood pressure, lymph congestion, nausea, cystitis, headaches, migraine, irregular periods, aches and pains, rheumatism, sprains, anxiety, depression, irritability, palpitations, cellulite, fluid retention, colds and flu, bites and burns. It soothes and reduces acne rosacea, eczema, dermatitis and diminishes scarring. Apply neat to burns to reduce the pain and inflammation, to lessen the scarring and reduce the shock. For period pains massage into the lower back and abdomen. For tension headaches and migraines, massage into the temples and the back of the neck. For insomnia use in the bath before going to bed and sprinkle a few drops on the pillow.

Rosemary
Is a stimulating oil with many uses including headaches, mental tiredness, migraine, memory loss, aches and pains, arthritis, rheumatism, debility, epilepsy, paralysis, mental stress, fluid retention, asthma, bronchitis,

alopecia and dandruff. It is helpful in the treatment of Candida albicans. Rosemary has a strong stimulant effect on the mind, clearing the head and clarifying thoughts. It can have an uplifting and antidepressant effect and is indicated for the sluggish and apathetic. Rosemary stimulates the circulation and the removal of toxins, and is therefore useful for varicose veins, arthritis, low blood pressure and poor circulation. Use as an inhalation for respiratory problems such as catarrh, colds, flu and sinusitis. Use in the bath to relieve exhaustion.

Base Oils

Generally speaking, essential oils should always be used in a dilute form. A few drops of essential oil are blended with base oil. Any vegetable oil will do- sunflower, almond, olive, wheatgerm etc. Do not use baby oil, which is a mineral oil. If you wish to keep the blended oil for more than a few weeks, use a wheatgerm base or add 10% of vitamin E oil or wheatgerm oil.

Revitalising Massage Oil
20 ml base oil
4 drops vitamin E oil
10 drops lemon oil
10 drops basil oil
5 drops black pepper oil

Relaxing Massage Oil
20 ml base oil
4 drops vitamin E oil
4 drops patchouli oil
5 drops ylang ylang oil
8 drops lavender oil
4 drops sandalwood oil

MAGICAL OILS

Magical oils can be used in several ways:
- In the bath – add two teaspoons of blended magical oil to the bath after it has run. Swirl it about in the water to ensure dispersion over the surface. As you get into the bath the oil will coat your skin, and the heat of the water helps its absorption. You will also breathe in

the vapours. For an oil bath do not use soap- treat it as a ritual, not a wash. A purification bath is a pre-requisite to any ritual, and you can add an appropriate oil to help you attune to the ceremony to come.

- Anointing – most magical groups anoint coveners as they enter the circle, during initiation rituals etc. Magical tools are anointed as part of their consecration.
- Vaporisation – all essential oils readily evaporate and may be used in the place of incense if this is more convenient. Bear in mind that in this case they represent the element of fire, rather than air, within the circle. Purpose made oil evaporators should be used.
- An oil may be used to 'seal' a doorway or window against negativity after a cleansing or exorcism has taken place. A suitable oil is smeared around the opening.

Do not take any of the oils internally. The oils are highly concentrated and can be damaging or even poisonous when taken internally.

Types of Oils
There are two types of magical oils that I use. The first type I make from herbs and flowers that I collect or grow; it is impossible to make essential oils at home, so I make infused oils (see below). The second types I make are blended oils, made with base oil and drops of bought-in pure essential oils added.

Making Infused Oils
Loosely fill a clear glass jar with freshly picked sprigs of herbs or flowers. Fill the jar with a vegetable oil (almond or sunflower is fine). Cover the top of the jar with a piece of muslin and leave on a sunny windowsill for about two weeks, stirring daily. Strain into a clean jar or bottle. This oil will keep for around 4-5 months in a cool, dark place. There is no need to dilute it any further for use, but you can blend together several varieties if you wish.

Making Blended Oils
The recipes below are for blended oils. They are formulated using 20 ml of base oil and the stated number of drops of essential oil. If you wish the oil to keep for longer than a few weeks you will have to use a base of wheatgerm oil, or add 20-30 drops of pure vitamin E oil to the blend. I have oils that have kept for years based on this prescription.

Pan
Patchouli 8, pine 2, cedar 10, juniper 4

Peace
Ylang ylang 6, lavender 6, chamomile 4, rose 2

Prophetic Dream
Frankincense 4, lemon grass 5

Dragon Oil
Frankincense 2, orange 5, lemon 4, patchouli 4

Demeter Oil
Myrrh 9, vetivert 6, oakmoss 3

Personal Blessing
Cinnamon 3, lavender 4, vetivert 5

Attraction
Orange 7, lemon 7, verbena 4, patchouli 5, rose 10

Aradia
Frankincense 5, sandalwood 5, myrrh 4, lemon 3, musk rose 20

Protection
Rosemary 3, geranium 4, cypress 4

Temple
Rosemary 3, frankincense 3, thyme 4

BATH SALTS

Bath salts can be made by adding the above combinations of essential oils, minus the base oil, to a handful of salt. Blend in with the back of a spoon. Use prior to ritual.

INCENSE

Soon after I began to study the properties and characters of all the trees, plants and herbs I learned how to blend incenses and oils for magical use and this became my speciality. Their power works on three levels. The first is the effect it has on the mood of the magician. Secondly, a perfume may have certain associations for the person who experiences it. If you associate certain perfumes with a ritual setting, it can induce the mood required and concentrate the mind on the task in hand; if you condition yourself to associate different perfumes with different rituals or deities this will act as a subconscious short cut. Thirdly, on a more profound level, is the effect of the *vibration* of the perfume. When we use plants for incense making we use the vibrational life force of the plant rather than its medicinal qualities or its perfume for the purpose of changing the vibration of the atmosphere to the level needed for a magical operation, not because it has a 'nice smell'.

Incenses are simply barks, resins, leaves, flowers and oils that are burned to release their fragrance and smoke. An incense may be one single herb or a blend of many. Each should be chosen for its attributes and correspondences. Traditional British incenses are made from wild herbs, flowers and barks that are gathered, dried and blended together at the correct season, and then thrown onto the fire. You can make useful incenses from shop bought ingredients, but really powerful incenses can only be made from ingredients you collect yourself.

DRAGON INCENSE

3 parts frankincense
1/8 part dragon's blood
½ part lemon peel
½ part orange peel
Few drops lemon oil
Few drops orange oil
Few drops patchouli oil

YULE

1 part cedar wood
1 part pine wood
1 part juniper berries
2 parts frankincense
Few drops orange oil

MORRIGAN

1 part musk crystals
¼ part dragon's blood

1 part yew wood
Few drops patchouli oil
1 part myrrh
½ part nettle leaves

EARTH MOTHER

1 part pine resin
1 part mandrake root
1 part rose petals
½ part patchouli leaves
Few drops patchouli oil

HERNE

3 parts oak bark
½ part yarrow
½ part betony
1 part pine resin
Few drops pine oil
1 part ash bark

ESBAT

3 parts white sandalwood
½ part orris root powder
½ part thyme
½ part poppy seeds
1 part white rose petals
1 part benzoin
2 parts myrrh
2 parts frankincense
½ part gardenia flowers

TRANCE INCENSE

1 part broom flowers
½ part broom seeds
2 parts crushed juniper berries
½ part foxglove seeds
1 part crushed sloes
1 part ragwort flowers
1 part mistletoe
1 part valerian root
1 part wild lettuce

SUCCESS

½ part marigold petals
¼ part orange peel
1 part red sandalwood
2 parts frankincense

HEARTH BLESSING

½ part orange peel
1 part rose petals
1 part juniper berries
4 parts frankincense
1 part lavender flowers
1 part sandalwood
¼ part dragon's blood

MIDSUMMER

½ part chamomile
½ part cinquefoil
1 part lavender
¼ part mugwort
1 part rose petals
¼ part St John's wort
¼ part verbena
½ part orange peel
3 parts frankincense
Few drops camomile oil
Few drops orange oil

ASTRAL PROJECTION

2 parts sandalwood
1 part mugwort
1 part benzoin resin
½ part dittany of Crete
½ part lemongrass
1 part frankincense

HECATE

1 part cypress
1 part mint
2 parts sandalwood powder
3 parts myrrh
Tiny amount of garlic oil
1 part patchouli leaves
Few drops patchouli oil

HEARTH GODDESS

3 parts frankincense
1 part sandalwood
½ part orange peel
Few drops lemon oil
Pinch dragon's blood
½ part rose petals
½ part lavender flowers

THE HERBS

Alder *Alnus sp.*
Alder is a soft wood favoured by wood turners. Use the pulverised bark in hot poultices for rheumatism. The fresh crushed leaves are soothing to chapped skin. A decoction of the bark makes an external lotion for bathing swellings. Alder wood, bark, dried leaves and catkins can be used in incense for the spring equinox, divination and scrying, planet Venus, fire, water and earth, and Pisces.

Alecost *Balsamita major*
The scented dried leaves can be added to potpourri.

Alfalfa *Medicago sativa*
An infusion of the stems and leaves are used as a general tonic. Alfalfa is associated with fertility, wealth and plenty, ruled by the element of earth. Alfalfa may be employed in a herb talisman, in an incense of earth. Use oil to anoint a green candle to attract money.

Anemone *Anemone pulsatilla*
Associated with the direction of the east, the element of air, sylphs, the spring equinox, Aphrodite in her aspect as goddess of spring and the vegetation god, the planet Mars.

Angelica *Angelica sp.*
The stems are candied for adding to cakes - cut into lengths, scrape off the tough outer covering and simmer in syrup (1 pint water to 1 lb sugar) until tender. Drain and dry in a cool oven. Sprinkle with sugar and seal in an airtight container. Angelica stems, leaves and seeds are good for the digestion, wind, and as a tonic. Use in an infusion. NB do not use if diabetic. Use for incenses at Beltane, Midsummer, fire, the Sun, and the direction of the south, healing, protection, cleansing, exorcism and purification. Use to purify the personal aura, the temple or sacred space and magical tools, as well as houses and work places.

Aniseed *Pimpinella anisum*
Crush the seeds and pour boiling water over to make an infusion for coughs and to aid digestion and prevent flatulence. Aniseed is ruled by the planet Mercury. Aniseed is a plant of air, the mind and thought and can help tune the consciousness towards psychic awareness. Use anise in the

ritual bath and to anoint the forehead for divination rituals. Evaporate the oil for divination, clairvoyance and prophetic dreams.

Apple *Malus sp.*
Apple wood is good for hand carving. Apples are rich in vitamins and minerals. As a treatment for fever, wash the apples, slice and boil gently until soft, strain and add honey or brown sugar. Eating a raw apple helps to neutralise toxins in the blood, benefits the gums and reduces cavities in the teeth by clearing away plaque deposits. Dried apple peel can be used to make a tea which eases rheumatic conditions. Apple peel eaten in small amounts can ease heartburn. Apple is considered the fruit of the Otherworld in British lore, where blossom, buds and apples grow simultaneously. To eat of the fruit of an apple given by the Queen of Elphame is an initiation into its mysteries. The tree blossoms in the spring, bears fruit at Lammas, and at Yuletide, apple trees are wassailed, and toasted with cider to encourage them to grow. Use apple wood and flowers in love and harmony incenses, also to invoke and honour the goddess in her many aspects.

Ash *Fraxinus sp.*
Ash wood is light and pliable and was used for spear shafts, shepherd's crooks, hay rakes, tent pegs and handles. It is the best wood for burning, whether green or seasoned. The bark may be employed in a decoction to for fevers and for arthritis. The leaves should be gathered in June, dried and powdered. An infusion of the leaves is used in the treatment of arthritis and gout. The fresh leaves can be used as a compress for infected wounds. Ash is used in incenses designed for astral travel, during the rites of passage of birth, death and first degree initiation and the festivals of Herfest, Coamhain, Ostara and Yule. Also in sun incenses or to purify the aura and infuse it with the vitalising, healing energy of the sun.

Avens *Geum urbanum*
Infuse the whole herb to treat diarrhoea. It is astringent with antiseptic properties, useful for inflammation of the gums.

Basil *Ocimum sp.*
Infuse a sprig in boiling water for nausea. It also has mild antiseptic powers. Use in love spells, to invoke sky deities and during initiation rites, in incenses of love, the planet Mars, Scorpio, fire and the deities Erzulie,

Krishna, Lakshmi and Vishnu. Basil oil is uplifting; it reduces tension caused by stress. It protects the family and the home, attracts money and wealth. Basil oil is also used clear the mind and to invoke courage and determination. Use basil oil in the ritual bath before initiation, to anoint the priest representing the god at Lughnasa and Herfest. The warriors at the Lughnasa games may be anointed with basil oil. NB. Do not use during pregnancy.

Bay *Laurus nobilis*
Though large quantities of the vapour are dangerous, small measures of bay leaves can be added to incense utilised for trance work, divination and prophecy. Tarot cards can be consecrated with incense which includes bay. Also use for cleansing the temple and magical tools and to magically "seal" doorways and windows against negativity. Bay is used sparingly in incenses to invoke the gods of healing, the element of fire, and the zodiac sign of Leo and the Sun.

Beech *Fagus sylvatica*
Beech wood is strong and hard, used for making clothes pegs and chair legs. Beech leaves make good stuffing for mattresses and pillows when you are camping. Beech is good wood for the fire. Very young leaves can be used as a salad green in the spring or made into a liqueur by packing them into a jar and covering them with gin. Leave for 2 weeks and strain off, then for every 1 ½ pints of gin add 1 lb Demerara sugar which has been dissolved in ½ pint boiling water. Mix well and bottle. The nuts can be eaten in the autumn, toasted and salted, as well as eaten raw. A salad oil can be produced by grinding the nuts in their shells in a blender, and straining the oil through a muslin bag. Use dried beech leaves, nuts and bark in incenses dedicated to thunder and sky gods, to consecrate magical books or to aid the concentration while studying magical scripts and alphabets and in planetary incense for Mars and Saturn.

Betony *Betonica officinalis*
Add to the incenses used in rituals of healing, and to invoke the deities of healing and medicine. Betony is sacred to stag-horned gods, such as Herne and Cernunnos. It can also be added to incense dedicated to the zodiac sign of Aries, the element of fire, and the planet Jupiter.

Bilberry *Vaccinium myrtillus*
Soak a few berries in boiling water. It is a reliable cure for diarrhoea and a variety of mild bowel complaints. It also makes an excellent gargle.

Birch, silver *Betula sp.*
Birch wood is hardwearing and waterproof. The bark can be peeled from the tree (never peel a whole ring round the tree, as this will kill it) and has been used for roofing, waterproof clothing, and even writing paper. The inner bark can be eaten. The twigs are used for birch brooms, the wood for pipes, dishes, clothes pegs, and the branches can be used for basket making. Use the thin twigs bound together to make a whisk for beating eggs and batters. On the fire, birch is hot and fast burning, so is best for kindling. Make the fresh young leaves into a tisane to aid gout and rheumatism. It is also a good spring tonic. Add to incenses of purification and protection, and incenses celebrating the passage of the sun, the winding up of summer and the turning of the seasons particularly at Beltane and Coamhain as well as rituals of the fertility of the land, Imbolc, the planet Venus, and the element of water. It may be added to incense for Otherworld travel, vision and divination.

Bistort *Polygonum bistorta*
The common name of bistort is derived from the Latin '*bis*' meaning 'twice' and '*torta*' meaning 'twisted'. This refers to the serpentine shape of the roots. Bistort was, and still is, traditionally eaten at Easter, boiled and then made into a pudding with eggs, butter, salt, and pepper and steamed in a basin. Apply an infusion externally to haemorrhoids. A decoction of the root may be used for diarrhoea, dysentery, jaundice, arthritis, rheumatism, coughs, and sore throats, as a mild sedative and as a mouthwash for ulcers. Bistort is primarily a power plant of the vernal equinox, Ostara. Bistort can be used in incenses for divination, especially in conjunction with frankincense.

Blackberry *Rubus sp.*
You can make an excellent tea by boiling the berries in a tiny amount of water till soft, sieve and pouring the resulting juice over soft brown sugar to make a delicious drink full of vitamins. Make the leaves into a tea to aid diarrhoea, bowel and urinary complaints by putting the dried leaves into water and bring slowly to the boil. Simmer for 5 minutes and then remove from the heat. Allow to steep for 10 minutes and then strain. This can

be drunk three or four times daily. Apply the leaf tea externally for acne and use as a gargle and mouthwash. As well as jam, you can make jellies, an excellent wine which is ready to drink in eight weeks, fruit fools and summer pudding. The shoots and stems can be used for basket making. Soak the stems and strip off the skin and thorns- try pulling them through an old wool jumper. Split into two lengthways and scrape out the pith. The pieces are then ready for weaving. The wood and petals are used in incenses at the autumn equinox and to consecrate the magical tool of the cup or cauldron. They can be added to incense dedicated to the planet Venus, the element of water and the zodiac sign of Aries.

Blackcurrants *Ribes nigrum*
Make a blackcurrant tea as for blackberries above. Full of vitamins and goodness!

Blackthorn *Prunus spinosa*
Blackthorn wood will burn green or seasoned, but emits plenty of sparks. The fruit of the blackthorn is called a sloe, and it is the ancestor of the cultivated plum. They are bitter but make a good jelly and an excellent liqueur called sloe gin. Just place the fruit (after they have had a frost on them) in a jar with an equal weight of sugar and cover with gin. Leave for two months then strain into a clean dark bottle. The wood, flower petals, dried leaves and sloes may be added to Samhain incenses and incenses dedicated to death aspects of the Goddess, particularly Ceridwen. It may be added to incense of the element of earth, the planet Saturn and used to consecrate mother of pearl, dark green malachite, and black banded agate. It may also be burned to invoke the bird totems of thrush and rook.

Borage *Borago officinalis*
The fresh or dried leaves are used medicinally. Use the fresh leaves to make a stimulant tea by pouring ½ pint of water onto 1 tsp dried leaves or 1 tbsp fresh leaves, cover and infuse 10 minutes, strain and sweeten with honey if desired. Borage is useful at times of stress, as it is a restorative for the adrenal cortex. A decoction of the flowers and leaves in wine can be used to stimulate the adrenals and increase the ability to cope during times of stress. It is particularly useful for someone who has been on steroids for any length of time, restoring the adrenal glands. It can be used for fevers and during convalescence, and for the treatment of pleurisy. It also stimulates the flow of milk in nursing mothers. The leaves are rich in mineral salts and

can therefore be used in a salt free diet. A poultice of the leaves can be used to soothe bruises and inflammations. A tea of the flowers (to aid menstrual problems and colds) can be made by adding 1 tsp dried flowers or 2 tsp fresh flowers in ½ pint boiling water, stand for 3 minutes. The cucumber-tasting flowers may be added to salads or crystallised for cake decoration. To do this drop the flowers in boiling syrup of 1 lb sugar to 1 pint water, leave for 1 minute and remove carefully with a slotted spoon, and lay them on a baking tray. Dry out in a slow oven. Add fresh flowers to summer drinks. The young leaves may be chopped and mixed with cream cheese as a sandwich filler. Said to impart courage, borage is used in the incense at Lughnasa, and to invoke aspects of the God such as Lugh and Llew. The incense can also be used in incenses to heighten psychic awareness during meditation and inner journeys. It can be added to incense dedicated to the planet Jupiter and the zodiac sign of Leo.

Broom *Cytisus sp.*
The twigs can be made into a besom. The flowering of the broom sweeps away the winter and is added to the incense at Beltane. It is particularly sacred to the Welsh goddess Blodeuwedd ("Flower Face") who was created from nine types of blossoms, including broom, meadowsweet and oak. Broom may also be added to strengthen incenses of cleansing and purification.

Burdock *Arctium sp.*
The leaves, roots and rhizome of the greater burdock are used. Burdock has been in use for centuries as a poultice for skin eruptions, ulcers and wounds (speeding up the healing), varicose veins, dry eczema and psoriasis. The whole leaves can be picked, made into a tea and used as a tonic and blood purifier and for cystitis. A decoction of the leaves makes a good wash for acne, eczema and psoriasis. Use externally as a poultice for sores and ulcers. The seeds can be infused to make a diuretic tea. An amulet may be made from the root, or the leaves used in incenses and spread around the house or temple.

Camomile/Chamomile *Anthemis nobilis/ Matricaria chamomilla*
The flowers are used to make a sedative tea, useful for insomnia. It also benefits the nerves and can be helpful in cases of hysteria. Gargle with camomile infusion for a sore throat and apply externally to promote the healing of wounds and to reduce any inflammations. In a cream, camomile

is useful for the treatment of cracked nipples. A herb of the sun, it may be used in incenses of regeneration, healing and protection. Camomile is one of the sacred herbs of Midsummer and may be thrown onto the festival fire. Add to planetary Sun incense and incense of the element of water. The essentials oils *Anthemis nobilis* (Roman) / *Matricaria chamomilla* (German) Chamomile, are middle note oils, and are soothing and calming, and can induce meditative states. Camomile is very safe, but best avoided during the early months of pregnancy.

Caraway *Carum carvi*
Use the whole herb to make a tea which is refreshing and a mild carminative. Make an infusion of the seeds as a mild carminative. The seeds can be added to cakes and bread. The Sun and Mercury, and the element of air rule it. Caraway is associated with the cycles of sowing and reaping and used to mark various stages on the wheel of life, such as birth marriage and death. Use at the beginning of new projects or their coming to fruition. Caraway is a herb of love, used in love attraction blends, or used as the anointing oil at handfastings to help lovers remain faithful. The rings may be consecrated with caraway oil. It is a herb of protection and purification and my be used to cleanse and seal the ritual area or home. NB: The oil may cause skin irritation

Carnation *Dianthus sp.*
A herb of celebration, carnation can be used in the handfasting incense and in incenses designed for joyful celebrations in general, where it will impart the energy of the sun. It can be added to Sun incenses, fire incenses, protection incenses, and used to invoke the direction of the South, and the festival of Coamhain or Midsummer.

Catmint *Nepeta cataria*
A tisane is calming and stress relieving. The leaves are mildly hallucinogenic and can be added to incense (or smoked) used to induce trances or used for shapeshifting work. Catnip may also be used to invoke cat or lion totems. It is ruled by the planet Venus and the element of water.

Cedar *Cedrus sp.*
The wood, which represents eternity, drives away ghosts and evil spirits and dispels negativity. It is used in incenses of Mercury and the Sun, the element of fire, to consecrate amethysts, sapphires and the magic wand, at

the festival of Herfest. The oil was used in the ancient world for incense and preservation in the embalming process. It is calming and useful for meditation, pathworking and trance work. .NB: Never take the oil internally. Do not use during pregnancy. Irritates sensitive skins

Celery *Apium graveolens*
The water in which celery has been cooked should be saved and drunk as a remedy against rheumatism. It is also a mild sedative and a mild diuretic.

Centuary *Erythrœa sp.*
The tea is a tonic and blood purifier. The dried aerial parts and flowering stems are used medicinally. Centuary is a gastric and digestive stimulant and may be used when these are required. It can be used to treat anorexia, dyspepsia and liver complaints. The herb of the healer centaur Chiron, incense of centaury may be used to dedicate you to the craft of herbalism, to aid in communication with other plant spirits and Chiron, the patron of herbalists. It may be added to incense of the Sun and fire, or used to invoke a horse totem.

Chervil *Anthriscus cerefolium*
Chervil can be infused as a tea to benefit the digestive system or to alleviate circulatory problems, liver complaints and catarrh. An external wash can also be used for inflamed eyes or as a beauty treatment for the skin. Use as a poultice for painful ankles, wrists and knees. It is used in incenses used to stimulate mental activity and clarity. It is sacred to the goddess Ceridwen and the festival of Samhain, and the mysteries of initiation. Use to become in tune with this Higher Self and to consecrate the cauldron. It is ruled by the planet Jupiter and the elements of air and water.

Chestnut, Horse *Aesculus hippocastanum*
The wood was previously used to manufacture cotton reels and chopping boards. It is good for hand carving, but useless on the fire for burning. The nuts contain saponin and may be used [like soapwort] as soap. Externally horse chestnut can be used for cuts and grazes, frostbite, ringworm and piles, rubbed on fresh or used in a salve. Peel and crush the nuts. Simmer in oil for 30 minutes and strain. Thicken the oil, over a low heat with beeswax, pour into clean glass jars and allow to set. NB Do not take horse chestnuts internally. Added to any incense chestnut will deepen the experience of the ritual or meditation in hand.

Chestnut, Sweet *Castanea sativa*
The wood is resistant to rotting and can be used for outdoor items such
as fencing, garden poles, railway sleepers, chair legs, charcoal and walking
sticks. Sweet chestnut should not be confused with the conker producing
horse chestnut. This one has autumn fruit in a spiny, round, green case
which contains two or three nuts. They are best peeled and roasted, though
they can be eaten raw, pickled and candied.

Chicory / Succory *Cichorium intybus*
The roots can be boiled and eaten, or dry roasted and made into a coffee
substitute or additive. The leaves are eaten as a salad vegetable.

Chickweed *Stellaria media*
This is one of the first green plants to flower in very early spring, and
the tiny white blossoms continue throughout the year. It can be eaten as
a green vegetable or made into a salve for sore and irritated skin. As an
ointment, poultice or externally applied infusion, chickweed is a remedy
for cuts, wounds, itching and irritation. It is useful for irritable eczema and
psoriasis. Internally it can be used for rheumatism.

Cinnamon *Cinnamonum zeylanicum / Cinnamonum lauraceae*
This makes a spicy tea, which cleanses the mouth and throat, is warming,
stimulating and cures nausea. Cinnamon raises magical vibration and
creates a peaceful energy; it is therefore useful for rituals of healing and
divination. It is a herb of the Sun, the element of Fire. Use in blends to
raise magical vibration and create a peaceful energy, healing and divination.
In sexual or tantric magic, cinnamon oil is used to anoint the body and
stimulates the male passion with sun energy. NB: Can irritate sensitive skin

Cinquefoil *Potentilla reptans*
Cinquefoil is good for treating fevers, reducing the temperature,
particularly with influenza, inflammatory fevers and those associated with
mucus. It can also be used to treat diarrhoea. As it is also an astringent
it can be used as a lotion to treat skin problems. The root has astringent
qualities which can be used as a mouthwash, and which supposedly secures
the teeth. No more than a pint of moderate infusion should be drunk
per day. During the Middle Ages cinquefoil had the reputation of being a
magical herb. It was widely associated with witches and believed to have
been used in various spells and in 'flying ointment'. Sacred to the Goddess

as Mother Earth, and is included in protection incenses, purification incenses for the home, temple, ritual space and personal aura. Add to a planetary incense for Jupiter, for the element of fire.

Clary Sage *Salvia sclarea*

Clary's best reputation is in the treatment of eye problems. An infusion from the seeds may be used to remove foreign matter painlessly from the eye. In water the seeds yield a mucilage which envelopes any particle of dust etc. which may be causing the irritation. The leaves can be used as a compress in the treatment of swellings, boils, ulcers and to draw out splinters. Clary sage essential oil is a relaxing aphrodisiac. Use in oils designed to attract the opposite sex, for love and harmony, also divination, prophecy and clairvoyance. It is ruled by Mercury, the Moon, and the element of air. It may be used to enhance visions within meditation. It has the power to protect clairvoyant sight and may be applied to the third eye chakra. NB: Causes drowsiness, so do not drive or operate machinery after use. Use only in small amounts and do not use at all during pregnancy.

Clove *Eugenia caryophyllus/ Carophyllus aromaticus/ Syzygium aromaticus*

The dried flowers and oil are all used medicinally. They contain volatile oil. Cloves are used to ease nausea, vomiting and flatulence. Clove oil is a powerful antiseptic and a local anaesthetic. Apply the oil to a tooth to allay toothache or put a clove into the mouth in contact with the tooth. Cloves help to ease the pain of childbirth, and women in labour may take wine in which cloves have been steeped. Clove essential oil is base note perfume distilled from the dried flower buds; clove oil is a strong antiseptic and local analgesic. It is ruled by the Sun and Jupiter, the zodiac signs of Sagittarius and Scorpio and the element of fire. Clove oil is utilised as a protection or to attract the opposite sex. It may be used at handfastings and to aid astral travel. NB: The oil can irritate sensitive skin.

Clover *Trifolium sp.*

Red clover makes a useful infusion for menopausal women, containing more phyto-oestrogens than Soya. Sacred to the Triple Goddess and fairies, clover is a visionary herb which connects with the Otherworld. Use in incense at Beltane, to consecrate the ritual pentacle and copper tools (such as herb knives). It is ruled by the planet Mercury and all four elements.

Coltsfoot *Tussilago farfara*
The flowers and leaves of coltsfoot contain the same properties. Coltsfoot
is widely believed to help chest and lung complaints, and the leaves may
be burned as an incense to help breathing. A tobacco of the dried leaves is
said to positively help asthma and breathing complaints, this can be mixed
with other dried herbs such as thyme, peppermint and camomile. Drinking
coltsfoot tea can help lung complaints, colds, flu and asthma. Powder the
leaves and use as a snuff for blocked sinuses. As a compress the leaves can
be chopped and mixed with honey to help inflamed and dry skin, ulcers,
wounds, bites, sores and varicose veins. Coltsfoot was also used by the
Romanies in herbal medicines, combined with liquorice, for coughs and
colds.

Comfrey *Symphytum officinale*
Comfrey was often grown in monastery gardens as a bone setting plant,
the mashed root sets hard like plaster. A compress made from the grated
fresh or dried roots, mixed with water can be applied to inflamed joints,
sprains, twists, bruises, burns and scalds. Comfrey can be used in the
treatment of arthritis and rheumatism in the form of infused oil which can
be warmed and applied to the affected area. An infusion added to the bath
water softens the skin. The leaves can be boiled and eaten like spinach,
or dipped in egg and flour batter and deep fried. Comfrey's primary use
is in healing, though it also has protective properties and may be used in
incenses and herbal amulets for this purpose. NB: Comfrey contains an
alkaloid which may damage the liver and may be carcinogenic when taken
internally in *extremely* large doses over an extended period.

Cypress *Cupressus sp.*
Cypress is a tree of death and mourning, sacred to the underworld deities,
the Fates and the Furies. Cypress may be used at funerals and memorial
services as it reminds us of the incorruptible nature of the spirit. At Yule it
shows us that the life spirit remains, even in the dark time. It is ruled by the
planet Saturn and the element of earth.

Daisy (English) *Bellis perennis*
Daisies are one of our most common plants and the fresh or dried flowers
may be used safely both internally and externally. For sore eyes use an
eyebath of daisy infusion. For bruises use a compress of the crushed
leaves. Chew the fresh leaves to relieve the pain of mouth ulcers. For

skin diseases such as eczema and for stiff necks, lumbago and general aches and pains, make a decoction and apply externally. Taken internally the decoction or infusion is useful in the treatment of heavy or painful menstruation. Add the flowers to the bath to refresh dull skin. Sacred to sun gods and goddesses and is associated with purity, innocence and faithful love, use in incenses to attract true love and bring back an absent lover. At the spring equinox daisies may be used to attract dryads to implore their help during the growing season. It is said that when you can put your foot on nine daisies, spring has really arrived. They may be used in incenses at rituals to greet the arrival of a baby or a young girl celebrating her first menstruation. They are ruled by the planet Venus, the sign of Cancer and the element of water.

Dandelion *Taraxacum officinale*
Though rarely eaten in Britain, dandelion is a popular foodstuff in the Continent. The young leaves can be eaten in salads or cooked like spinach. The roots make an acceptable coffee substitute- pick in the autumn, wash them and pat them dry with a clean towel, then dry roast them in a hot oven until easily broken, grind and use as filter coffee. A tea made from the leaves is a fairly strong diuretic, but does not rob the body of potassium as conventional diuretics do. Pour 1 pint of boiling water onto 1 oz fresh leaves. Cover and infuse 10 minutes. Sweeten with honey if desired and drink a small wineglassful three times a day. Dab the white juice from the flower stems directly onto acne and spots. The flowers are an obvious sun emblem, and a plant of bright energy and vitality. The dried petals may be added to sun incenses to increase their power, to divination incense, used at Beltane. Dandelion is ruled by the planet Jupiter, the sign of Sagittarius and the element of air.

Dill *Anethum graveolens*
Known as one of the 'St. John's Eve' herbs, dill was valued as a protection against witchcraft. Dill seeds infused in wine were considered to be an aphrodisiac and magicians traditionally used dill in magical spells. Use as an incense to clear your mind and strengthen your personal focus. It can be added to incense for protection, for cleansing the sacred space and is a sacred herb of Midsummer. It can also be added to incense for the planet Mercury, the element of fire or air, and for the festival of Beltane.

Elder *Sambucus nigra*

The word 'elder' is derived from the Anglo-Saxon word '*aeld*' meaning 'fire', because hollowed elder branches were once used to kindle fires by blowing through them. The generic name '*sambucus*' is derived from the Greek '*sambucu*', a musical instrument, as the Greeks and Romans made flutes from its hollow stems and a triangular stringed instrument from the hardwood. Push the pith out of young shoots to make whistles and flutes. The wood is useless for burning. The elder is a tree associated with witches and the Crone aspect of the Goddess, and it is often treated with great caution and surrounded with warnings as a result. Elder blossoms were worn at Midsummer and twigs were woven into a headdress at this time to enable the wearer to see spirits.

The elder is one of the most common and useful of our hedgerow shrubs. It has tough wood, edible berries, medicinal leaves. Every part of it is useful. Elderflower water is good for sore eyes, as a skin cleanser, just place a flower head in a glass and add boiling water. An infusion of the flowers helps reduce fevers, tones the mucous linings of the nose and throat, increasing resistance to infection, chronic catarrh, allergies and Candida. Infusions of the flowering tops help reduce the severity of hay fever if taken for some months from local bushes before the season. The infusion is also useful for arthritic conditions, removing toxins from the body. The berries used in a decoction are mildly laxative and have been taken for rheumatism. The berries can be used to make teas, wines, preserves and in baking. The bark can be used for headaches, to promote labour and as a poultice. It can be used as a diuretic for use with kidney and heart problems, and the leaves and flowers can be used in drinks, poultices and salves. The leaves can be used fresh or dried and are best collected on a warm day in spring or summer. Added to salves of beeswax and olive oil they are useful in healing skin irritations, bruises, cuts and sprains. When boiled in linseed oil the leaves are an external remedy for haemorrhoids.

Elder flowers are used to make elder flower water, an astringent good as a skin toner. An infusion can be made that is beneficial to boils and skin irritation by infusing the dried flowers for an hour. The flowers made into a cream are good for all skin types but especially for mature and sallow skins. It softens the skin; smoothes wrinkles, fades freckles and soothes sunburn.

The sweet blossom can be collected in June and make a good fixative for herbal incenses. The flower heads may also be dipped in batter and deep fried and dipped in sugar as a Midsummer treat. All parts of the elder may be used in incenses dedicated to the planet Venus, the element of air, Earth and Crone Goddesses.

Fennel *Foeniculum vulgare*

Fennel is one of the oldest known plants cultivated in this country. It was held in high esteem by the Romans. The men took fennel to increase their stamina and courage whilst the ladies took fennel to prevent obesity. The Romans also ate fennel shoots as a vegetable. An infusion of the crushed seeds is a well known remedy for digestive complaints such as flatulence, colic, loss of appetite and stomach pains. They stimulate the appetite and aid digestion. Fennel is also useful in the treatment of anaemia and is of benefit when added to gripe water for babies. The infusion will increase the flow of milk in nursing mothers. Make a compress of the infusion to treat blepharitis (inflammation of the eyelids) or tired eyes. Recent studies have shown that fennel can reduce the effects of alcohol on the body. Fennel oil is a stimulating, cleansing oil which is used for purification and protection against evil influences. It may be a component of the anointing oil for initiation, Lughnasa or Midsummer. NB The oil is not to be used before exposure to the sun, as fennel is phototoxic. It should not be used on sensitive skin.

Feverfew *Tanacetum parthenium* / *Chrysanthemum parthenium*

A tisane is good for headaches and migraines, to relive arthritis and promote restful sleep. It has to be taken for 2-3 months before the full benefit is felt, and only works on those whose symptoms are relieved by heat. An infusion of the leaves rubbed over the skin will act as a natural insect repellent. It can be used as a mouthwash for inflamed gums or following a tooth extraction. It can also be taken as a mild laxative. A poultice of the leaves can be used for the treatment of bruises, bites, stings and acne.

Fir (Silver) *Abies alba*

The fir is sacred to the Goddess as both mother and patroness of childbirth, and its incense is used to bless and renew a woman after childbirth. The wood and needles can be used for the fire or incense at women's rites, particularly those connected with the Mother aspects of the Goddess. The Silver Fir is ruled by the Moon and the element of earth and the sign of Sagittarius.

Flax *Linaceae. Sp.*
Take the infusion morning and evening, sweetened with honey,
for the treatment of catarrh, bronchitis, urinary infections and
pulmonary infections. It can be used externally for boils, ulcers, cuts
and inflammations. Use the poultice for pleurisy and other pulmonary
conditions, especially when combined with mustard. Use also alone or
with marsh mallow root for boils, swellings and inflammations. Apply the
boiled seeds directly to festering boils. The oil extracted from the seeds
is known as linseed oil. It has soothing and lubricating properties. It can
be used to treat tonsillitis, sore throats, coughs, colds and constipation. It
can be mixed in equal quantities with lime water and used to treat scalds,
burns and sunburn. Take the whole seeds as a laxative. Flax may be used
in incenses of the planet Mercury and the element of fire and be thrown
onto the fire at Coamhain.

Fumitory *Fumaria officinalis*
The tea is a laxative. The infusion can be used in the treatment of arthritis,
water retention and liver complaints, especially jaundice. Fumitory infusion
can also be used externally for the treatment of eczema. It can be made
into a lotion to help fade freckles and to ease sunburn. NB: if taken
regularly for an extended period fumitory is known to have severe sedative
and hypnotic qualities. Fumitory has connections with the inner earth's
spirit and underworld. It is also a herb of Samhain and can therefore be
used to help lend material form to spirits of the ancestors attracted to the
sacred circle at this time.

Garlic *Allium sativum*
Garlic is a powerful antiseptic and is useful for coughs (particularly
whooping cough), colds, influenza, bronchitis and asthma. Taken regularly
garlic is said to regulate the intestinal flora. It can be used for the treatment
of diarrhoea, stomach cramps, flatulence, sluggish bowels and Candida.
Taken regularly garlic can also be used as a general blood tonic to help
reduce cholesterol and lower blood pressure. There is also evidence
to suggest that garlic may be of benefit on reducing the symptoms of
rheumatism and arthritis. An excellent source of iodine, garlic is of benefit
to those suffering from an under active thyroid. Externally garlic can be
applied it insect bites, boils and unbroken chilblains. Garlic was used by the
Greeks to invoke Hecate. This was done by placing a clove of garlic on a
small pile of stones at a crossroads.

Gorse *Ulex eurpaeus*

A tea of the fresh flowers is a diuretic. It was formerly burned at Midsummer and blazing branches were carried round the herd to bring health to the cows and good luck for the rest of the year. It is ruled by the Sun and the element of fire. The flowers may be used as a purifying agent, taken as a tea or scattered in the ritual bath.

Hawthorn / Whitethorn / May *Crataegus monogyna*

In May the hedgerows are white and fragrant with hawthorn blossom, and in the autumn, red with the abundant haws, the fruit of the hawthorn. Hawthorns are often planted as hedging and will keep out both animals and people. The wood can be used for door knobs, mallet heads and tool handles. Hawthorn wood burns reasonably well on the fire. The young leaves in early spring are very tasty eaten straight from the bush, with a mild, nutty flavour. Children used to call them 'bread and cheese' and nibble them on the way to school. You can also add them to soups, stews and pies. The flowers make a delicate white wine. Hawthorn berries are a tonic to the heart and circulatory system; professional herbalists us them to balance the functioning of the heart in a gentle way, either stimulating or depressing its activity. They can be used as a long term treatment for heart weakness or palpitations. They can be used to treat high blood pressure, angina and arteriosclerosis. NB: self prescription is not recommended.

For the Celts the flowering of the hawthorn heralded the festival of Beltane, and the turning of the wheel of the year from winter to summer a time of growth and fertility. It is said that the scent of the hawthorn is reminiscent of female sexuality, perhaps the sexual flowering of the Goddess. Both the Turks and the orgiastic cult of the Roman goddess Flora had hawthorn blossom as an erotic symbol. The flowers and leaves may be used in Beltane incenses, for Great Rite and Sacred Marriage incenses. It may be added to Mars planetary incense.

Hazel *Corylus avellana*

Hazel twigs are cut in the spring and used to support peas and other climbing plants in the vegetable garden. Any forked stick can be cut for a divining rod, and a longer forked piece used for a walking stick or stang. Hazel wood burns well. Ready for picking in late September- though you will have to beat the squirrels and birds to them- hazels can be found growing wild in the hedgerows. They should be stored in their shells, in moist sand, and kept until the following spring by which time the flavour will have improved. They can be eaten raw, toasted and used in various dishes. High in protein, they repay the effort expended in gathering them. The wood and ground nuts are added to incenses designed to invoke wisdom, and engender true visions and inspiration and at the festival of Herfest to represent the fruition of what has gone before and the culmination of the work. Hazel wood may be added to incense of the planet Mercury and the element of air.

Heather *Calluna vulgaris*

The whole plant may be used to make besoms. Heather blossoms can also be used to make a tonic tea. In northern parts of Britain people often added the tips of flowering shoots to herbal drinks and beer to purify the blood. When used externally in an infusion, heather benefits the complexion and rids it of freckles. Sacred to the goddess of Midsummer, use also in incense of third degree initiation, shamanic initiation, Midsummer (Coamhain), the planet Venus and the element of water.

Holly *Ilex aquifolium*

Holly wood is suitable for carving, particularly statues of warrior gods. The wood is good on the fire, green or seasoned. Holly has many herbal uses, being used either fresh or dried. The leaves can be infused to help in the treatment of catarrh, pleurisy, fevers and rheumatism. They are also slightly diuretic. The infusion helps by inducing sweating. The berries can be dried and powdered and used externally to stop bleeding. NB: holly berries are purgative and should not be used internally by an inexperienced person. Added to incense used for protection against negativity and for counter-magic against witches, sorcerers and evil spirits. It is sacred to Crone aspects of the Goddess, such as the Cailleach Bheur and the Morrigu. It is especially associated with sky and thunder gods such as the Holly is a tree of warrior magic and spiritual strength. Use at the winter solstice (Yule), in Saturn and Mars planetary incenses, the element of fire, or to invoke robin and dog totems.

Honeysuckle *Lonicera caprifolium*

The thin shoots of honeysuckle can be used for basket making. An infusion of the flowers can be used as a treatment for coughs, catarrh and asthma. The warmed infused oil, obtained from the flowers, can be used for treating chilblains. To improve bad circulation, which causes chilblains, it should be rubbed into the hands and feet. Add the flowers to Beltane,

Midsummer and Lughnasa incenses, and at the rite of the harvest and Samhain. Add to incense of the planets Jupiter and Mars, the zodiac sign of Cancer, the element of earth, and the goddess Ceridwen.

Hops *Humulus lupulus*
Recommended by the Roman writer Pliny as a garden plant and vegetable, by the eighth century hops were used throughout most of Europe in the brewing industry because of their clearing, flavouring and preserving qualities, although the British people resisted their introduction. Initially Henry VIII banned them, but during the sixteenth century they became more widespread and by the late seventeenth century their bitter flavour and preserving qualities were being recognised. The infusion makes a sedative and calming tea which can be used as a general tonic, an appetite stimulant and the treatment of digestive problems. It can also be used in the treatment of jaundice and menstrual cramps, as well as being used to stimulate the flow of milk in nursing mothers.

Horehound, White *Marrubium vulgare*
Horehound cough remedies were once very popular. The leaves were used by milkmaids to wash out pails and churns and the dried calyxes make useful wicks for oil lamps. For coughs, colds and catarrh, the leaves may be infused in boiling water. Used in an incense horehound will keep the mind clear and focused and foster the free flowing of the intuition. It can be used in incenses for exorcism, temple and aura cleansing. Add to Mercury planetary incense and incense to invoke the element of air.

Horsetail *Equisetum arvense*
Make a decoction with 1 oz herb to 2 cold pints water steeped for 4 hours, then simmered for 20 minutes. Apply to the skin to treat acne. Use the whole plant as a pot scourer.

Hyssop *Hyssopus officinalis*
Good for coughs and catarrh, make hyssop tea by pouring 1 pint of cool water over ¼ oz dried hyssop flowers. Cover and leave overnight. Strain and sweeten with honey, if liked. Take a small wineglassful three times a day. Hyssop tea is also calming, and can be used in compress for bruises. Add to incense of purification, to dispel negativity in personal meditation and in ritual. Add to incense of the planet Jupiter, the element of fire and the zodiac sign of Cancer.

Iris *Iris florentina / Iris germanica*
Use iris petals or root (called orris root) powder in incenses dedicated to the planets Venus and the Moon, **the** element of water. Orris root may be added as a fixative to incense and for spiritual protection and to connect with the Higher Self.

Ivy *Hedera helix*
The leaves may be made into a soothing ointment for tired muscles, to relieve sunburn and as a general skin tonic. It may, however, cause an allergic reaction with sensitive skin. The ointment or infusion can also be used externally to help disperse toxins and fluid trapped within the body as in the case of cellulite. Infuse in rose water and rub on the temples to relieve headaches. NB: do not use internally. A plant of regeneration and symbol of eternal life, use ivy leaves in incense for the planet Saturn, for the element of water, at Yule, at the rebirth of the God and the year and at initiation rituals.

Juniper *Juniperis communis*
A tea made from the berries is a diuretic. Juniper represents justice, use crushed juniper berries or leaves in incense for the planets Mars, the Sun and Saturn, for the element of fire, the zodiac sign of Aries. Use also in healing incense and at Samhain to drive out the old year, and at Yule the time of new life and rebirth. Juniper oil is a disinfectant, and is used to drive away negativity, evil spirits and disease. It stimulates and revitalises the psyche and emotional energy levels; use after being 'drained' by daily contact with a number of demanding people. It is invaluable for healers and health professionals in this regard.

Lavender *Lavendula officinalis*
A very dilute tea makes a good pick-me-up and is said to help dizziness and vertigo. For a relaxing bath to ease aches and pains, pick a few sprays of lavender, tie them together and place them in a hot bath while the water is still running. Place lavender flowers between the sheets and towels in your linen cupboard, and sew into sachets to scent your drawers. Use in incenses for the planet Mercury, the element of air. Lavender purifies, heals and cleanses. Add to incense for calm meditation and to bring peace and harmony in the home, or at difficult discussions and meetings. Add to Midsummer incense. Lavender essential oil is the most versatile and safest of all the oils, valuable in healing a large number of conditions. It is

a general tonic during and after illness. Used in an evaporator it stimulates the brain. It helps balance emotional extremes caused by stress, shock and worry.

Lemon
Add the juice of half a lemon to warm water to cure hiccups. It is ruled by the planets Neptune and Venus and the element of water. Use in oils dedicated to psychic and emotional work. Use also in oils for love, attraction and sexual rituals, including the Great Rite.

Lemon Balm *Melissa officinalis*
This refreshing tea helps reduce fevers and high temperatures. Lemon balm is a hardy, herbaceous perennial native to southern Europe. Use in incense of the Moon, the element of water, the zodiac sign of Cancer, healing incenses, particularly to heal emotional problems. The oil is cheering, good for hysteria, shock, and nervous tension. It releases tension, relieves depression, is uplifting and joyful. Use when you need to bring peace and harmony to a situation. It is used in oils employed in spells and rituals designed to attract love and money. It may also be employed for cleansing, purification, and driving out negativity. It is a useful insect repellent for those outdoor rituals. NB: Do not use during pregnancy.

Lemongrass *Cymbopogon citratus also C. flexuosus*
A refreshing oil, lemongrass acts on the nervous system. It is ruled by the planet Mercury and the element of air. It is used in oils used for psychic development, clairvoyance and divination.

Lemon Verbena *Lippia citriodora/ Aloysia citriodora*
The tea is a mild sedative, aids dizziness, helps the digestion and is cooling in hot weather. Put 6 leaves in a teapot, pour on ½ pint boiling water and infuse 5 minutes. Strain. It is not hardy in our climate, but I grow the small shrub in my polytunnel and it would do equally well in a greenhouse or conservatory. It loses all its leaves in the winter, but re-greens along the same branches in the spring.

Lime / Linden *Tilia europaea*
The wood can be used for fine carving, boxes and kitchen chopping blocks. The suckers can be used for basket making. It makes poor firewood. Tea from the fresh leaves is relaxing and good for tension

headaches. Use externally as a wash for acne. The fresh yellow flowers in June smell of honey. Use in incenses of divination, healing and restoration, when working with magical scripts and alphabets and the planet Jupiter.

Liquorice Root *Glycyrrhiza glabra*
Recent research has shown that liquorice has a pain killing effect on stomach complaints such as ulcers and that prolonged use increases blood pressure. Liquorice has a strong stimulating action on the adrenal glands. The increase in adrenal steroid hormones results in an anti-inflammatory action and is therefore useful in the treatment of arthritis and rheumatism. Make into a tea for peptic ulcers, coughs and colds. NB Should not be taken by people suffering from high blood pressure.

Lovage *Levisticum officinale*
The flavour of the stems and leaves resembles celery, and they can be added to soups and stews. The hot seeds can be used on breads and biscuits. An infusion of the seeds or root is used in the treatment of colic, indigestion and flatulence. It is a stimulant and helps with the removal of waste and toxins from the body. The cooled infusion can also be used as a gargle. A strong decoction can be added to the bath water as a natural deodoriser. NB: Lovage should note be taken by pregnant women or people suffering from kidney problems. Lovage added to the bath leaves you physically cleaned and revitalised. It can be used in the bath of purification before any ritual. An infusion of the leaves can be used to wash and cleanse magical tools and the working space.

Mallow *Malva sylvestris* **Marsh Mallow** *Althaea officinalis*
The leaves can be cooked like spinach, but use only perfect specimens. In Egypt they are used to make a soup called *melokhia*. The seeds can be eaten fresh, and have a nutty flavour. The starchy roots of the marsh mallow were once eaten as a sweet treat, though the confection of the same name today is made from sugar and gelatine. Both the common and musk mallow have similar properties. They both contain mucilage which makes them useful for the treatment of coughs. The leaves and roots can also be applied in poultices or made into ointments for the treatment of bruises, wounds, cuts, stings and burns. Make an infusion of 1 oz leaves to ½ pint boiling water to ease indigestion and acid stomachs. The mallow has connections with love and the petals can be used as confetti at

handfastings. They can also be dried and added to the incense or used to decorate the ritual cup at this time.

Marigold *Calendula officinalis*
The flowers can be eaten in salads. It is ruled by the Sun, the element of fire, the zodiac sign of Leo and is sacred to sun gods and goddesses. Use in the ritual bath before the solstices and equinoxes, or rituals of divination. Use marigold petals in incense dedicated to the Sun, the element of fire, the star sign of Leo, and to invoke Sun Gods. Marigold is a herb of healing and protection, and can also be added to incense for prophetic dreams, love, divination, to consecrate divinatory tools such as crystal balls, and at Ostara, Herfest, Coamhain and Yule.

Marjoram or Oregano *Origanum vulgare.*
Add fresh leaves to salads, stews, soups, sauces and casseroles. The tea relieves flatulence. The dried leaves can be sewn into pillows to promote sleep. They were used in brewing before the advent of hops. The fresh leaves can be rubbed over furniture to polish it. The plant is antiseptic and an infusion soaked into a cloth makes a soothing poultice. Add to the bath water as a pick-me-up. Add to incense dedicated to the planet Mercury, the element of air, and the zodiac sign of Aries, a herb of protection that repels negativity and fosters happiness. It is sacred to the Goddess of Love and may be used to invoke her in all her aspects, use in love incenses and also at weddings and handfastings. It is used in incenses used in healing rituals designed to comfort the bereaved, and may be used to unblock and activate the heart chakra. The oil is comforting and good for anxiety, insomnia, and irritability. Marjoram stimulates both the body and the mind, but is an anaphrodisiac- it puts off potential lovers!

Meadowsweet *Filipendula ulmaria / Spiraea ulmaria*
Flowering all summer long, meadowsweet has a wonderful scent, like new mown hay, which is preserved when the plant is dried. It was a favourite wedding plant and received the folk name of 'bridewort' became popular because it was often used in bridal garlands and posies for bridesmaids. It was also frequently strew in the church, on the path to the church and in the home of the newlywed couples. The flowers were used to flavour bride ales, port, claret and mead. The leaves flavour summer drinks. In rural area meadowsweet was used to produce a herbal tisane which was used for the treatment of head colds. The dried aerial parts of the whole plant are used

medicinally. The infusion may be used to treat heartburn, acid stomachs, gastritis, peptic ulcers, diarrhoea, fevers, rheumatism, gout, flu, kidney and bladder complaints, insomnia and as a painkiller to rid the body of excess fluid. To make a skin tonic place the flowers in rainwater or distilled water and soak for twenty four hours. The root can be boiled to make a strong decoction to treat sores and ulcers. Use the flowers in incense dedicated to the planets Venus and Jupiter, the element of water, the zodiac sign of Gemini, sacred to the Summer Goddess and may be used at Beltane and Coamhain. Use also in incense for love, marriage and handfasting, fertility and plenty.

Mint *Mentha species*
Mints are a general tonic and an antispasmodic. They have antiseptic and anaesthetic properties. A mild infusion acts as a sedative whilst a stronger infusion acts as a stimulant and a tonic. Take for colds, coughs, catarrh insomnia and dyspepsia. Chew a mint leaf to freshen your breath.

Mistletoe *Viscum album*
Add to incense dedicated to the planets of the Sun and Jupiter, the element of air, healing incense and incense to aid divination and prophetic dreams. Use also in the incense of Coamhain and Yule, when it is a plant of fertility and rebirth. NB: the berries are poisonous.

Mugwort *Artemisia vulgaris*
The infusion is used in the treatment of painful and irregular menstruation and the menopause (often in equal parts with pennyroyal). It can also be used for indigestion, upset stomachs, depression, nerves, hysteria, tension and rheumatism. There is some evidence that mugwort is an anti-epileptic. The tea relieves sickness. NB: mugwort should not be taken during pregnancy. At the Celtic festival of Midsummer girls would wear garlands and girdles of mugwort whilst dancing around the Midsummer bonfires. These were later cast into the fire as a protection for the coming year. Mugwort is also a herb of clairvoyance and may be taken as a tea to aid divination. It may be used as an incense or the fresh leaves rubbed onto the crystal ball. It can be placed by the bed or used in a dream pillow to aid prophetic dreams. Used in the bath mugwort will refresh and revive.

Mullein *Verbascum thapsus*
Take a wineglassful of the tea three times s day to relive gout. Add the

leaves and flowers to incense dedicated to the planet Saturn, the element of water, and to invoke the deities Circe, Odysseus, Jupiter and Crone aspects of the Goddess. Add to incense of protection, courage, and to attract the opposite sex. Use in the Samhain blend for ancestor contact, or any incense used in rituals or meditations designed to gain ancestral or ancient knowledge.

Myrtle *Myrtus communis*
A tea made from the leaves is useful for coughs and colds. It also eases flatulence, sinusitis and psoriasis. It can be used externally as a douche for vaginal discharge. An ointment, made from the flowers and leaves, is used for eczema, psoriasis, bruises and acne. The Romans dedicated the plant to the Goddess Venus. They used it as a decoration at festivals, feasts, weddings and celebrations. Northern brides wear myrtle as a bridal wreath, in honour of Freya, the love goddess. Use in incense dedicated to the planet Venus and the Moon, the element of water, the Goddess in all her aspects, and is employed for prophecy, love, fertility and marriage, death and regeneration.

Nettle *Urtica dioica*
Nettles make good eating, though this may seem surprising. In the past, country folk made puddings, soup and beer from nettles. Pick them in the spring, as they are too tough after the beginning of June. Cooking destroys the formic acid that causes the stinging sensation. They can be boiled as spring greens, or better still, eaten in a soup with potatoes, onions and other vegetables as desired. Nettle tea is very good for rheumatism and helps remove uric acid deposits in the joints. Nettles are rich in vitamins and minerals and make one of the best teas for treating gout and rheumatism. It can be used to regulate menstruation and stimulate the flow of milk in nursing mothers, during and after the menopause to supply essential nutrients and calcium. Nettles are excellent in the treatment of eczema, particularly childhood and nervous eczema. An infusion taken daily will help the circulation. It also makes a good gargle for mouth ulcers and sore throats. A decoction made from the root may be used as a general hair tonic, or a hair tonic can be made from young nettles simmered in water for two hours. This can be bottled and kept for use as required. A decoction of the aerial parts is used to cleanse the circulatory system. The stop nosebleeds a cotton wool ball should be soaked in nettle juice and inserted into the nostril. A compress may be used to treat acne,

alopecia and eczema. Add to incense dedicated to the planet Mars, the
element of fire. Nettle is a herb of healing and protection, and is used to
dispel negativity. It may be used in incenses for Underworld journeys, and
rites of birth, initiation and death.

Oak *Quercus robur*

Oak wood is useful for a variety of purposes, for making wooden pegs,
buckets, barrels and charcoal. Ink is made from its galls. The wood can be
used for fencing, gates, wooden roof tiles, wheel spokes, and ladder rungs.
Oak is slow burning, good for keeping the fire going. Acorns have been
used as food for humans and animals since early times, though as nuts
they are rather bitter and disappointing. They can be toasted and added to
cakes or and dry roasted and ground as a coffee substitute. Use the wood
or bark at Beltane; the flowers and wood at Coamhain; leaves or wood at
Lughnasa; acorns at Lughnasa and the wood at Yule. Also add the wood
and bark to incense dedicated to the planet Jupiter, the element of fire and
chief gods.

Parsley *Petroselinum crispum / P. satirum*

Rich in vitamin C, the tea is a diuretic. Use in incense dedicated to the
planet Mercury, the element of air, and Death aspects of the Goddess.
Parsley is associated with death aspects of the Goddess, the Underworld
and gaining ancestral knowledge. Use also in Herfest and Samhain incense.

Pine *Pinus sylvestris*

Pine wood is made into trugs. All conifer trees contain a resinous
substance. If the bark cracks, then it will secrete a resin to seal the wound.
It is antibiotic and antifungal. Use the needles, wood and resin in incense
of the planet Mars, the elements of earth and air, the spring equinox,
fertility, regeneration and new beginnings. Pine may also be used for
purification, cleansing and dispelling negativity. Pine essential oil is used
for cleansing the home, temple and aura. It is also very healing and boosts
levels of physical energy. It is ruled by the planet Mars and the element of
air. It may be used in spells to attract money and material goods.

Poplar *Populus sp.*

Use in incense against disease, to bring protection and help with
endurance, to connect with the Higher Self and hear the spirit within. Use
in planetary incense of the Sun and Saturn.

Poppy, Field *Papaver rhoeas*

This common red poppy is not narcotic, unlike the opium poppy *Papaverum somniferum*, which can occasionally be found growing wild in Britain. Red poppies once grew among the crops, before the advent of selective weed killers, and so are sacred to goddesses of fertility and the harvest. Add the petals or seeds to incense of fertility, luck, to attract money and love, to honour the Harvest Goddess. You can collect the seeds straight from the dried 'pepper pot' poppy heads and use on breads, cakes and biscuits.

Primrose *Primula vulgaris*

The flowering of the yellow primrose is one of the heralds of spring. The flowers can be eaten in salads, or crystallised for cake decorating. Primrose tea, made from the leaves and flowers, is good for rheumatism, arthritis, gout and migraine, as well as insomnia if taken at bedtime. Add to incense of purification and protection, to incense designed to attract love and glamour, at the festivals of Ostara and Beltane and to honour all goddesses of the spring and love. Use also to attract fairies, and at the initiation of a bard. It is ruled by the planet Venus and the element of earth.

Raspberry *Rubus idaeus*

These can often be found growing wild as garden escapes, though the plant is indigenous to the British Isles. They are best eaten raw with cream, though they do make wonderful jam and wine. The leaves and fruits tone the uterine muscles during pregnancy, but should not be used during the first trimester. Use as a gargle for tonsillitis, mouth ulcers, sores, conjunctivitis, burns and small wounds.

Reed *Phragmites communis*

When the stems are accidentally broken, they exude a sweet sticky gum which hardens and may be eaten as a sweet. In some ancient cultures, such as the Egyptians, the reed bed was seen as the entrance to the underworld, from which the sun was reborn. Because they are filled with air or spirit reeds are associated with the speaking of the spirits. They are a symbol of royalty and sun gods. Reeds are ruled by the Sun and the element of fire.

Rose *Rosa* sp.

The single pink blossoms of our native wild rose or dog rose (*Rosa canina*) flower at Midsummer. The fruits are orange-red hips which are used in the commercial production of rose hip syrup. They have to be handled carefully as their insides are full of pointed hairs which can cause irritation to sensitive skins- a fact exploited by generations of schoolboys who used them to make itching powder. Roses are edible, and the petals have been used to make jam, wine, vinegar, sweets, Turkish delight and rose water, as well as perfumes and cosmetics.

Red roses are ruled by Jupiter, damask roses by the planet Venus and white roses by the Moon. All fall under the element of water. The white rose represents purity, perfection, innocence, virginity and the Maiden Goddess, while the red is earthly passion and fertility, the Mother Goddess. Add rose petals to incense for spells and rituals of love, passion, sexuality and sensuality, seduction and marriage, the Great Rite and handfasting. Use at the festival of Beltane.

The essential oils is made from *Rosa centifolia* (Absolute) or *Rosa damascena* (Otto). It is useful for women, treating impurities in the womb, irregular periods and depression. It is ruled by the planet Venus and the element of water, and is used for spells of love, attraction, marriage and sensuality. It brings about a calm, peaceful atmosphere and induces harmony.

Rosemary *Rosemarinus officinalis*

The tea is very stimulating, as is adding fresh rosemary leaves to the bath. The infusion can be used for the treatment of depression, insomnia, anxiety, nervous migraines, rheumatic pain and aching joints. The tea can be taken daily as a tonic. It can also be used as an antiseptic gargle or mouthwash. Externally it can be used to heal wounds, bruises, strains and bumps. It stimulates the circulation and eases pain because it increases the blood supply to the area where it is applied. Rosemary is a circulatory and nervine stimulant. It tones the digestive system. When such problems as headaches and dyspepsia are caused by nervous tension rosemary is a suitable remedy. Ruled by the Sun, the element of fire, and the zodiac sign of Aries, healing, love, marriage, births, funerals and memorial services, for protection and to dispel negativity and evil, to keep a lover faithful, for love spells and spells designed to retain youth. Rosemary essential oil has a strong stimulant effect on the mind, clearing the head and clarifying thoughts. Rosemary can have an uplifting and antidepressant effect.

Rowan or Mountain Ash *Sorbus aucuparia*

The branches can be made into hoops, baskets and tool handles. The brilliant orange-red berries are best picked in October, though they can still be found clinging to the shrubs until January. They make an excellent jelly-

150

boil the fruit in a little water, then add 1 pint of water per pint of juice and boil till setting point. An infusion of the berries makes an antiseptic gargle for sore throats, inflamed tonsils and hoarseness. A decoction of bark or rowan jelly is used for diarrhoea and vaginal irritations. NB: Eating the raw berries can cause stomach upsets. Rowan is ruled by the Moon and the element of water associated with witchcraft, protection, divination and the dead. The berries and leaves can be dried and burned as an incense to invoke spirits, familiars, spirit guides and elementals, to ask for their help when seeking visions, particularly at Samhain. The berries can also be used in an incense to banish undesirable entities and thought forms. The incense is burned whilst seeking visions.

Rue *Ruta graveolens*
Rutin, a substance extracted from rue, was used during the Second World War to treat high blood pressure. Rutin tea is still available in health food shops. The infusion may be used to bathe tired eyes. NB: rue should only be used under qualified supervision as it contains toxic properties. Avoid totally during pregnancy. The fresh sap may irritate sensitive skins and cause dermatitis. Rue banishes negative energies and may be used in exorcism and purification incenses. It is ruled by the Sun and the element of fire and the sign of Leo.

Saffron *Crocus sativus*
An aphrodisiac used in incense for love, marriage and handfasting. It lifts the spirits and may be used during divination. Though given to the sun by the astrologer-herbalists, for its golden stamens and dye, to the ancient people saffron was sacred to the Moon Goddess. It may be used in incenses to honour her. It is ruled by the element of fire and the sign of Leo.

Sage *Salvia officinalis*
Sage tea relives headaches, hot flushes and menopausal symptoms. The tea is also good for sore throats and coughs and can be used as a gargle. It is a tonic and good for the liver. Pour ½ pint water over a handful of freshly chopped leaves. Sweeten with honey of liked. Ruled by the planet Jupiter, the element of air, associated with wisdom, prophetic dreams and warding off the evil eye, sage is a herb of purification and its smoke may be directed to cleanse the aura, the working area and magical tools. The oil is useful for the treatment of stress and depression. NB: do not use the oil when pregnant and use it sparingly as sage oil can be toxic if over-used.

Skullcap/ Scullcap *Scutellaria galericulata*

An uncommon wild plant in Britain, which grows along rivers and ponds, skullcap is a sedative, and makes a very relaxing tea, useful in times of stress.

Sorrel *Rumex acetosa*

The old herbalists called sorrel cuckoo's meat, since they believed the birds used it to clear their throats. The leaves can be used to remove rust marks from linen and stains from the hands. The leaves appear early in the year and can be picked in February. Cook them in butter until they are pureed and add cream. Add the chopped leaves to soups. To make sorrel vinegar, pack the washed leaves in a jar and cover with white wine vinegar. Sorrel aids the kidneys and benefits the digestion. The tea cools fevers and is a good blood tonic in early spring; used as a gargle it benefits sore throats. Use as a poultice for inflammation. It is a herb of Venus. NB. Sorrel should not be used frequently as it contains oxalic acid.

St. John's Wort *Hypericum perforatum*

St John's wort is used in the treatment of depression. A red oil is obtained from the flowers and leaves of St. John's wort. Externally the oil can be applied to bruises, wounds, varicose veins, ulcers and sunburn. NB: the oil should not be taken internally unless under qualified supervision. The oil is phototropic and can cause skin irritation if exposed to direct sunlight. The flowers can be used to make an infusion for the treatment of anaemia, rheumatism, headaches, nervous conditions, asthma, bronchial catarrh, irregular menstruation, depression and insomnia. A couple of spoonfuls of the infusion is said to prevent bed wetting in children. One of the many herbs which gain special powers at Midsummer, when it should be collected for magical purposes, it is used in the Coamhain incense or thrown on the Midsummer bonfire. It can be used in incenses cleansing the working area, working tools or the person. It repels negativity and can be used in purifications and exorcisms. It is ruled by the Sun, the element of fire and the sign of Leo. It is sacred to sun gods, particularly Baldur.

Tansy *Chrysanthemum vulgare/ Tanacetum vulgare*

Once widely grown, tansy was used in the kitchen and still room. The leaves were served at Easter, and used to flavour omelettes. During the Middle Ages tansy was a popular herb in monastery gardens as it was used as a strewing herb because of its antiseptic properties. It was also used as a substitute for the spices nutmeg and cinnamon which were very expensive. A traditional use of the herb was in tansy pudding, a rich custardy dessert or a bread or dough cake, called tansy cake, which was eaten at Easter. During the Lenten fast tansy tea was considered to be an excellent tonic and stimulant. . It can be used in the bath or as a facial steam for mature or sallow skins. NB: Tansy can be an irritant to sensitive skins. It should not be taken internally in large amounts owing to some toxic constituents which can be a violent irritation to the stomach. It should not be taken by pregnant women.

Thyme *Thymus vulgaris*
The generic name *'thymus'* comes from the *'thymon'* which means 'to fumigate' as thyme was used as an incense to drive away insects. At midnight on Midsummer's night the King of the Fairies is said to dance with his followers on thyme beds. It is an ingredient of many recipes dating from around 1600, which supposedly allowed one to see the fairies. The tea is useful for treating insomnia, chest complaints and irregular periods. An infusion of the leaves is good for hangovers, a general tonic, poor digestion, flatulence, over indulgence, loss of appetite, nausea, nervousness and depression. Sweetened with honey it can be used for sore throats, coughs, colds, flu, whooping cough, menstrual problems, asthma and bronchial problems. Externally it can be used in the bath or facial steams for spots, acne, cuts, sores and wounds. Thyme leaves and rosemary infusion can be used as a hair rinse for dandruff. Eating the raw leaves helps with the digestion of fatty foods. For a relaxing bath to ease aches and pains, pick a few sprays of lavender and thyme, tie them together and place them in a hot bath while the water is still running. Thyme may be used as an incense to help focus personal energies and gain the strength to face difficulties ahead. It is also a herb of purification and protection and can be used to purify the working area. It is ruled by the planet Venus and the element of air and used for cleansing, purification and to engender courage. It is helpful for closing down the psychic senses when experiences and visions become overwhelming.

Valerian *Valeriana officinalis*
The young leaves can be boiled as greens in the spring. The generic name is derived from the Latin *'valero'* which means 'to be in health' or 'powerful' and is a reference to the medicinal properties of the plan. Witches have long employed valerian for bonding with their cats, and for attracting cat

familiars (totems or allies). The Wildfolk were often thought to take cat disguises and valerian is used to attract some types of fairy allies. The root is used medicinally. It is employed to treat insomnia, cramp, intestinal colic, period pain and rheumatism. It is useful in the treatment of all nervous disorders including hysteria, vertigo, migraine, palpitations and stomach cramps. It reduces pain, induces sleep and minimises stress and strain. The tea is a mild sedative, often drunk for emotional distress. A decoction of the root is used as a facial wash and soothing bath herb.

Vervain or Simpler's Joy *Verbena officinalis*
Vervain is one of the sacred plants of the druids, used in lustral water for purification and in divination brews, and gathered at the heliacal rising of the Dog Star Sirius at Lughnasa. The Romans took it back to Italy, and called it *Britanica* and used it as a ritual cleansing plant. One of the sacred herbs of Coamhain and used at Samhain, it will cleanse and purify it as well as raising vibrations. It is sacred to poets and singers and heightens the consciousness and intensifies clairvoyant powers. Beginners sometimes confuse this with lemon verbena because of the botanical name, and I once discovered an oil on sale at a psychic fair called 'Vervain' which was actually lemon verbena. Vervain does not have a lemony smell!

Violet *Viola odorata*
Not to be confused with the odourless dog violet, the sweet violet is quite common in shady places. In the past they were often used in puddings and sweets. To crystallise violet flowers, powder a teaspoon of gum Arabic and place in a jar with rosewater. Leave 3 days. Paint this mixture onto violet flowers with a soft brush and sprinkle with caster sugar. Dry in a warm place on a wire rack and store in an airtight container. For a soothing tea for bronchitis and colds, pour ½ pint boiling water onto 1 tsp dried violets. Infuse for 5 minutes. Strain and sweeten with honey if liked. Mix with lavender to attract a new love. Violets are associated with the twilight, a magical 'time between times', when the Otherworld is closer and it is easier to slip into. Violets are ruled by the planet Venus and the element of water.

Walnut *Juglans regia*
A slow growing tree which is becoming increasingly rare; the wood is excellent for carving and cabinet making. The generic name '*juglans*' comes from the Latin '*Jovis glans*' which translates as 'Jupiter's nuts'. Best picked after late October if you want ripe nuts, or pick green in July for pickling.

Boil the husks with honey and water for a gargle for sore throats. The tea made from the bark is a stomach tonic and can be used as a gargle for sore throats or as a mouth wash for ulcers. An infusion or decoction of the bark may be used to treat diarrhoea and to dry up breast milk.

Willow *Salix* species.
The young stems can be soaked and used for basket making. The black willow (*Salix nigra*) is used in an infusion as an anaphrodisiac (the opposite of an aphrodisiac). The white willow (*Salix Alba*) contains salicylic acid, a natural aspirin, and was used to treat headaches and rheumatism, and it sometimes seems that the Goddess placed the tree in the damp places where rheumatism is more common to provide the cure. Place the shredded bark in ½ pint cold water, bring to the boil, simmer 2 minutes, turn off the heat and stand 15 minutes. Willow incense can be used when working on the feminine side of your nature, the Goddess and the gentle rhythms of the moon and Nature's cycles.

Woodruff *Galium odoratum / Asperula odorata*
Press the leaf rosettes of woodruff between the pages of a book, and as it dries it will develop a sweet scent. You can use this as a bookmark in you Book of Shadows, or to scent drawers and linen cupboards. The flowers can be added to drinks. In Germany it is gathered on May Day to make a seasonal drink called May Bowl.

Wormwood *Artemisia absinthium*
Used to flavour the liqueur absinthe, wormwood is a bitter herb used to expel worms, but wormwood is dangerous of overused and can damage the heart and its internal use is not recommended- please don't experiment with this. You can hang some in cupboards to deter moths and insects, or add to incense of Artemis and Diana. It can be used externally in an infused oil or salve for lumbago, sprains and bruises, but again, continued use is not recommended.

Yarrow *Achillea millefolium*
A fern-like plant that grows in shady places, the leaves can be used in salads or cooked as a vegetable. The tea is a tonic and diuretic, useful for relieving high temperatures. The non woody parts of the stems, or sometimes the flowers only, are used medicinally. The tea aids digestive problems, fatigue, cystitis, haemorrhoids, incontinence and regulates the

menstrual flow. It induces perspiration, lowers the temperature, helps colds and cleanses the entire body. A salve helps ulcers and varicose veins, a decoction helps wounds, chapped skin, eczema, and rashes and a mouth wash will calm inflamed gums. Yarrow stems bleeding. For slow healing wounds apply a compress of yarrow. Yarrow is sacred to the Horned God and to the male principle. Yarrow tea may be used when working on aspects of masculinity and for connection with the God. Yarrow is one of the sacred herbs of Midsummer. Yarrow incense can be used to promote divination and clairvoyance. It is ruled by the planet Venus and the element of water and is sacred to Cernunnos, Herne and Pan.

Yew *Taxus baccata*
A yew fence post is said to outlast iron. Yew was used for making bows, small carvings and bowls. The small, twiggy branches can be used for basket making. Yew is a tree of death, but one which promises regeneration from that death. It is sacred to Underworld aspects of the Crone Goddess like Hecate and Banbha, keepers of the spirits in Her Underworld womb. It is ruled by Saturn and the element of water. NB Yew berries and needles are highly poisonous.

Chapter 8
TIDES OF THE YEAR

The tides of the year weave a magical web which twines about us; the life cycles of humankind, animals and plants are intimately bound together. Our ancestors sought to understand these mingled threads, and to read the patterns they made, patterns that were translated into the famous Celtic knotwork designs that are full of meaning. The task of the shaman or wise woman was to understand this many layered pattern, to comprehend the significance of the arrival of the cuckoo and the swallow, the rising of the Pleiades, the blossoming of the May, and the mournful autumn song of the robin. They noted which birds fed on which trees, what animals did at each time of year, which plants bloomed or matured in each season - not as isolated or unrelated events but integral parts of the whole picture. At different times certain things came to the fore in the pattern of the web, like the flowering of the oak at Midsummer. They would note how the woodpecker runs spirally round its trunk at this time, beating on its bark to call the summer storms. How, at midwinter rare mistletoe produced berries on the oak, like semen from the Lord of the Forest, and the red breasted robin perched atop the holly, still green in the depths of winter and red berried with the colour of life and blood. In this way the shaman or witch sought to work with, rather than in spite of natural cycles, recognising that everything had its place in the natural world.

The purpose of their rituals was to maintain this configuration and to prevent it returning to the primal chaos from which it emerged. The Pagan's Wheel of the Year- the marking of the seasonal festivals- is all about the ebb and flow of energy; pouring into the land during the spring and draining out again in the autumn, maintaining a natural balance; a time to receive, a time to pay out. This is something not well understood nowadays – where dark, death, winter are deemed to be evil and unwanted, rather than a necessary part of the whole. For the Pagan death is not the end but part of the ongoing cycle of rebirth.

We forget just how far the turning of the Wheel of the Year determined the activities of humankind, planting in the spring, praying for good weather to nurture the crops during the summer, harvesting in the autumn, and resting in the winter, telling stories around the hearth fire to keep the threatening dark at bay.

At first the Celtic year had just two seasons called simply winter (*Geimredh*) and summer (*Samhradh*). During *Samhradh* food would be varied and plentiful, but during the winter half, careful management of stored produce would be necessary to supplement the few vegetables could that survive the frosts. Towards the end of this season, unless the harvest had been particularly good, all these stores would have been largely consumed. Who knows what would happen if the weakened sun was not reborn at the winter solstice? What if the days continued to diminish until cold and death overtook the world completely? Only the return of good weather and the greening of the land could save the population from starvation and signs of the changing season would be eagerly awaited.

Later, as understanding of the seasons became more sophisticated, it was divided into a fourfold year. *Geimredh* was now the first quarter beginning with Samhain (what we know now as Halloween). Then followed *Earrach* (Spring), *Samhradh*, and finally *Foghamhar* (Autumn). Within this framework, several festivals were celebrated. It is unlikely that they took place on specific dates as ours do, but were probably calculated according to natural signs, such as the first full moon after the blossoming of the hawthorn at Beltane or at the heliacal rising of the Dog Star at Lughnasa.

Later the year was divided into months, much as we know it today. The Celts measured time by the movement of the sun and the moon, with months always beginning on the same phase of the moon. According to Pliny this was fixed to the sixth day after the new moon. The Celtic names for the months reflected their close bond with nature. Names like Stay Home Time, Time of Ice and Time of Winds leave us in little doubt of the general mood. There were gentler months too. Cantlos, the time of singing, fell around what we now call September and came to contain the harvest festival known to modern Pagans as Herfest, the Autumn Equinox (or Mabon to US Pagans). Rather than naming individual days they called those that fell during the waxing moon *Mat,* a time of growth and receiving, and those that fell in the waning moon *Anmat,* a time of reduction and payment, showing a subtle understanding of the ebb and flow of energies.

Each month, there are things we can do to feel a part of nature as the ancients did. *Samnios* was Summers End and fell around October. Go blackberry picking and make wine or jam. At Beltane (the beginning of May) you could gather hawthorn blossoms and make a tea, then meditate for a while to get in touch with the feminine side of yourself. Deck your house with greenery to celebrate the vegetation spirit and the return of life to the earth. Make Beltane cakes and roll them down a hillside. Light a ritual fire and scatter the ashes on your garden as a fertility rite.

THE CELTIC MONTHS OF THE YEAR
Based on the Gaulish Coligney calendar inscribed on sheets of bronze.

SAMIONOS – seed fall (Samhain) — October/ November (includes Samhain)

DUMANNIOS- darkest depths — November/ December

RIUROS- cold time — December/January (Includes winter solstice)

ANAGANTIOS- stay home time — January/February (Includes Imbolc)

OGRONIOS- time of ice — February/March

CUTIOS- time of winds — March/April (Includes vernal equinox)

GIAMONIOS- shoots show — April/May (Includes Beltane)

SAMIVISIONOS- time of brightness — May/June

EQUOS- horse-time — June/July (Includes summer solstice)

ELEMBIUOS- claim time — July/August (Includes Lughnasa)

EDRINIOS- arbitration time — August/September

CANTLOS- song time — September/ October (Includes autumn equinox)

JANUARY
The month of January is named after the Roman god Janus, a two-headed deity who looks backwards to the past and forwards to the future. He guards the gateway of the year, following on after the December festival of the Saturnalia, the wild revels in honour of Saturn.

Every culture celebrates the New Year, and here in the west, this is reckoned to be in January, though this has not always been so. Until the introduction of the New Gregorian calendar in 1752 in Britain the New Year officially began in March. In ancient Babylon it was celebrated between March and April, while in ancient Egypt it was linked with the flooding of the Nile in July. In Europe it was marked at various times between the winter solstice and the spring equinox.

Traditional New Year celebrations always include elements of death and rebirth. There is a muffled peal of funeral bells on New Year's Eve until midnight, when the muffles are removed, and a loud, clear peal allowed to ring out across the skies, ringing out the old and ringing in the new. The passing year is pictured as an old man or Old Father Time (Saturn), complete with scythe and hour glass, who gives way to the New Year Baby. This is a very ancient theme, re-enacted in many folk customs. In the mummers plays the Fool dies and is brought back to life by the medicine man.

The symbolism is very clear- one cycle has ended and another begun. It makes sense that this is celebrated around the time of the solstice when the sun dies and the sun (son) is reborn. For twelve days he grows and gains the attributes he needs to conquer the dark, until on January 1st the New Year King is ready to begin his reign. He grows and develops within the Wheel of the Year, reaches his peak with the summer solstice, and dies again at the winter solstice. I can hear some of you saying 'but isn't the Pagan new year at Samhain (31st October)?' Well, some think that the Celts celebrated their New Year at the end of October, beginning and ending the year with the dawn of winter. However, this is by no means proven, and the evidence is quite slim. The survival of folk customs seems to imply that the solstice and calends of January are far more convincing candidates.

Whatever our individual paths, we have to acknowledge that a lot of energy, thought power- and therefore magic- is directed into the celebration of New Year. The festival has only ever had a thin veneer of Christianity over it, and nearly all of its customs and lore are obviously Pagan. In Scotland, of course, the celebrations are more important than Christmas. The day is called Hogmanay when fires are lit and good luck attends drinking pure water, though the festival is better known for people drinking plenty of whisky and beer. The chief custom is first-footing, based on the idea that whatever happens within the dawning of the New Year foreshadows what will happen for the rest of it. The first person to step over the threshold should therefore represent good fortune. He should be whole and hearty, male and dark (i.e. saturnine). Red-haired men and women are deemed unlucky. In some parts of Scotland if women broke the taboo boys would be called upon to perform the rite of 'breaking the witch'. The first foot must bring with him gifts that represent fire, food and wealth for the coming year in the shape of coal, bread and money.

Because what happens at New Year indicates the trends of the rest of the year, it is considered a good day to make resolutions. For the same reason it is unlucky to be unemployed on New Year's Day and you should be careful to keep some money in your pocket. If you eat well today you will be assured of food for the rest of the year. The giving of New Year presents was an old custom arising from the same principle as first footing, while Druids distributed mistletoe on this day. However, no one would give away a light on New Year's Day as this symbolised giving away the household luck. Washing clothes would wash a life away, and no iron object should be parted with.

On Twelfth Night (which some say is the 5th and some the 6th January) there was a traditional celebration with Twelfth Night cake, decorated with red and green knots, yellow bows and flowers. There was a bean and pea inside- whoever discovered the bean was king, and whoever discovers the pea was queen, of the revels and presided over the games, mumming plays and dances.

Everyone also had a turn at the wassail bowl full of Lamb's Wool (a spiced drink), taking a piece of toasted apple from the wassail and eating it, before drinking the health of all present. The word 'wassail' comes from the Saxon *wass hael* meaning 'good health' and actually refers to the large bowl used for the toasting. In the evening the apple orchards were wassailed, the trees' roots drenched in cider while they were serenaded with songs and exhortations to fruit well in the autumn. Shots would be fired or horns sounded to scare off any evil spirits that might want to damage the crop. On returning home the wassailers often had to answer questions or riddles before they would be let back in.

After the festive season it was time to get back to work and prepare for spring. On 7th January, St Distaff's Day (there is no such saint), spinning was resumed and on Plough Monday, ploughs and other tools were blessed for the coming year and the corn dolly was ploughed into the first furrow.

Here in Britain, January is often the coldest month of the year, with the land wrapped in a blanket of frost and ice. The daylight hours are short, and it seems to be a bleak time, an in-between period of waiting after the excitement of Christmas and the winter solstice, and before the welcome return of warm weather in spring. Only a hundred years ago, it might have meant a lean and hungry time if the stored harvest had not been abundant enough to see the village through the winter. Food and fuel to stave off the winter cold was essential for survival, and the weakest members of the community would often die during January and February. In the Anglo Saxon Chronicle, January was called the *Wul-manoth* ('wolf month'), because the death bringing cold prowls around the settlements like a hungry wolf. The Celts called it *Anagantios* – stay home time- the ideal time to catch up on all those indoor pursuits like writing, storytelling, painting, crafts, composing, making music and so on, which is one of the reasons that the festival of Brighid, goddess of inspiration, falls during *Anagantios*.

In the bleak month of January, there is very little green around, apart from the evergreen trees and shrubs, like conifers such as the pine, fir, juniper, yew, spruce and larch, which produce cones instead of seeds or nuts, and have needles instead of leaves, and the holly which is able to grow in shade and low light. Its berries are ripe in January and provide much needed food for birds and deer. The old Pagans thought that all evergreens were magical since they could endure through the cold time when all other plants died. They carried the life of the vegetation spirit through winter.

In early January the ploughs were brought out and blessed to ready them for their work during the year. You can do this with your own gardening tools, even if they don't amount to much more than a trowel and a watering can; the important thing is that they will help you benefit from the year's harvest and it is a ritual preparation for the task. It doesn't seem a very promising month in the garden, but it is during January that the first seeds of the year go in. In a propagator you can plant broad beans, lettuce, spinach and summer cauliflowers. If you are not sure what happens during each season, try keeping a notebook this year, and record what flowers, animals and birds you see each week, what the weather is doing, and how the energy of the season feels.

Deep beneath the earth's icy mantle many creatures sleep through the chill to conserve their meagre stocks of energy, and these include bats, tiny dormice, insects such as earwigs, ladybirds, droneflies and moths, as well as all of our native reptiles like the adder, grass snake and lizards, as well as frogs and toads. The hedgehog hibernates through the coldest time of year. He often comes out at Imbolc to see whether it is warm enough yet to wake up, if not he returns to his sleep. Contrary to popular opinion, the squirrel does not hibernate but stays in his nest and only goes out to visit his hidden supplies of nuts; those he forgets often sprout and this is one way by which the oak is spread.

Some animals, such as the mountain hare, camouflage themselves to hide in the winter snow by turning their coats white for the season. The northern stoat turns white for the winter, except for the black tip of its tail. Its beautiful coat is then called ermine, and is the reason the animal is cruelly hunted and killed. In the south of the country, where it is slightly warmer, the stoats remain brown, and you might even come across a half white and half-brown one.

Though Mother Nature seems to be asleep in January, she is actually busy preparing for the spring. Several animals begin mating and breeding in January, encouraged by the lengthening daylight hours. Trout are spawning and badger breeding starts mid January and lasts into March. Mating can last for up to half an hour and may be repeated over several nights. The female may give birth to up to five young, but there are usually three, of which only two may survive. They spend their first few weeks in a cosy nest being suckled by the sow. By summer the cubs are weaned and venture out to feed and play. Foxes also mate in January and the vixen excavates several new and disused earths until she finds one she thinks suitable. Sometimes one dog will have several vixens, and the younger vixens in such a social group may not breed, but help to look after the young of others, finding food and hiding them when necessary.

One of the Goddess's messengers this time of year is the mistle-thrush. He screeches in a sad way when the weather is at its worst. The robin too sings his heart out in order to protect his territory during a time of scarce food. Meanwhile the rooks, in pairs now, circle the grey skies. Water birds can suffer when the water is frozen, though the water is usually warmer than the land and a good place to spend the winter.

FEBRUARY

With February the year noticeably begins to turn towards spring. The bare arms of winter trees begin to redden with sap and the first snowdrops poke their heads from the cold earth. Animals begin to shake off their winter sleep and emerge from hibernation. Young lambs are born and nurtured. During February we notice that the days are lengthening and the sun grows stronger as Brighid, the sun maiden, brings back the light. The year is awakening, all bright, new, and pure, an innocent waiting for life to mark it.

The Roman feast of Februa (giving its name to February) took place during this month, when the women would undergo purification after parading through the streets carrying candles. The Roman festival was Christianised as Candlemas, a time for blessing the candles for the church and seen symbolically as the time when the Virgin Mary was purified after the birth of Christ.

Imbolc (Imbolg, Oimelc) is one of the four festivals of our Celtic ancestors celebrated by modern witches. It begins the second quarter of the winter half of the year around 2nd February. It is the time of awakening and celebrates the very first stirrings of spring. It is the time of first lambing and one of the translations of Imbolc is 'ewe's milk', showing that birth and nurturing exists even in the depths of winter. In Gaelic the word means 'in the belly' and refers to the quickening of life in the womb of Mother Earth. It is the festival when the Hag of Winter is transformed into the Spring Goddess, renewed in her virginity. All the evergreen decorations of Yule were burned as a symbolic banishment of winter.

At Imbolc she was said to use her white wand to "breathe life into the mouth of the dead winter"; meaning the white fire of the sun awakened the land. An old poem stated; *"Today is the day of Bride, The Serpent shall come from the hole."* An effigy of the serpent was often honoured in the ceremonies of this day, making it clear that Brighid had aspects as a serpent goddess. As the serpent sloughed its old skin and was renewed, so the land shook off winter to emerge restored; the snake symbolised the cycle of life. When Brighid's cult was suppressed, then St Patrick had indeed banished the snakes (Pagans) from Ireland. However, Brighid's popularity was so great that the church transformed her into a saint, allegedly the midwife of Christ and the daughter of a Druid who was converted to Christianity by St. Patrick, and who went on to found the Abbey of Kildare. Maybe she has the last laugh, as there are even now many more places in Ireland named after Brighid than Patrick.

St Valentine's Day is celebrated on 14th February. He is the patron saint of sweethearts, though the choice is a strange one since he was a Christian priest beheaded by Romans in 280 CE. When the church suppressed the Pagan Lupercalia (February 15th) festival in 494 CE St Valentine was celebrated instead. The Lupercalia was a Roman festival of youth and fertility, echoing the seasonal mating activities of the natural world. Young people chose their sweethearts by drawing lots for each other. Since then, it has been the day for lovers and love magic.

Though February is often the coldest month of the year, beneath the surface Mother Nature is renewing herself. By the end of the month the sun is beginning to warm the soil enough to encourage the new shoots to push through. The snowdrops, often called 'Fair Maids of February', are not native plants but are naturalised in many parts of the country. They symbolise the Maiden Goddess of spring and you can place a bunch on your windowsill to invoke her blessing.

One of the loveliest signs of spring is the catkins of the pussy willow breaking their buds and hanging silver in the light. There are also catkins on the hazel; little lamb's tails dangling in the breeze, by some trick of Mother Nature just when the real lambs come along.

The shining white papery bark of the silver birch really stands out in the barren woodlands, and it is not surprising that it is one of the totems of February. It is one of the earliest trees to come into leaf, taken as a signal to start sowing in agricultural communities, making it an important symbol of regeneration and fertility. In the Nordic tradition the birch (*Beorc, Byarka*, or *Berkana*) is a symbol of Mother Earth and represents the feminine powers of growth, healing and the natural world. Silver birch is associated with purification, since white is believed to drive away the dark, and its branches are used in a country ritual for driving out the old year by beating the bounds of the village.

The blackthorn flowers before its leaves appear, and brightens the hedgerows with its starry white blossoms. It is called 'the mother of the woods' because it is the first tree to bloom.

The garden starts to come alive with bulbs pushing through the ground. Several seeds can be sown this month, including celery, tomatoes and lettuce in seed trays in the greenhouse or on the windowsill. Prick out the vegetables sown last month. Sow parsnips directly into the ground. Bring in strawberry pots into the greenhouse or conservatory, and feed with potash for an early crop.

Snow often covers the ground and there is little fresh food to be found. In February our ancestors would have been be using up their stored produce, but might have been lucky enough to find some early spring greens like chickweed (*Stellaria media*) which is one of the first plants to return. Imbolc is sometimes called 'the time of the green shoots' and any young edible shoots are good at this time to remind us that the earth is about to blossom. If you have no access to wild or garden shoots, try making some of your own. Take some mung or aduki beans and place them in a jam jar with some blotting paper soaked in water. Pierce the lid of the jar and turn it occasionally until the beans have sprouted.

In February, activity amongst birds increases, with rooks noisy in the fields and blackbirds scrapping in the hedgerows. Birds are in full song this month, calling for mates; legend has it they choose their partners on St Valentine's Day. Listen and you may hear the nuthatch, tawny owl, robin, skylark, sparrow, starling, song thrush, blue tit, great tit, wood pigeon and wren, all piping romantic ballads. They begin to nest this month, with ravens being among the first, building in the same trees every year. The raven's croak is distinctive, and the bird has been known to mimic human speech, giving it an association with prophecy and oracular utterance. The Irish phrase 'raven's knowledge'; meaning to discover secrets. The Druids took omens from the flight of ravens.

Though frogs and toads are still hibernating at the start of the month, they will be spawning by the end of it. Frogs, which spend winter on land, return to ponds in February.

Keep your ears pricked and you will hear foxes barking this month. On mild February days the moles get busy, making hummocks in lawns and meadows. They are digging tunnels underground to search for juicy worms, and when all the worms have gone the moles move on and the tunnels are left abandoned; they do not take up permanent residence. If they get too troublesome, you can put old perfume bottles down the holes- they can't stand the smell and move on. Moles are wonderfully suited to their habitat, with broad, flat front feet like shovels.

MARCH

The Celts called this month *Cutios* - time of winds- and we still say that March comes in like a lion and goes out like a lamb- i.e. it come in raging but goes out mildly. According to one proverb, if it's not stormy and windy the first three days in March, it's saving itself for the three borrowing days at the month's end. Farmers considered that the winds of March dried out the fields and made the soil right for seeding. However, there is also likely to be plenty of rain and even some snow and several sharp frosts during the month.

During March we can feel the energy is building as the days become warmer with promise. We celebrate the vernal equinox around March 21st, the first true day of spring. The days and nights are now equal in length- twelve hours of night and twelve hours of day, though the light is gaining as we move towards summer. It is a time of hope and renewal when the sun shines brighter. On Easter Day people would climb the nearest mountain or hill to see the sun dancing at dawn 'in honour of the resurrection of Christ'.

There are many vegetation gods who are reborn around the time of the spring equinox such as Attis, Adonis, Osiris and Dionysus. They die and are reborn each year. These gods are usually the son of a god and a mortal woman, a saviour who saves his people. He is the vegetation, dying each year (at harvest) to be reborn in the spring. In ancient Rome, there was a ten-day rite in honour of Attis, son of the great goddess Cybele, which began on March 15th. A pine tree, which represented Attis, was chopped down, wrapped in a linen shroud, decorated with violets and placed in a sepulchre in the temple. On the Day of Blood or Black Friday, the priests of the cult gashed themselves with knives as they danced ecstatically, sympathizing with Cybele in her grief and helping to restore Attis to life. Two days later, a priest opened the sepulchre at dawn, revealing that it was empty and announcing that the god was saved. This day was known as Hilaria or the Day of Joy, a time of feasting and merriment. Mmm, now where I have I heard that story before...? Easter is fixed as the first Sunday after the full moon following the spring equinox, betraying its Pagan origins.

Witches call the equinox Ostara, and welcome the return of the Spring Goddess from her long season of winter sleep. Ostara or Eostre is a Saxon Goddess of Spring and the Morning Redness. Some descriptions say that she is hare-headed. She is only mentioned once in Old English literature, by the Venerable Bede (679-735) in *De Temporum Ratione*, which stated that April was called *Eostremonath*, due to the fact that the Heathen Anglo-Saxons worshipped and held ceremonies during that month in honour of Eostre. She may have been a sun maiden and possibly a version of Sol's daughter since her name is similar to Ausrine, the Baltic daughter of the sun.

The hot cross buns eaten on Good Friday were thought to be very powerful and some would be saved and kept tied in a bag hung from the kitchen rafters until the next Good Friday. It was thought that a portion of such a bun could cure any illness in man or beast. Eating buns marked with a cross, representing the four directions, the solar year and the four phases of the moon, was a traditional food at Pagan celebrations of the spring equinox in the ancient world, and was adapted into Christian custom.

Another essential Easter food was eggs, which were forbidden during Lent. At the equinox hens begin to lay again, and wild birds are mating and nest building. It is a symbol of new life. The ancient Egyptians and Romans gave each other presents of eggs at the spring equinox as a token of resurrection. Christians adopted the egg as a symbol of the resurrected Christ. It was common to give children hard boiled eggs dyed red as the symbol of Christ's blood and it was thought that this would keep them healthy for the coming year. Eggs blessed by the church were holy gifts. There were also games based around dyed and painted eggs rolled down hillsides until they broke and were eaten. In this case the egg represents the passage of the sun.

The early spring was anciently marked as a time of purification, ready for the coming year. Houses are spring cleaned and the body is also cleansed with tonic herbs. It is a good time to undertake a detox diet. Try cutting out all meat, dairy, wheat, sugar, caffeine and junk food, and eat only wholefood for two weeks. You will be amazed by how much more energised and light you feel. Traditionally, spring herbs, such as tansy and gorse, were used to purify the body after winter to prepare it for the new life cycle of spring. Cleavers (*Gallium aparine*) make a good spring tonic and ground ivy (*Glechoma hederacea/ Nepeta glechoma*) in the ritual cup honours the Spring Goddess. Pick a handful of gorse flowers, rinse gently and put them in a teapot with some boiling water to make a cleansing Ostara tisane.

The snake sloughing its skin and appearing 'reborn' is a powerful symbol of renewal at this time of year. The ancient symbolism is perseveed in folk customs and the popularity, at Easter, of bistort (*Polygonum bistorta*), also known as Snake Root, Easter Giant, Snakeweed, Dragon Wort, Easter Ledges and English Serpent Tree. The common name of bistort is derived from the Latin '*bis*' meaning 'twice' and '*torta*' meaning 'twisted'. This refers to the serpentine shape of the roots and accounts for many of its local names. Bistort was, and still is, traditionally eaten at Easter. In the north of Britain an annual contest is held to find the best Easter-ledge pudding.

Spring arrives this month in a blaze of sun coloured flowers like dandelion, celandines, daffodils and coltsfoot, which used to be called son-afore-the-father, since the flowers appear before the leaves. Country folk used to make a soothing smoking mixture for chesty conditions from the furry leaves, and it still makes one of the best herbal tobaccos.

The woodland and hedgerow trees seem hazed with green as the leaves begin to unfurl, providing fodder for animals. The tree totem of the spring equinox is the alder, which symbolises the power of fire and spring to reclaim the land from water and winter. Alders can be seen fringing streams, rivers, and lakes: the first trees to start colonising the land around watery places. The power of the alder's fire to free from water is also used by Craft herbalists to treat conditions caused by water and damp such as rheumatism, where a pulverised poultice of the bark is used. The fire of alder has a drying effect and the bark boiled in water is used to staunch bleeding, reduce inflammations of the throat, mouth and gums, reduce swellings and breast engorgement.

March is the start of the gardening year when we prepare the ground by digging, manuring and mulching. Onion sets and early potatoes can be planted out, and when the shoots come through they are earthed up to prevent frost damage. Straight into the ground, sow parsnips, radish, spring onions and carrots. Start making a trench for your peas and beans by digging a ditch, and fill it with manure, compost and leaf mould.

We blessed the seeds during the Ostara ritual and they are planted during March. In a propagator sow leeks, lettuce, Brussels sprouts, red cabbage, tomatoes, peppers, chillies, aubergines and summer cauliflower. You can also grow mustard and cress on the windowsill (I bet you did this at school). Just put some damp kitchen towel in a box, sprinkle on the seed and sit back and wait for crunchy salad.

The appearance of toads in their accustomed haunts is a good sign that the bad weather is over for the year. They seem to posses an instinct that tells them when no more hard frosts are due. Look out for adders coming out of hibernation after around five months of inactivity. The males will be the first to emerge, but our only native venomous snake is shy and retiring – so don't expect them to advertise their presence. They will be hungry too, so it is unfair to disturb them unnecessarily.

This year's badger cubs have spent their entire lives underground but now the older ones are ready to discover the world above ground. In some northern areas or after a severe winter the cubs are still newborn and will not emerge for some weeks. Young brown rats from last year are now beginning to leave the nest to establish new colonies, so if you are not keen to encourage them, keep your garden tidy. Another animal that has lately become a part of the British countryside is the mink, which will be beginning to breed in this month. Mink are not native and their aggressive feeding habits can devastate native species of small animals as they attack nests and eat young and eggs. Fox cubs are born at the end of March in a litter of four to five. They are born blind with short, dark fur. The vixen stays with the cubs while the dog fox provides the food. The young are fed for three weeks on mother's milk, then scraps of meat.

It is around this time that we expect to see hares boxing, as the mating season gets underway. They do box at other times of year, but tend to be hidden from view either by the long winter nights or the long summer grass. The brown hare is only sociable during the mating season which extends from December into early summer, though it is traditionally thought of as being in March ('mad as a March hare') when they gather in fields to indulge in 'boxing' activities. Bucks may fight each other aggressively, or females (does) may fend off unwanted attentions. They stand on their hind legs and strike with their forefeet, sometimes leaping into the air to strike at the belly of the opponent. Hares were sacred to the ancient British who associated them with moon deities and deities of the hunt. Killing and eating the hare was taboo, except at the spring festival, when a ritual hunt and consumption was name. Until the end of the eighteenth century an Easter Monday hare hunt took place in the Dane Hills, near Leicester led by the mayor and corporation together with hunters and hounds. This hare was associated with Black Annis, a fearful hag said to live in a cave in the hills known as Black Annis's Bower, which she had gouged out of the hillside with her own claws.

If we have an exceptionally warm March them we can expect to see the first butterflies, such as tortoiseshells, red admiral, burnet moths and tigermoths. Insects like honey bees and the common wasp are waking up and becoming more active.

Rooks breed early in the spring, building their rookeries in social groups high in the trees before the leaves are out. At this time they will join together in noisy flight displays. The rookeries are bowls of sticks, lined with leaves and moss. The female builds the nest, while her mate brings the materials.

APRIL

The first day of the month is April Fool's Day. This originates in the Pagan Roman festival of the Hilaria which marked the official end of winter with jollity. April also celebrated the return of Persephone to earth from the underworld.

The dandelion is in full bloom; its golden flowers are associated with solar energies, bright life force and vitality. Dandelion leaf tea may be taken to enhance psychic powers and the flowers may be added to divination and sun incenses. The traditional time to make dandelion wine is St. George's Day, April 23rd. St. George may well be a Christianised version of a sun/light god who overcame winter and blight, symbolised by the dragon he fought. He was popular all over Europe as a figure of spring and light. The Catholic Church demoted him from saint status in 1969.

April showers bring a flurry of new growth, and this month is one of the best for wild flowers, with lilac ladysmocks, marsh marigold, herb Robert, cow parsley, lords and ladies, garlic mustard, stitchwort, campion, and violets, windflowers and pale primroses carpeting the woodlands. And of course, this is the best month for dandelion flowers; traditionally, you should pick them on St George's Day to make your dandelion wine. In damper places, you can find white flowered ramsons, or wild garlic.

This is a busy month in the garden. Plant peas straight into the ground, but be aware of the old gardener's advice and plant 'one for the mouse, one for the crow, one to rot and one to grow'. Sow dwarf beans under cloches outside, and this is a good time to establish an asparagus bed and plant out bought in crowns, put in your maincrop potatoes, sow beetroot, carrot, kale, kohl rabi, lettuce, parsnips, peas, spring onions, rocket, spinach and chard. Start hardening off vegetables planted last month by opening the cold frame during the daylight hours. In the greenhouse sow your herb seeds, cucumbers and sweetcorn, and make up your hanging baskets, but don't put them out till the beginning of June to avoid frost damage. Hang up sticky yellow fly traps.

In Scotland the first day of April is Huntigowk Day, a gowk being a cuckoo or the person being sent up as the April Fool. April is the cuckoo's month, and when its distinctive call is heard, then spring is really deemed to have arrived, bringing the warm weather with it. It was once widespread, but much of its habitat has been destroyed in recent years, The male and female birds look alike, though the female may be browner. The plumage is grey, with the under-parts lighter in colour and darkly barred. The legs are yellow and the head is small with a thin bill.

Traditionally the bird only appears in Britain when all the Pleiades are in the sky; between 14th April and June 24th. Special cuckoo fairs were held during April to welcome it. It was often mentioned in early Celtic poetry, and its importance is reflected in the number of place names in Britain derived from it, such as Cuckoo Bush Mound and Cuckoo Bush Hill in Nottinghamshire.

Cuckoos bring good luck or bad luck, depending on what you are doing when you first hear them it is lucky to hear them if standing on grass, but bad luck if on barren ground. When you first hear the cuckoo, whatever you are doing you are fated to do for the rest of the year-so if

171

you are in bed you will become ill and bedridden. According to a Gaelic verse it is a bad omen to hear a cuckoo with no food in your stomach. In Yorkshire if a cuckoo calls repeatedly it means rain. If you turn the money in your pocket over when you hear a cuckoo, or spit on it, it will last the year.

If the call comes from the right, it is good luck for the year, make a wish and it will be granted, unlucky from the left. In Wales it is thought to be unlucky to hear the cuckoo before 6th April, but very lucky to hear it for the first time on 28th April, a whole year's prosperity will be in store. To hear the bird after August is very unlucky, more so to hear it in September or October when it should have left for warmer climates.

Swallows and other migrants like the yellow wagtail arrive as welcome summer visitors and many other birds are breeding, including tawny owls, blue tits, and great tits. The woodpecker can be heard drumming on trees. The birds are busy nest building, the animals are mating. Grey squirrels litter in April too as do field mice and rats.

MAY

This is the loveliest and most magical month of the year in many ways. Beltane is the real coming of summer, marked by the flowering of the hawthorn and the rising of the Pleiades. It is generally celebrated on Beltane Eve since, for the Celts, the day began at nightfall and ended at the next nightfall- darkness before light. They believed that Beltane Eve was the darkest night of the whole year. By now, the sun is in Taurus, the extended hours of daylight are very noticeable, and the weather is getting much warmer. There is blossom on the fruit trees and the earth has greened over. Migrating birds arrive in Britain and begin to build their nests.

Summer follows the death of winter. Death and rebirth is a theme enacted in many seasonal mumming plays and the May Day dance of the Padstow 'Obby 'Oss. The evening before, the village is decorated with green branches and flowers. The sinister black 'Oss, led by the Teaser, parades through the town to the accompaniment of drum and accordion. Now and then the drum falls silent, and the 'Oss gradually falls to the floor, only to rise again. At midnight the 'Oss dies, only to be reborn next summer.

Another familiar May Day custom is the may pole, a phallic symbol thrust deep into the belly of Mother Earth to bring fertility to the land. It is also the world tree or *axis mundi*, connecting the three realms.

172

The dance around the maypole with some dancers circling sunwise, some widdershins, suggests a dance of death and rebirth.

The name of Beltane, meaning 'bright fire' is derived from the Celtic God Bel or Beli the 'bright one', god of light, fire and death, the Sky Father who impregnates the Earth Mother. Until recently in Britain, fires were lit on hilltops on May Day to celebrate the return of summer. It was the custom to jump over the fire- young people to attract lovers, travellers to ensure a safe journey and pregnant women to secure an easy birth. The ashes were then scattered on the fields.

The two great Celtic festivals of Beltane and Samhain centred around the needs of cows. At Beltane cows were taken up to their summer pastures after being driven through the ashes of the Bel fire to purify and protect them. At Samhain, they were brought down to sheltered winter feeding grounds. In Scotland, the *caudle* was spilled on the ground, a milk offering for protect of the herds. The cow is the avatar of many mother goddesses symbolising the power to give birth, to protect, love, feed and nurture. It often represents Mother Earth, while the bull represents the fertilising Sky God.

The Pleiades (in the constellation of Taurus the Bull), which rise at Beltane, were also known as 'the Doves', the sacred birds of Venus/Aphrodite. Doves are emblems of faithfulness as they pair for life; a pair of doves was a traditional wedding gift. Doves were associated with all queens of heaven and mother goddesses, symbolising the soul or breath that was derived from the Mother.

The blossoming of the apple trees mark the return of the Summer Goddess, but perhaps the most significant herald of the season is the flowering of the hawthorn. It is said that the heavy scent of the hawthorn is reminiscent of female sexuality, perhaps the sexual flowering of the Goddess herself. May Day used to be celebrated by people going off to the woods 'a maying' carrying back fresh branches and shoots. Magically, the hawthorn is a doorway to the Otherworld. Solitary hawthorns growing on hills or near wells were considered to be markers to the world of the fairies. Any human who slept beneath one, especially on May Eve, was in danger of being taken away to the land of the Sidhe. Hawthorn is so potently magical that it is forbidden to bring it indoors except at Beltane. It is wound about with the mysteries of the Goddess and should be treated with great care.

In many areas still, the May Queen is crowned with flowers, and she sometimes has a male counterpart in Jack-in-the-Green, or the Green

Man. She represents flowers and new growth; he represents the death of winter and the rebirth of summer. She is covered in flowers; he is covered in ivy, holly, birch, poplar, and fir greenery. In ancient times they would have been appointed by the village as representations of the Goddess and the God and their performance reflected on the well being of the community; their ritual coupling or *hieros gamos* ensured fecundity for the coming season. In some places the king and queen are still called 'the bride and groom'. Villagers also performed sympathetic fertility magic by disappearing into the forest together, liaisons that were called 'greenwood marriages'. Any children born of them were considered to be sired by the God, and thus were surnamed Robin's-son, Hob's-son or Hod's-son.

In England, May Day was called Robin Hood's Day in mediaeval times. The character of Robin Hood appears at the Abbot's Bromley Horn Dance which is now a September custom, but it seems to have been transferred from Beltane. Robin is a name often applied to forest spirits, such as Robin Goodfellow, and Robin Hood may once have been a stag god, Lord of the Forest. The roebuck acquires his new red coloured coat at Beltane.

Mother Nature is bursting with life during May. The woods are swathed in clouds of bright bluebells, the hedgerows are white with cow parsley, hawthorn, oxeye daisies and comfrey. Meadows are gold with buttercups and horse chestnut candles adorn the lofty trees.

We can still get frosts in May, and the weather is changeable- it can be warm and sunny or cold and wet. Don't put out any tender plants till June, no matter how tempting it seems. By now you should be harvesting salad leaves grown under cloches or in the greenhouse. Keep sowing more lettuce, radish, parsley, basil and peas so that you can crop throughout the summer. Put out your outdoor tomatoes, leeks and sweetcorn. Pinch the tops out of your broad beans to encourage them to bush out. In the greenhouse you can sow annual flowers and herbaceous perennials, cardoons, marrows, courgettes, autumn cauliflower, calabrese and kohl rabi. Cover emerging carrot shoots with fleece to deter carrot fly. Take cuttings from perennial herbs like bay, rue and rosemary. Plant tomatoes, peppers, aubergines, chillies and cucumbers in grow bags in the greenhouse. Harden off plants grown under cover.

Bird activity is intense in May, and they seem to sing all day and most of the night. It really is the bird's month. The song of the skylark may be heard, the thrush, robin, blackbird, cuckoo (in May he sings all day), and wren in chorus at dawn and dusk. Several migratory birds return this month including the corncrake, spotted flycatcher, red backed shrike and nightingale, coinciding with a greater supply of insects in the warmer weather. The courting and nesting season is in full swing. Towards the end of the month the singers start to become more and more silent as the young are hatched and they become busy feeding their broods of chicks.

During May we start to see more insects flying in the warmth, including the cockchafer, green tiger beetle, green harestreak butterfly, the orange tip, small heath, common blue, peacocks, tortoiseshells, and brimstones, the damsel fly and crane fly. The May Fly emerges from the water, after having spent two years in the larval stage, and lives for a single day, dying after depositing its eggs.

JUNE

Every ancient religion had its own customs and traditions associated with Midsummer. These appear in the lore of Greece and Rome, the myths of the Norse, the Maya, the Aztecs, the Slavs, the writings of the ancient Egyptians, and the Old Testament of the Jews, while the Celts has a large collection of myths associated with Midsummer. Vestiges of these festivities can still be witnessed today. The time of light and warmth, summer and growth is here. We naturally feel more joyful and want to spend more time in the open air.

There are a number of customs associated with Midsummer, most of which celebrate the light and encourage the power of the sun with sympathetic magic in the form of bonfires, rolling wheels, circle dances and torchlight processions. Because the energy of the sun infuses the whole of nature, it is a potent time for gathering plants, seeking healing or practicing divination. Every self-respecting witch takes the opportunity afforded by the magic of Midsummer to collect a good supply of herbs to preserve for use throughout the year. At the end of this time any herbs left over should be thrown onto the Midsummer bonfire.

Midsummer fires once blazed all across Europe and North Africa. They also warded off the powers of bane, blight, dark, death and winter. A branch lit at the fire was passed over the backs of animals to preserve them from disease.

In Britain it was the custom to visit holy wells just before sunrise on Midsummer's Day. The well should be approached from the east and walked round sunwise three times. Offerings, such as pins or coins were thrown into the well and its water drunk from a special vessel. This is also the season of necessary rain and the time of thunderstorms. This is the time when the Earth Goddess is fertilized by the life-giving rain, or by the lightening flash of the Thunder God. However, another form of this sacred marriage takes place at the summer solstice Neolithic people would gather outside Stonehenge to witness this *hieros gamos*. As the sun rises behind the heel stone a phallic shadow is cast into the circle and touches the so-called 'altar' stone inside the circle which represents the Goddess womb, consummating the marriage of earth and sky.[23] In the Craft the fertilization of the Goddess by the God takes place when the wand is plunged into the cauldron, representing the womb of the goddess.

Though the summer solstice marks the zenith of the sun and day of longest light it is also a day of sadness, because from this day the light begins to decline, the days shorten and though this is Midsummer we are moving inevitably towards winter.

Mother Earth is in the full flush of her maturity, soft and ample, foliage is lush and the perfume of flowers fills the air. The woods are full of traveller's joy, woody nightshade, and bramble flowers, the meadow full of poppies, fat hen, mayweed and campion. The tree totem of the month is the oak tree, its roots extend as far underground as its branches do above, making a perfect symbol for a god whose powers royally extend to the heavens, middle earth and the underworld equally. In Ogham the oak is '*duir*' meaning 'door' in Gaelic (the word for door and oak, and perhaps Druid, come from the same root in many European languages), perhaps because a door made form oak offers protection and solidity and because oaks often marked boundaries; or perhaps because the oak is the door to knowledge and marks boundaries of a different kind. The oak flowers at Midsummer and marks the door opening on one side to the waxing and on the other to the waning year. It stands at the turning of the year. The male flowers are long catkins and the female flowers globes. Each flower ripens into an acorn, so called from the Danish word '*korn*' meaning 'oak-seed'.

Other Midsummer flowers include the dog rose, a plant of the Summer Goddess, along with the frothy white elder blossom. A single head of elder flowers infused in a cup of boiling water will make a tisane that can be drunk to contact the Goddess. At Midsummer foliage and flowering is at its fullest just before fruiting begins. This makes it the ideal time to gather herbs and flowers. An eleventh century Anglo Saxon medical text described gathering vervain at Midsummer to cure liver complaints. [24] Other customs included decking the house (especially over

23   Terence Meaden, *Stonehenge, The Secret of the Solstice*, Souvenir Press, London, 1997
24   G. Storm, *Anglo-Saxon Magic*, 1948

the front door) with birch, fennel, St. John's wort, orpine, and white lilies. Even churches were decorated with birch and fennel. Yellow flowered St John's Wort, an emblem of the sun, was gathered on the Eve and made into garlands. Yarrow was also gathered for medicinal purposes and to be used in marriage divination by young girls. By placing a bit of the herb under her pillow, she would dream of her future husband.

This month plant out celery in trenches prepared with manure, courgettes, runner beans and other vegetables raised under cover. Inspect the brassicas for signs of caterpillars, pick them off and protect the plants with fleece if necessary. Cut down pea plants that have been harvested but leave the roots in the ground as they help to fix nitrogen in the soil. Your new potatoes should be ready to harvest. Keep pinching out side shoots on your tomato plants, and remember to water the greenhouse copiously. You should stop cropping asparagus now if you have it, in order to let it recover and grow for next year.

Breeding continues unabated throughout June, with moorhens, nightjars (listen for their 'churring') pheasants, puffins, shags, skylarks, house sparrows, song thrushes and mute swans. Mammals such as the vole, hedgehog and dormice are also mating, and young red deer and row deer are born. More insects are seen, honey bees swarm, stag beetle, green hairstreak and cinnabar moths, elephant hawk moths, peppered moths, puss moths, bush crickets and grasshoppers. In the water, carp are spawning as are minnow, stickleback, tench, and our native lizards are laying eggs.

Birds are more silent now, being busy with parenthood, and the woods are full of fledglings. The baby cuckoo, laid in the nest of another bird, is almost ready to leave the nest of its foster parents. The bird song changes before becoming silent- the cuckoos note falters and the nightingale's voice becomes harsh. Only the late arriving migrants are still in full song, like the nightjar. You will see ducklings following their parents on lakes and streams, and note that the male bird has lost his fancy plumage after mating.

In the pond the tadpoles are acquiring their legs, but still have their tails. This will be absorbed into the body and by the end of June the young frogs will be ready to leave the pond. The vast majority will die in the jaws of birds and cats, or under cars.

JULY

According to Pliny, the Celtic year began in July [25] the corn is ripening to gold in the fields, and the heat is hot and sultry, because in July the Dog Days begin.

Our Anglo-Saxon ancestors called July mead-month, referring to the blossoming meadows. This is the month for hay making, and the cutters used to be a familiar sight in the fields with scythes. July meadows are still starred with wild flowers, where the farmer's weed killers haven't poisoned them. Weeds are a bigger problem now, since things are not allowed to balance themselves out naturally.

I always think of the late summer as the purple time, because this is the predominant colour of wild flowers- self heal, buddleia, heather, dead nettle and willow herb. Meadowsweet is flowering, along with yarrow, plantain, vetch and many of the grasses, rushes, and there are berries on the bilberry, flowers on the field bindweed, meadow buttercup, holly, ragwort, stinging nettle, traveller's joy, pineapple mayweed, enchanter's nightshade and the water lilies.

Harvest and dry lavender flowers. Cut off the old leaves of strawberries after they have finished cropping. Prune summer fruiting raspberries after harvesting, cut the canes that have borne fruit and leave the new wood which will bear the fruit next year. Earth up celery. Harvest vegetables as soon as they are ready, and preserve any surplus (see Kitchen Witchery). You can sow beetroot, fennel and chard. Keep dead heading flowers to encourage them to keep producing blossoms. Pinch out runner beans when they have reached the top of their canes.

Several creatures continue to breed throughout July, including housemartins, hedgehogs, house mice, wood mice and yellow necked mice. Sand lizard lay eggs, and young slow worms are born. Badgers begin collecting bedding for the winter and the roe deer is in rut.

Most birds are silent now and many are preparing for migration before the end of the month. Cuckoos are already starting to leave. A few still sing, like the soaring skylark, the yellow hammer and swallow. Robins start to compete for territory.

There are lots of butterflies about now including small tortoiseshells, whites, meadow browns, commas, red admirals, peacocks and skippers.

---

25   John King, *The Celtic Druids' Year*, Blandford, London, 1995

AUGUST

The month begins with the festival of Lughnasa, or Lammas. It celebrates the fruition of the year's work with the weaning of calves and lambs, the ripening of the corn and the first apples, pears, bilberries, blackberries and grapes. An old custom was to pick the first apples and make them into a drink called Lammas Wool (see recipes). In Ireland Lughnasa is sometimes called Bilberry Sunday. It was once believed that these fruits should not be gathered until Lughnasa or ill luck would result.

In parts of Ireland the nearest Sunday to Lughnasa was known as Cally Sunday. It was the traditional day to lift the first new potatoes. [26] The man of the house would go out to dig the first stalk while the woman of the house would don a new white apron and prepare to cook them, covering the kitchen floor with green rushes in their honour. In some localities the first potatoes were eaten with cabbage and bacon, in others with fish, but for most of the cottagers of the west the favoured dish was one known variously as *ceallaigh,* cally, colcannon, *bráightin* or poundy. This consists of boiled potatoes mashed, mixed with butter or milk, and seasoned with onion, garlic or cabbage. The family would give thanks that the 'Hungry Month' of July was over, as the harvest had begun. It was believed that if you ate a good meal on Cally Sunday that you would not go hungry for the next twelve months.

It was the custom to hold Lughnasa celebrations at a hill or harvest mound. These were seen as wombs of the Goddess from which life sprang and returned to at death. Sometimes these were artificially constructed, such as Silbury Hill. A later survival may have been the turf towers constructed at Lammas in Scotland. If possible take a trip onto a hill at Lughnasa. Make the walk an act of meditation. Take off your shoes and feel the earth beneath your feet.

Despite the fact that August is often the hottest month, according to Celtic lore Lughnasa is the last day of summer and the start of autumn. The days of growth are over and the harvest begins. The Flower Maiden become the harvest mother and at Samhain will become the Cailleach. In some parts of Ireland this was symbolically re-enacted with the burial of the flowers. Each person would climb the Lughnasa hill wearing a flower and these would be thrown into a hole at the summit, and then covered with earth.

Late July and month of August are traditionally times for fairs; the weather is warm and the ground suitable for travelling. Many traditional

26   Older varieties matured later than modern ones when new potatoes are lifted in June.

Lammas/Lughnasa fairs are still celebrated today. In bygone times a visit
to the Lammas Fair was the main public social event of the year, and for
young people it was an exciting opportunity to meet prospective romantic
partners. Couples would join hands through a holed stone, such as the
ancient Stone of Odin at Stenness, and plight their troth for a year and a
day. Many such temporary unions became permanent arrangements.

In Norse lore, the Dog Star Sirius, which rises with the sun at
Lammas, is called Lokabrenna ('the Burning of Loki' or 'Loki's Brand'). Sif
was the wife of Thor, the god of thunder. She had beautiful golden hair
until Loki cut it all off for a prank. Thor was so angry that he wanted to
kill the trickster, but Loki was able to persuade the dwarfs to make some
magical hair for Sif, which once it touched her head, would grow like her
own hair. It is clear that Sif's hair is the golden corn, which is cut and
regrows with the next year, making her a corn or harvest goddess. Her
husband is the thunder god who brings the fertilizing rain to the earth in
the summer, to make it grow. Loki, usually described as a god of wildfire
and heat is associated here with Sirius and the heat of the Dog Days,
which causes the ripening and subsequent cutting of the grain.

By August, the wildflowers are going over a little, though there
are still plenty left if it has not been too hot and dry. They include teasel,
purple loosestrife, fleabane, watermint, angelica, bellflower, bird's foot trefoil,
lady's bedstraw, pink clover, yarrow, field scabious, and melitot. The flower
of Lughnasa for me is the rosebay willowherb, pink in the field margins
and waste ground. A few heads of meadowsweet linger on, while yarrow,
nipplewort, yellow hawkweed and blue skullcap begin to seed. I use yarrow
for winter colds and dip fresh heads of meadowsweet in batter and fry
them for a summer treat. Deadly nightshade and woody nightshade bloom
in the hedgerows and the white trumpet flowers of bindweed rampage
throughout the hedges. Red poppies stand in the field's edges along with
wild camomile or scented mayweed, which make a calming tea. The tall
spikes of mullein are in full bloom. They are called hag tapers, since they
are sacred to the Death Goddess and were dipped in tallow and burned
at funerals. As well as flowers we now have fruits, since the harvest
begins this month. There are blackberries on bramble, conkers on the
horsechestnut, acorns on the oak, nuts on the hazels and poisonous fruit
on the yew.

In the garden, August is a month of harvesting and weeding,
having barbecues and picnics, sitting back with a glass of something nice

and admiring all your hard work paying off. If you really want to, you can plant more salad crops.

During August winter bird visitors start arriving, including the redwings, barnacle goose, and turnstones. There are pheasant chicks in the woods and other young birds are maturing now, including goldfinches, chaffinches, and the tawny owls. The cuckoo is silent now and the young birds, reared by strangers, will leave after the adults for warmer climes. This is the month when birds fall silent and go into moult and gain their new coats ready for winter. The only sounds to be heard are a few notes from the goldfinch, or a plaintive cry from willow warblers. The robins recover first and by the end of the month most birds will be back in song. The cutting machines are busy in the fields scenting the warm summer air with hay. Birds such as jays, jackdaws and finches swoop down to feast on the gleanings.

You might also hear the sound of crickets in the grass at this time. They make the sound by rubbing their back legs together. There are various types, including the oak cricket, the dark bush crickets, and the speckled bush crickets. On the insect front, certain moths appear around this time, such as the brown hawker and the common darter. You might find caterpillars of various butterflies on plants just now, including those of peacocks and small tortoiseshells. Over ponds and canals, the neon coloured damsel flies flick in and out, little moorhen chicks swim, and the sedge warblers nest at the base of the reed mace. Waterhen chicks are growing fast into adolescence.

SEPTEMBER

In Celtic lore this is the month of *Cantlos* – song time- when the Autumn Equinox marks the completion of the harvest which began as early as mid June with the hay cutting. Light and darkness stand in balance, with equal hours of night and day; but the darkness is gaining, and with it, barren winter. We must look to the storing up of the provisions and the bounty of the earth. We give the Lord and Lady sincere thanks for what they have given to us, but also recognise that this is the time when the Lord leaves us as he dies with the cutting of the last sheaf of corn and begins his journey through the underworld. This is a time of great transformation.

Until recently the seasonal harvesters would elect a Harvest Lord empowered to negotiate with the farmer over terms and conditions on behalf of his fellows. As a symbol of his office, he would wear red poppies and bindweed around his hat. He would be served first at mealtimes and addressed as 'My Lord'. Originally in ancient times, he would have been the Sacred King, elected for symbolic marriage with the land.

The corn harvest was fraught with tension. The weather might ruin the harvest, the work was hard and the final capture of the Corn Spirit was hazardous. The Corn Spirit had to be treated carefully to ensure a full rick. As late as the beginning of the twentieth century, the harvesters followed customs that would have been familiar to the ancient world. The corn was cut in decreasing circles, the Corn Spirit ever retreating into the remaining ears. There was a reluctance to be the one to cut the final ear and the be the captor of the spirit, so sickles were thrown at it from a safe distance. The final severance is called 'Crying the Neck' or 'Mare'.

The last stalks were woven into a corn dolly or kern maiden, sometimes called the Ivy Girl, which embodied the spirit of the corn and was kept to ensure fertility. It was often tied with red thread as a form of protective magic. Sometimes the corn dolly was given a chair of honour at the harvest feast and would either be kept in the farmhouse until the next harvest or buried in the field with the crop sowing.

The expansive, active part of the year is over and it is time to turn inwards. Each festival of the year in its eternal spiral can be viewed as an initiation into a new mode of consciousness. At Herfest we enter into the death of the God. Through that death comes transformation, regeneration and rebirth. It is only through this process that spiritual illumination comes. At Herfest we enter the Underworld part of the cycle of the wheel as the God enters the Underworld until his rebirth at Yule. It is the time for Otherworld travel and the exploration of the self. However, this it the time when, deprived of the external light, we encounter the inner illumination.

By September the wild flowers look a little tired and ragged though there are still a few around, with all the mints and watermints in bloom, cotton-weed, sea convolvulus, horned poppy, sweet Alison, flixweed, sea starwort, sea holly and the autumn crocus, a British native nicknamed 'Upstart' from the way it bursts from the ground in the autumn. If we are lucky the warm weather continues well into the month but there are definite signs that autumn has arrived, with plants going to seed. There are hips on dog rose, berries on spindle tree, and fluffy seedheads on traveller's joy.

This is the harvest month, a time of plenty with an abundance of foods available. On misty September mornings it is time to go mushroom hunting. Get a good field guide; though few are deadly poisonous, some can upset your stomach, some are hallucinogenic like the liberty cap, and many are simply unpalatable. Some of the most pleasant are shaggy caps best stewed in milk, giant puffballs roasted whole in the oven and the giant horse mushroom, one of which can fill a frying pan on its own. Check carefully for maggots though.

On the way back you can search for wild food in the hedgerows. Hazel nuts are good to eat raw, or add to salads, soups, bread and cakes. Nuts are a Celtic symbol of concentrated wisdom. The hazel has connections with the festival of Herfest; it represents the fruition of what has gone before and the culmination of the work. Hazels should play a part in the Herfest festival and may be made into ritual cakes.

The hedgerows are bright with many fruits in September, not the least the blackberry, a sacred plant of the Celts. A taboo on eating blackberries exists in Celtic countries, in Brittany and Cornwall the reason given is that the blackberry belongs to the fairy folk. The five petalled flowers associate the blackberry with the Goddess, and the fruit, which appears green at first, then red and finally black, symbolises her three aspects and the completion of the cycle. Blackberries provide the wine at Herfest, which marks the end of the harvest.

Elder trees and their black fruits are associated with witches and the Crone aspect of the Goddess, and often treated with great caution and surrounded with warnings as a result. Collect your acorns for coffee (roast them in the oven and grind them) and collect sweet chestnuts and walnuts to preserve them in vinegar. Collect the bluish pea-like berries of the buckthorn to make syrup.

It is the harvest month in the garden too, and this must be completed before the first frosts, the food prepared, stored and preserved for the dead time of winter to come.

Potatoes need to be lifted, left on the soil for a day or two to dry out (not in the rain) and then sorted through and packed in paper sacks out of the light and frost. If there are any uneaten runner beans left on the vines, I usually leave them for seed, as I really don't like them frozen- for me they must be eaten small and fresh. Other peas and beans can be frozen or dried. Allow them to ripen in the pods, then open the pods, leave the seeds in, and hang them up in a well ventilated shed to dry out. They will need soaking overnight before cooking. Onions should be lifted and laid on the ground for a week or two if the weather is good enough. Otherwise I spread them out in the polytunnel to dry out and tie them together in strings and hang them in the still room. I pickle all the little ones. Leave celery until it has had a frost on it, and leeks, and brassicas remain where they are, pick as and when you want them. I store carrots where they are – in the ground, by cutting off the green tops and covering with a layer of straw. Whenever I want any, I just go and pull them, fresh and crunchy, and much better than frozen ones. They last till March or April like this. Herbs can be dried or frozen. Squashes should be stored in a cool, dry place. They will keep for many months.

The robin is in full songs, and other birds are staring to join in after their August silence. Some will fly off for the winter. You might be lucky enough to still see some butterflies if the frosts do not come too early- red admirals, tortoiseshells and peacocks.

OCTOBER

The hours of light have diminished; the days are short. The harvest has been gathered in, leaves fall from the trees and animals ready themselves for hibernation. The powers of growth and light are in decline, seemingly ready to fall into their long winter sleep. The powers of darkness and cold begin to gain ascendancy.

Every year, on October 31ˢᵗ, we celebrate All Hallow's Eve, when the ghosties and ghoulies are supposed to come out from under the bed and the cracks in the woodwork. We hollow out pumpkins and turnips, put lighted candles in them and place them in the windows. There is a delicious frisson of light-hearted fear in the air.

For the Celts any boundary was important magically. The time when one season passed to another was particularly tricky, especially the two hinges of the year, Beltane and Samhain, when the Otherworld came very close. Samhain is the pivotal point of the year itself, when one year passes to the next, and the doors between the worlds stand open. The Celts believed that because the veils between the worlds are thin at this time, the spirits of the ancestors were close; hence the idea of ghosts issuing forth at Halloween. Indeed, the whole period between Samhain and the rebirth of the sun at the winter solstice (around 21ˢᵗ December) was a tricky time when spirits were abroad, it was their period of the year. So Christmas too was a popular time for ghost stories and legends- think of the Christmas stories of Dickens and M.R. James, with their strong supernatural element. Because the veils between the worlds are thin at this time, the spirits of the ancestors are close, and instead of being avoided they are sought for their wisdom and guidance.

To celebrate the full circle of existence we must recognise the reality of decline and death as natural events, not something to be ignored

184

or swept under the carpet. It is these energies we pay our respects to at Samhain; but we must always remember the new life to come.

The Celtic inhabitants of the Isle of Man still celebrate Hogmanay at this time. All household fires were put out on Samhain Eve, and the population would gather on a nearby hilltop where a large bonfire would have been prepared the previous day. There they would wait in silence and darkness until the hour was past between the seasons and the spirits which roamed abroad had departed. Then the sacred needfire would be lit by the Druids. The time of danger past, everyone would celebrate and make merry. When the dawn came, each family would then take a torch from the sacred fire to rekindle their own hearth fire from, thus marking an ending and a beginning: the end of summer, and the beginning of winter. The fires themselves were a means of purification, of expelling evils. Cattle were driven through the ashes to free them from disease. The fire was sympathetic magic to encourage the weakening sun. Samhain fires were lit until quite recent times in the Highlands and in Wales, where people would jump through the fire, and when it had burnt down, rush away to escape the 'black sow', the death goddess, who would take the hindmost. The bonfires of early November pre-date the supposed festival of Guy Fawkes by thousands of years.

At Samhain the cattle were brought down from the summer pastures to the safer winter ones. Any beast that could not be kept through the winter would be slaughtered. This is one of the reasons Samhain was called 'the festival of the dead'. It may have been that some of the animals would have been ritually sacrificed to propitiate the powers of winter (like Irish offerings at Samhain to the Formorians, gods of blight), and to feed the spirits of the dead that came to visit the Samhain feast. To this day a traditional Scottish food at this time is blackbread and oatcakes mixed with blood instead of water. Possibly one of the animals would have been made 'scapegoat', carrying all the evils of the previous year.

Winter in ancient times was hard. Animals for which there was not enough fodder would have to be slaughtered. Many people would die; the old, the sick, the very young. If the harvest had been poor even the strong would not survive. Death was always close.

At this time too plant life withers and dies, the earth will shortly become bare. However, ivy, holly and other evergreens carried the spirit of life throughout the winter, and promised the renewal and rebirth of the spring. It is at Samhain that the significance of the whole wheel becomes apparent - without the decline to death, there is no re-birth, no new growth. To have new life, there must be decline and death. At this time, the Goddess is in her Crone aspect, the wise old woman who imparts wisdom. She is also the Death Goddess, who brings winter to the land and enfolds her tired children in her cloak of death to await another dawn.

In Scotland, the Cailleach Bheur ('The Blue Hag') strides across the land, beating down the vegetation with her staff and hardening the earth with frost. When her season has fully set in she brings the snow. As spring approaches her power begins to wane, until at Beltane (1st May) she gives up her struggle, flinging her staff under a holly tree, and this is why no grass can grow there.[27] She then shrinks to a grey stone to wait until her season comes again. It is said that if anyone can find her staff they will have the power of destiny over the human race. She is one of the clearest examples of the folk survival of a winter crone goddess. She is styled the daughter of Grianan, the winter sun (the Celts thought that there were two suns, the winter and the summer).[28] She is reborn each Samhain, the start of winter, and proceeds to blight the earth with snow and cold. She has been known to turn into a wild boar, an ancient symbol of approaching winter. In Greek/Roman and Irish myth the wild boar kills the vegetation god.

The leaves are starting to change colour now- on the horse chestnut they are shaded with orange, the maples turn yellow, the guelder becomes crimson, the cherry red, the sycamores purple, and the beeches blaze with copper; the God of summer goes out in a blaze of glory. The first frost will bring them all tumbling down, leaving the trees bare for winter.

Flowers are scarcer every day though all the nettles are still in flower, dog violets and milkwort in the woods. The motherwort continues to bloom and is used for curing heartburn, and chamomile, which should be collected for tea. Now is the time I gather crab apples for jelly and rose hips and haws for syrup and wine. After the first frost I will pick my sloes for sloe gin. This month I collect all the seeds I can from the garden, to ensure a good supply for planting next year. Some are edible, like poppy, nigella, sunflower and pumpkin. Harvest what remains of apples, pears and other fruit and move frost tender plants into the greenhouse or conservatory.

The young birds and animals are nearly grown now and seagulls arrive inland for the winter. Wasps have left their nests, but a few are still

27   D.A.Mackenzie, *Scottish Folk-Lore and Folk-Life*, London, 1935
28   *ibid.*

about, feeding on the last flowers of the season, the ivy flowers. Look around and you will find the chrysalises of moths and butterflies, and spiders coming indoors. Not many birds sing now, except the robin and the wren who were once said to be husband and wife, ruling the waning and waxing year. Other singers include the missell thrush and the song thrush. The cries of the owls are heard at night before they fall silent at the end of November. The song thrushes and skylarks are also vocal now, while house martins and swallows leave for warmer climes. Winter visitors like the waxwing arrive. Rooks are seen circling and flying in the rough autumn winds.

Insects are getting sleepy with the cold. Many creatures begin their winter hibernation including bats, dormice hibernate, hedgehogs, earwig, ladybird, drone fly, burnet moth, garden tiger moth, herald moth, wasp queen. In the water, however, from late November female salmon lays eggs and dies soon after. Trout are also spawning and seal pups are born at this time of year. The red deer is in rut.

NOVEMBER

The beginning of November is all All Saints' Day in the Christian calendar. It was customarily a day for practical jokes, hiding farm implements, letting animals out of their pens, and blocking chimneys. Soul- caking was traditional, going from door to door asking for money or food in return for a song, originally to pay for prayers for the dead. Every house had to make a quantity of soul cakes to give to each visitor. Some of these cakes were kept for many years, and thought of as lucky. The tradition may derive from the Pagan practice of putting food out for the dead.

Bonfire Night, on 5th November, ostensibly celebrates the foiling of Guy Fawkes plot to blow up the houses of Parliament, but probably dates back to the Samhain fires. At Lewes in Sussex an image of the pope is burned, while at Ottery St Mary blazing tar barrels are carried through the streets by brave men, signifying the driving out of evil. It is said that this day was a festival of Thor.

The fields have been ploughed and where it was gold with corn it is now brown and black. Bonfires of leaves and garden refuse making the air smoky. In the garden, tidy up and make everything secure for winter. Repair and clean the greenhouse, and check stored produce for signs of rot. Finish the winter digging and manure your ground well. Then you can sit back and look at the seed catalogues for next year.

Now there are no insects around in the garden. Flies have either died or tucked themselves up to hibernate in warm corners. Males wasps and bees die with the cold but the females hibernate till the sun warms up in the spring and they will hatch out new colonies. Snails huddle together for the winter under piles of dead plants or woodpiles- they hate the cold. They glue themselves together and withdraw into their shells. Newts and lizards hibernate, as does the water vole in his little streamside hole. The hedgehog curls up in log piles, and sleeping too are badgers, mice, squirrels and butterflies. Wood mice may be driven into sheds and out buildings. You can recognise one by his pale underbelly, unlike his house mouse cousin.

The squirrels are busy collecting nuts, and if they collect a lot it is a sure sign that there is a hard winter ahead. They hide nuts all over the place and usually forget where they have put them, so the stores shoot in the spring and make new little forests. They love pine nuts, acorns, beech mast and fungi. They were once hunted on November 30th, St Andrew's Day.

All the harvest is in and there are pheasants in the stubble. When the frosts come, the weeds and hedgerow flowers will die back. The butterflies will be gone soon, though the red admiral is last seen, feeding on ivy flowers. Peacock butterflies may sleep in hollow tree trunks till spring, while tortoiseshells seem to prefer to winter in the corners of houses.

Bird summer visitors have flown south for the winter, only to be replaced by winter visitors from the cold north lands. There is nothing more eerie than the calls of geese on the wing.

DECEMBER

These are the darkest days of the year, if not always the coldest. There are only six hours of daylight by the winter solstice, and the attentions of the ancient priests were directed to reviving the sun. To many the sun was, or represented a god, and the diminishing of his warmth and light over the winter months was seen as his sickness and decline towards death. It was important to banish the darkness before the sun disappeared forever. For the ancients, the rebirth of the sun was by no means certain. Humans believed that they partook in the cycle of the wheel, their actions affecting it. Their efforts and rituals were needed to turn it, and ensure the regeneration of the god. Unless prayers were said, ceremonies performed, sacrifices made there would be no return of the sun, no summer, and no harvest.

Winter was a dangerous time, not only from the threat of death by cold or starvation, but because between the dark days of Samhain and Yule the dead walked the land. It was a time for ghosts, werewolves, vampires and the Wild Hunt. Charms and spells were needed to protect people, animals and property; fire was needed to push back the darkness. In Greece a black bull, wreathed in yew was sacrificed to Hecate to appease the dark spirits. Yew is an evergreen still associated with the solstice, it is known as a tree connected with the spirits and with death.

St Lucy or Lucia ('Light') was an Italian 'saint' who evolved from the legend of the Roman goddess Lucina, a Pagan deity of light and childbirth whose festival was the winter solstice. St Lucy's festival is on 13th December is very popular in the northern countries, where it is called 'little Yule' and probably gathered to itself all the remaining customs of a pre-Yule festival in Pagan times. The house was cleaned, all spinning and weaving had to be finished, and candles were made. The youngest daughter rose before dawn, dressed in white and wore a crown with nine candles waking the family with cakes in the shape of sun wheels. All the lights and candles are lit. She is called the Lucia Bride (*Lussibruden*) who brings blessings of light and food as a representative of the Goddess. In some places the Lucia bride rides in a procession accompanied by the Star Boys dressed as trolls and monsters (representatives of winter blight).

17th December was the start of the Roman seven day Saturnalia, honouring Saturn, the god of crops and time (who makes his final appearance of the year as Old Father Time at our New Year) trapped by his son Jupiter (Zeus) beneath the earth. It is interesting that one god is trapped beneath the earth while one is in the sky. Originally perhaps they were warring twins in the manner of the Holly and Oak King ruling dark and light halves of the year. This is given further credence by the fact the festivities involved the sacrifice of an ass by means of a holly club. The dark of winter before the solstice was regarded by the ancients as a time of chaos, reflected in the topsy turvy nature of the celebrations when the masters became slaves and the slaves, masters. Some of this was preserved in the later Xmas custom of the Lord of Misrule. The Romans decorated with greenery and gave presents- customs later adopted by Christians.

Around 21st December we celebrate the winter solstice, the festival of *Yul* or 'wheel', the darkest day of the year. It has been celebrated since the dawn of time, from the Roman Saturnalia and the Saxon fire festivals to the new Christian festival of Christmas, the birth of Jesus Christ Solstice means the sun 'stands still', and the winter solstice in our northern hemisphere occurs when we are tilted at the furthest point from the sun. It is the shortest day and the longest night of the year; after the solstice the sun grows stronger and the days lengthen, until its zenith at the Midsummer solstice, the longest day and shortest night.

Fire is the brother of the sun, so fires were lit at the solstice to encourage (by sympathetic magic) the sun to strengthen and begin the long climb back to Midsummer. Around the fire would dance shaman dressed in deer skins and antlers, goat hide and horse head skulls and masks. Red was worn to give strength to the sun.

The sun was reborn from the Underworld or the womb of the Goddess. Several Neolithic burial chambers, such as the one at Newgrange, are orientated to the midwinter solstice. A shaft of light from the rising sun illuminates the inner chambers and appears to re emerge from it as though rising from the cave womb of the Earth Goddess. According to legend the sun god Lugh is buried at Newgrange i.e. it is both his tomb and womb of rebirth. Spirals carved around the entrance depict the path of the sun, spiralling down to death and out again from its rebirth.

In the northern hemisphere many gods of the sun and light are said to have been from a cave, for example Mithras, the Persian god of light was born in a cave on December 25th. Zeus the chief god of the Greeks was born in a cave on the darkest night. The Cretans maintained he was born every year in the same place with flashing fire and a stream of blood.

The Celts regarded the sun that rose on the day before the solstice as a shadow sun, the real sun being by abducted by Arawn the king of the underworld. In a year of thirteen lunar months of twenty eight days there is a day left over, the Nameless Day, a time of chaos, a crack between the worlds. The sun was reborn on the solstice as a babe of Ceridwen.

To keep alive the vegetation spirit houses were decorated with evergreens, holly, ivy and mistletoe. Evergreens had great power as they could withstand the winter death. The mistletoe was called 'the druids' plant'. As it grew not on the ground, but on the branches of a tree it was considered very magical. The berries were regarded as the semen of the host tree, or by some the semen of the Lord of the Trees. The most sacred mistletoe grew on the oak (a rare occurrence). The oak was the chief tree of the druids. Around the midwinter solstice, preferably on the sixth day of the moon, the druid would cut the mistletoe from the oak in one stroke with a golden sickle. The mistletoe was used to strengthen the sun god in His weakened state.

Amongst the Celts, warfare had to cease at the time of the winter solstice and mistletoe cutting. This is why we see the solstice as a time of peace and goodwill, and the Christians subsequently adopted this. Formerly Christian cathedrals and churches would lay mistletoe on the altar for the twelve days of Christmas and in some cities, such as York, a general pardon would be proclaimed at the gates.

Trees and evergreens played a large part in the solstice celebrations. In Scandinavian and other northern countries, including some Celtic ones, evergreen trees were decked with lights. The Romans decorated pine trees with images of Bacchus.

The waning half of the year was the season of the Holly King. The custom of holly decoration was carried on into the Christian era although it was not to be brought in until Christmas Eve or allowed to remain after twelfth night. The ivy is a symbol of life and rebirth as it remains green throughout the winter and for its spiral growth.

Though there is little fresh food available at this time, unless it is imported, Yule remains the time of great feasting and merrymaking, when special foods, such as sweets, costly spices, liqueurs and spirits, are brought out to celebrate the rebirth of the sun and impart a little cheer in the depths of winter.

During December you will appreciate evergreens in the garden. It is a good time for contemplating the structure of the garden, and planning any changes you need to make in the layout. Keep checking the greenhouse and the plants stored there for winter.

Don't forget to feed the birds in bad weather. The birds are quiet this month, only a few still sting, notably the robin, which is why he is the bird of Yule.

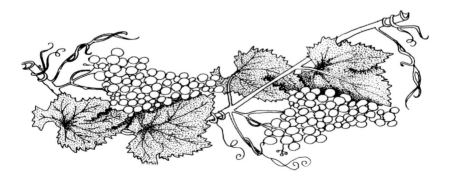

APPENDIX 1

Plants specially protected in Great Britain:

A. scabra	Bristol Rock-cress
Ajuga chamaepitys	Ground-pine
Alisma gramineum	Ribbon-leaved Water-plantain
Allium sphaerocephalon	Round-headed Leek
Althaea hirsuta	Rough Marsh-mallow
Alyssum alyssoides	Small Alison
Apium repens	Creeping Marshwort
Arabis alpina	Alpine Rock-cress
Arenaria norvegica	Norwegian Sandwort
Artemisia campestris	Field Wormwood
Atriplex pedunculata	Stalked Orache
B. falcatum	Sickle-leaved Hare's-ear
Bupleurum baldense	Small Hare's-ear
Carex depauperata	Starved Wood-sedge
Centaurium tenuiflorum	Slender Centaury
Cephalanthera rubra	Red Helleborine
Chara canescens	Bearded Stonewort
Chenopodium vulvaria	Stinking Goosefoot
Cicerbita alpina	Alpine Sow-thistle
Clinopodium menthifolium	Wood Calamint
Coincya wrightii	Lundy Cabbage
Corrigiola litoralis	Strapwort
Cotoneaster cambricus	Wild Cotoneaster
Crassula aquatica	Pigmyweed
Crepis foetida	Stinking Hawk's-beard
Cynoglossum germanicum	Green Hound's-tongue
Cyperus fuscus	Brown Galingale
Cypripedium calceolus	Lady's-slipper
Cystopteris dickieana	Dickie's Bladder-fern
D. gratianopolitanus	Cheddar Pink
Dactylorhiza lapponica	Lapland Marsh-orchid
Damasonium alisma	Starfruit
Dianthus armeria[1]	Deptford Pink
Diapensia lapponica	Diapensia
Eleocharis parvula	Dwarf Spike-rush
Epipactis youngiana	Young's Helleborine
Epipogium aphyllum	Ghost Orchid
Equisetum ramosissimum	Branched Horsetail
Erigeron borealis	Alpine Fleabane
Eriophorum gracile	Slender Cottongrass
Eryngium campestre	Field Eryngo
F. pyramidata	Broad-leaved Cudweed
Filago lutescens	Red-tipped Cudweed
Fumaria reuteri	Martin's Ramping-fumitory
G. ciliata Fringed	Gentian
G. uliginosa	Dune Gentian
G. verna Spring	Gentian
Gagea bohemica	Early Star-of-Bethlehem

Gentiana nivalis	Alpine Gentian
Gentianella anglica	Early Gentian
Gladiolus illyricus	Wild Gladiolus
Gnaphalium luteoalbum	Jersey Cudweed
H. northroense	Northroe Hawkweed
H. zetlandicum	Shetland Hawkweed
Hieracium attenuatifolium	Weak-leaved Hawkweed
Himantoglossum hircinum	Lizard Orchid
Homogyne alpina	Purple Colt's-foot
Hyacinthoides non-scripta²	Bluebell
Lactuca saligna	Least Lettuce
Lamprothamnium papulosum	Foxtail Stonewort
Leersia oryzoides	Cut-grass
Limosella australis	Welsh Mudwort
Liparis loeselii	Fen Orchid
Lloydia serotina	Snowdon Lily
Luronium natans	Floating Water-plantain
Lychnis alpina	Alpine Catchfly
Lythrum hyssopifolium	Grass-poly
Melampyrum arvense	Field Cow-wheat
Mentha pulegium	Pennyroyal
Minuartia stricta	Teesdale Sandwort
N. marina	Holly-leaved Naiad
Najas flexilis	Slender Naiad
O. caryophyllacea	Bedstraw Broomrape
O. militaris	Military Orchid
O. reticulata	Thistle Broomrape
O. simia	Monkey Orchid
O. sphegodes	Early Spider-orchid
Ononis reclinata	Small Restharrow
Ophioglossum lusitanicum	Least Adder's-tongue
Ophrys fuciflora	Late Spider-orchid
Orobanche artemisiae-campestris	Oxtongue Broomrape
Petroraghia nanteuilii	Childing Pink
Phyllodoce caerulea	Blue Heath
Phyteuma spicatum	Spiked Rampion
Polygonatum verticillatum	Whorled Solomon's-seal
Polygonum maritimum	Sea Knotgrass
Potentilla rupestris	Rock Cinquefoil
Pulicaria vulgaris	Small Fleabane
Pyrus cordata	Plymouth Pear
Ranunculus ophioglossifolius	Adder's-tongue Spearwort
Rhinanthus angustifolius	Greater Yellow-rattle
Romulea columnae	Sand Crocus
Rumex rupestris	Shore Dock
S. cespitosa	Tufted Saxifrage
S. germanica	Downy Woundwort
S. hirculus	Yellow Marsh-saxifrage
Salvia pratensis	Meadow Clary
Saxifraga cernua	Drooping Saxifrage
Schoenoplectus triqueter	Triangular Club-rush
Scleranthus perennis	Perennial Knawel
Scorzonera humilis	Viper's-grass

Selinum carvifolia	Cambridge Milk-parsley
Senecio paludosus	Fen Ragwort
Stachys alpina	Limestone Woundwort
T. scordium	Water Germander
Tephroseris integrifolia ssp. *maritima*	South Stack Fleawort
Teucrium botrys	Cut-leaved Germander
Thlaspi perfoliatum	Perfoliate Penny-cress
Trichomanes speciosum	Killarney Fern
V. triphyllos	Fingered Speedwell
Veronica spicata	Spiked Speedwell
Viola persicifolia	Fen Violet
W. ilvensis	Oblong Woodsia
Woodsia alpina	Alpine Woodsia

Select Bibliography

AA, *Book of Britain's Countryside*, Midsummer Books, London, 1998

Anderson, William, *Green Man*, Harper Collins, 1990

Arnold, James, *Country Crafts*, John Baker Ltd, London, 1968

Baker, Margaret, *Folklore and Customs of Rural England*, David and Charles, 1974

Billson, Charles, *County Folk-lore I: Leicestershire and Rutland*, Folk Lore Society, 1895

Boland, Maureen & Brigit, *Old Wives Lore for Gardeners*, The Bodley Head, London, 1976

Bord, Janet and Colin, *The Secret Country*, Paladin, London, 1978

Branston, Brian, *The Lost Gods of England*, Thames and Hudson, London, 1957

Buczacki, Stefan, *Fauna Britannica*, Hamlyn, London, 2002

Campbell, Joseph, *The Way of Animals Powers*, Times Books, London, 1984

Cooke, Ian, *Journey to the Stones* Men-an-Tol Studio 1987

De Menezes, Patricia, *Crafts from the Countryside*, Hamlyn, London, 1981

Elkington, John & Hailes, Julia, *The Green Consumer Guide*, Victor Gollancz Ltd, London, 1988

Franklin, Anna, & Lavender, Sue, *Herb Craft*, Capall Bann, Chieveley, 1995

Franklin, Anna, Familiars- *the Animal Powers of Britain*, Capall Bann, Chieveley, 1998

Frazer, James, *The Golden Bough* The Macmillan Press Ltd 1976 [First published 1922]

Gordon, Lesley, *A Country Herbal*, Peerage Books, London, 1980

Graves, Robert, *The White Goddess* Faber and Faber, London, 1961

Green, M. *Gods of the Celts*, Allan Sutton, Gloucester, 1986

Guest, Charlotte, and Jones, J. [trans.], *Mabinogion*, University of Wales Press, 1977

Hemphill, Rosemary, *Herbs for All Seasons*, Penguin, London, 1975

Henderson, George, *Survivals in Belief among the Celts*, MacLehose, 1911

Holt, J.C., *Robin Hood*, Thames and Hudson, London, 1991

Jani Farrell Roberts, *The Seven Days of My Creation*, iUniverse, Lincoln, 2002

Lansky, Vicki, *200 Fabulous, Frugal Uses for Baking Soda*, Rodale Press, n/d

Mabey, Richard, *Flora Britannica*, Sinclair-Stevenson, London, 1996

Mabey, Richard, *Food for Free*, William Collins, Glasgow, 1972

Mabey, Richard, *Plants with a Purpose*, Fontana, London, 1979

Murray, Margaret, *The Witch Cult in Western Europe*, Oxford University Press, 1971 (1921)

Newdick, Jane, *Sloe Gin and Beeswax*, Charles Letts & Co Ltd, London, 1993

Nichols, Ross, *The Book of Druidry*, Aquarian, London, 1990

Pennick, Nigel *Natural Magic*, Lear Books, Earl Shilton, 2006

Seymour, John & Sally, *Self Sufficiency*, Faber and Faber, London, 1973

THE PATH OF THE
SHAMAN
Anna Franklin

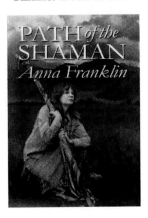

The Path of the Shaman is book two in Anna Franklin's *Eight Paths of Magic* series, exploring the role of the shaman, the mediator between the world of humankind and the world of spirits. This book explores, from the perspective of native British shamanism, the shamanic cosmos, the web of power, the shamanic crisis and becoming a shaman, healing and soul work, as well as working with the spirits of the land, plus animal and plant allies.

"I was moved beyond words by the beginning of this book. It reminded me of my traumatic numinous experiences which I have studiously tried to forget. It woke in me those vestiges of that path which I did not wish to traverse. I learned more, understood more and recognized more than I had before."
New Moon Reviews

£12.95 ISBN 0-9547534-4-5

For details and special offers visit www.learbooks.co.uk

THE PATH OF THE PRIEST AND PRIESTESS

PAGAN RITUAL

Anna Franklin

Pagan ritual, whether it is an act or worship or magic, employs a specific series of stages, using symbolism and ceremony, to create a sacred place and state of consciousness whereby the participants are put in touch with forces outside themselves – the Gods. Step by step, we weave together the disparate threads of time, place and people using the beliefs, words, symbols, movements and intent of those involved to make the ritual pattern, a pattern by which we "establish a link and cultivate a dialogue between the microcosm and the macrocosm". Ritual is a two way exchange between the microcosm (us and through us, our world) and the macrocosm (the greater Cosmos and the powers of the Gods).

£11.95 ISBN 97809547534

For details and special offers visit www.learbooks.co.uk